THE STORY OF A COURAGEOUS MAN
WHO WITNESSED HISTORY . . .
AND HELPED MAKE IT

 From his time as a young firefighter in the South Bronx, to his controversial years as president of the Uniformed Firefighters Association, to his term as New York's Thirtieth Fire Commissioner under Mayor Rudolph Giuliani, Thomas Von Essen faced many challenges during his thirty-one years in the FDNY. But nothing could have prepared him, or his department, for the devastation of September 11, 2001. Many of the 343 firefighters lost were Von Essen's friends and colleagues, men whose exemplary lives contributed to his love of the department and taught him about the value of self-sacrifice in the service of others.

In this moving memoir, he provides an insider's look into the tragedy and its harrowing aftermath. Yet *Strong of Heart* is more than a haunting retelling of that day. It is also an uplifting tale of one man's search to rise above tragedy and find hope in the legacy of those great men, including Chief of Department Pete Ganci, FDNY chaplain Father Mychal Judge, and head of special operations Ray Downey. And it is an homage to the amazing and often unsung acts of heroism that the Bravest perform every day.

Acclaim for
THOMAS VON ESSEN
and
STRONG OF HEART

"Manages the neat trick of not joining
the avalanche of bargain-basement pieties
about September 11. His exquisitely tormented
relationship with the department he served
for thirty-one years as firefighter, union president
and commissioner gives rich texture to the book. . . .
He is a born memoirist: irreverent, observant,
self-critical and possessed of an elephantine
recall of jokes, grudges and telling moments. . . .
With grace, humor and honesty . . .
he also deftly shows how one person's life
has swung on the hinges of history."
New York Times

"Thousands of World Trade Center survivors
have gripping firsthand stories,
but few of these stories have the scope
and bitter poignancy of Thomas Von Essen's . . .
a heart-wrenching memoir . . .
The world is awash with books on September 11.
This is one of the best."
Barnes & Noble.com

STRONG OF HEART
LIFE AND DEATH IN THE FIRE DEPARTMENT OF NEW YORK
THOMAS VON ESSEN

ReganBooks

AVON BOOKS
An Imprint of HarperCollinsPublishers

The author is donating a portion of the proceeds from this book to the Fire Safety Education Fund of the Fire Department of New York.

CREDITS—Text: Photographs on pages 10–11 by NYPD Photo Unit; photograph on pages 68–69 courtesy of the author; illustration on page 186 by anonymous; photograph on pages 218–219 by Doug Mills/Associated Press; map on page 326 courtesy of the FDNY; illustration on page 270 by anonymous (This illustration was left at many firehouses throughout the city as a message of sympathy. The artist is unknown). **Insert:** Photographs on pages 1, 2 (bottom), 3 (top right, bottom), 4 (bottom), 5, 9 (bottom), 14 (bottom), 18–19, 20, 21, 24–25, 28, 29, and 32 (top) by FDNY Photo Unit; photographs on pages 2 (top), 3 (top left), and 7 (bottom) courtesy of the author; photograph on page 6 (top) by Todd Maisel; video image on page 6 (bottom) by Steve Spak; photographs on pages 7 (top), 8, 10–11, 12–13, 15, 16–17, 22–23, and 26–27 by NYPD Photo Unit; photograph on page 9 (top) by the Mayor's Office; photograph on page 14 (top) by the White House; photograph on page 30 by Peter Arnell; Photograph on page 32 (bottom) by Al Freni.

AVON BOOKS
An Imprint of HarperCollins*Publishers*
10 East 53rd Street
New York, New York 10022-5299

Copyright © 2002, 2003 by Thomas Von Essen
ISBN: 0-06-055664-1
www.avonbooks.com

First Avon Books paperback printing: September 2003
First HarperCollins hardcover printing: August 2002

Printed in the U.S.A.

10 9 8 7 6 5 4 3 2 1

*This book is dedicated to
the children left behind on September 11;
and to my own children and grandchildren,
who gave me some comfort in the
face of so much sorrow.*

The bravest are surely those who have the clearest vision of what is before them, glory and danger alike, and yet notwithstanding, go out to meet it.

—THUCYDIDES

STRONG OF HEART

CONTENTS

PART THREE: BE NOT AFRAID

ACKNOWLEDGMENTS

Writing this book has been an adventure on a par with my days as a young firefighter. More than once, I've felt as if I were crawling down a long dark hallway, scared of what I'd find when I came to the end, thinking of turning back and wondering why the hell I wasn't doing something else.

As in those days, I never would have been able to complete the journey without the help of many other people.

I'd like to thank the following friends and colleagues who generously provided insight, advice, memories, and inspiration: Richie Sardiello, Werner Van Elsing, Lee Ielpi, Tom Kelly, Frank Pampalone, Marty Henry, Jim Ginty, Marty Doherty, Jack McDermott, Joe Daley, Dennis Smith, Billy McLaughlin, Ed Koch, Tom Regan, Richie Brower, Henry McDonald, Howard Safir, Rudy Giuliani, Michael Regan, Ray Goldbach, Beth Petrone, Tara Stackpole, and Addie LaPiedra.

At the FDNY, Frank Gribbon provided statistics, videotape, and records. The wise Tom Fitzpatrick shared many memories and was generous enough to read several drafts of the manuscript. Lynn Tierney, my former colleague and close friend, did those things and more, spending several dozen hours with me going over the manuscript, providing detailed memories, keeping me from making major factual mistakes, and in general improving the book in immeasurable ways. There is no adequate way to thank Lynn for her generosity and friendship. Her influence is on every page.

Thanks to everyone at ReganBooks and HarperCollins, especially Judith Regan. She not only helped me to tell my story, but her insight, concern, and philosophy of life aided me in many other ways. Aliza Fogelson's editorial work greatly improved the book, and her unwavering dedication, spirit, and sense of humor added enormously to the whole experience. Angelica Canales was also wonderful and really helped me get through this grueling project.

Matt Murray was much, much more than just a collaborator. He was sensitive, with great insight and intuition. Early on he realized how much I loved the firefighters and tried to get that message out in the book. He immersed himself completely in the FDNY and my life. I especially thank him for all his effort.

In my family, my brother Fred Von Essen recounted tales of our youth. My children, Pam, Erica, Marc, and Tom, all sat for interviews; Pam also read multiple drafts and provided plenty of her typically incisive commentary and advice. I love and thank them all. My brother Roddy shared hours' worth of memories, obtained videotape, phone numbers, and laughs, and performed whatever odd jobs I asked of him, as always. My wife, Rita, provided reminiscences, comments on the manuscript, and delicious Italian meals—and tolerated, with good humor, all the boxes of records on the floor and piles of papers on the dining room table for months. Without her love, support, and forbearance, none of the other good things in my life would have happened.

FOREWORD

I've loved the FDNY my whole life. Like a lot of young boys, I always looked up to firefighters, especially because one of my uncles was in the fire department and four were in the police department. When I was very young, one of my childhood memories was of my uncle Eddie, one of my mother's younger brothers who was a firefighter in Brooklyn, being thrown from a ladder truck going to a fire. He was seriously injured and the doctors thought he might not be able to walk again.

My mother took me to Kings County Hospital to visit Uncle Eddie. Despite his tremendous pain, all he talked about was returning to work. And he did. He recovered and had a long career in the fire department, got injured twice more, and then retired as a captain. Even as a young boy, I understood that this was not a regular job. This was a job for heroes.

As mayor, I went to hundreds of fires and met thousands of firefighters. They remain the bravest men I know. Tom Von Essen is a firefighter's firefighter.

Although we both attended Bishop Loughlin High School in Brooklyn at the same time, I didn't meet Tom until I was running for mayor of New York City. I got to know him when I was elected mayor and Tom had emerged as the respected president of the Uniformed Firefighters Association, the main labor union of the New York City Fire Department.

In 1996 I chose Tom to be the city's fire commissioner. The choice surprised a lot of people, since Tom was the head of the firefighters union and thus had been on the other side of the negotiating table. But from that vantage point, I recognized Tom's dedication to the department and his excellent leadership skills. He never let the city down. He reformed a department that had remained largely unchanged since its inception, and his attention to detail regarding safety training and response time saved countless lives. Under Tom's command, civilian casualties fell to record lows.

One of the department's saddest days was the Father's Day fire of 2001. Three firefighters were killed in the tragedy. I prayed that this would be the last time Tom and I would stand together at a firefighter's funeral. I only wish that were the case.

The horrible events of September 11 forever changed New York City and its fire department. The FDNY lost 343 men—more in a single day than the department had lost in the last hundred years. I'll never forget seeing Tom on that day, his face frozen in sorrow.

Tom was with Ray Downey, Pete Ganci, Father Mychal Judge, and Bill Feehan as they set up the board that the department uses to plan its emergency response. They're all gone; he's still here. He wanted to stay with his men, but I needed him with me to help, to advise the public, to relay information about evacuation, and to coordinate the rescue with the police commissioner and the director of Emergency Services. He was outside when the first tower collapsed, was nearly crushed and covered in debris, and walked north to find us. Tom knew that the firefighters he'd seen moments before, men he loved and respected for years, could not have fared well as they rushed in while everyone else rushed out.

For as much as America has learned about the FDNY, one story that hasn't been told enough is that September 11, as awful as it was, involved by far the greatest rescue in American history. More than 25,000 people were safely evacuated from the towers, almost entirely due to the courage and professionalism of the best-trained fire department in the world. Tom tirelessly consoled the countless grieving families and boosted the morale of the workers trying to dig out from under.

Over the next few months I was impressed and even awed by the way Tom held his shattered department together. He was indefatigable and wonderfully compassionate, never succumbing to the unbelievable pressures put on him in the wake of the attacks. Tom Von Essen was ready to lead when the department he loves needed him most.

It is crucial to maintain a sense of humor when dealing with a catastrophic situation and the person who was best at that was perhaps the person most affected by the tragedy. Whether cracking jokes with President Bush after his Ground Zero visit or poking fun at us for finally using forks after a week of eating with our hands, Tom kept our spirits up even as his own heart was breaking. In addition to his humor, Tom's gift for telling it like it is makes him a natural storyteller.

I've spoken at far too many funerals for firefighters. At the end of every eulogy, I ask everyone there to stand and applaud the departed hero, so the family can feel

XX   THOMAS VON ESSEN

the strength of the emotion. Tom deserves that same applause, the acknowledgment due to a true hero and a fine man.

—Rudolph W. Giuliani

STRONG OF HEART

PROLOGUE

SUNDAY, JANUARY 6, 2002

My family is in the middle of a dark church and the priest is drizzling Holy Water on the forehead of my granddaughter, Julia, and talking about the Father, the Son, and the Holy Spirit. Julia wriggles happily in my daughter's arms.

All I want to do is get out of here.

The memories hit me as soon as we walked in. The last time I was here, it was a Friday night, at the end of the longest week I can remember. The church, nearly empty today, was overflowing. People spilled into the aisles and along the back wall. On the right, pew after pew was filled with Franciscan monks in their brown robes. On the left, up front, sat Mayor Rudolph W. Giuliani, hunched over and looking weary. My wife and kids sat nearby. I had barely seen them in days.

By the altar, in an open casket, lay the body of Father Mychal Judge.

The white-haired priest was one of our chaplains, a genial and soothing presence at major fires who had become one of the most beloved figures in the New York City Fire Department.

To me, he was simply a close friend, one of the best I had. I wasn't a devout Catholic, as I had been when I was small, but Father Judge had been that rare kind of priest who radiated goodness and made the old Bible stories relevant to the world I know, in a way that made me want to believe. As fire commissioner, I had spent many long hours with him, seeking his advice and, at times, reassurance. On my darker days over the years, he had sent me dozens of encouraging cards and notes. He had become a close friend to my whole family and had baptized Julia's two-year-old sister, my first grandchild, Rita. He was supposed to have baptized Julia, too.

On too many nights, Father Judge and I had found ourselves sitting in a hospital emergency room, trying to find the words to tell some widow or mother that her husband or son had just died fighting a fire. In the middle of chaos and sorrow, we often exchanged knowing glances in search of strength. Usually he was the one giving it, and I was the one taking. I knew I was supposed to be a comforting presence at those times, but I was always a wreck on the verge of tears. Not Father Judge. He would stay calm and soothing as he took the hands of the families and spoke to them. He seemed able to suck the pain and worry and fear out of them and absorb it into himself, to take on the burdens of others and bring them relief.

Looking down at him in his casket, I wished I could do the same. The ruddy, robust face I knew so well had taken on a bluish hue that I recognized as the color of death. His features were twisted into a pained, unfamiliar grimace. It felt like a knife in my heart.

Thinking back to that awful night, I realize that four months have already passed. But the wound feels as fresh today as it did then.

Only the Monday before the wake, on a warm, sunny September morning that was the last purely happy day I can remember, I had seen Father Judge celebrate mass at an event that had been very emotional for me. He had come to bless a firehouse in the South Bronx, the home of Ladder Company 42 (where I had worked for nearly sixteen years) and Engine Company 73. The dilapidated building I'd known had been completely renovated, and we were at a ceremony—the fire department likes a lot of ceremony—to rededicate it.

I was there alongside the mayor and our chief of department, Pete Ganci, to cut the ribbon. Dozens of my old friends and colleagues, men I'd worked with thirty years earlier like Jimmy Ginty and Werner Van Elsing, had come back to sit alongside the younger guys who ran the house now.

"We come to this house this morning to celebrate renewal, rejuvenation, new life," Father Judge had said, roaming a little restlessly on the makeshift altar that was set up on the floor normally reserved for the rig. "We come to thank God for the blessings of all the years that good work has been done here. We can never thank God enough for the reality of the lives we have."

He asked us to pause and think of some small blessing in our lives.

I had many. I had my wife, my four kids, two granddaughters, and a grandson on the way. I was happily employed as commissioner of the nation's largest fire department, overseeing 11,000 firefighters who work in

240 stations across the city, 3,000 EMTs and para-medics, and 2,000 civilians—about 16,000 in all. I'd spent more than thirty-one years in the department.

As a firefighter here, I had reveled in the camaraderie that came from being with the guys, whether we were bullshitting around the kitchen table or crawling down smoky hallways on our hands and knees. Working in the union for years, I had made friends all over the department. I knew hundreds on a first-name basis, including some of the greatest people I've ever met.

Being commissioner had felt a little weird at first. Tommy Von Essen, a former "can man" from the Bronx and union president, given the job of running the entire department? Nothing like that had ever happened in the department before. I almost felt embarrassed to call myself "commissioner." I never used the title when answering my phone, never felt comfortable working behind the commissioner's broad desk in a spacious corner office. I preferred to use the desk in a little closet-sized office that was off to the side, where I was crammed in between stacks of files and papers as if I were the commissioner's clerk.

But if I'd been a little uncertain in the beginning, I knew I'd done a good job over the last five and a half years. Sure, I'd had some ugly run-ins with some of my chiefs and with the union leaders. At times I'd been accused of pigheadedness, micromanaging, and vindictiveness—not *completely* unfairly. But I'd also worked long hours to improve safety for our guys; to make their bosses, the fire chiefs, more accountable; and to continue to improve the best department in the world. Because of my willingness to take on tough fights, and the hard work and support of my team, we'd been able to upgrade the equipment and training of our men, improve safety for both firefighters and citizens, and bring the number of fire fatalities across our entire sprawling city to a fifty-year low.

It had been the best, most rewarding job I'd ever had.

If there was any melancholy in the air that morning, it was largely because we had been through a rough few months. Three firefighters had been killed in a fire on Father's Day, and another had died of a heart attack while on a job in August. Dealing with deaths, talking to the widows and children, handling the pain I felt in wanting to help, had always been the hardest part of the job for me.

With summer inevitably giving way to fall, moreover, the end of my job was in sight, which made me a little wistful. Mayor Giuliani's term ended at midnight on December 31, and it was all but certain that I wouldn't be sticking around to work for the next mayor. With the Giuliani era winding down, and the focus shifting to the upcoming election, a lot of us in the administration were spending these last days starting to plan our futures and remembering old times.

There was some solace in our imminent departure, of course. With less than four months to go, I figured that with any luck I wouldn't have to endure any more fatalities on my watch.

The ceremony that morning stoked my nostalgic feelings. Father Judge talked to us about change, about how the current group of guys, from the mayor to the commissioner to the chaplain to all the firefighters, was only one piece in a long continuum. We would all be forgotten in a hundred years, he reminded us. It was enough that the great spirit of the department was, for now, in all our hands. We had taken it like a baton from those who came before us, and we had to hand it off to those who would follow. That kind of change, he said, was hard, but it was good and healthy and natural. The way he described our job, it was a calling.

"Good days, bad days, up days, down days, sad days, happy days, but never a boring day on this job," Father Judge said. "You do what God has called you to do. You show up, you put one foot in front of another, you get on the rig, you go, and you do the job, which is a mystery, and a surprise.

"*You have no idea when you get on that rig—no matter how big the call, no matter how small—you have no idea what God is calling you to.*"

The next morning, I was driving south on the FDR Drive on the east side of Manhattan when the first hijacked plane slammed into the north tower of the World Trade Center. Along with hundreds of firefighters, on duty and off, active and retired, I raced to the scene. Not long after I got there, the second plane hit.

Like everyone else, I saw the twin towers come crashing down later that morning. Like everyone else, I was swept by waves of sadness, revulsion, confusion, and shock.

For those of us in the fire department, though, the attacks brought a special horror and grief. We lost 343 men, nearly half as many in one day as the 774 we had lost in all the years since the modern fire department was formally constituted in 1865. The disaster took top commanders—including my close friends Chief of Department Ganci and our number two executive First Deputy Commissioner Bill Feehan—veteran chiefs and officers, and brand-new probationary firefighters, or probies, with just a few weeks on the job.

In the end, more than one in ten people who died at

the World Trade Center that day were firefighters, men who had not been in the buildings when the planes hit but who raced to them afterward. Survivors told us that while they had been going down the stairs, they had passed our guys going up.

In a matter of minutes, the department I loved, to which I had devoted my life, was decimated.

Among the dead and missing were over a hundred men I had worked with or known on a first-name basis. One of the first to die was Father Judge, who had been ministering in the lobby of the north tower.

Instantly, permanently, I felt a grief that was overwhelming, overpowering. So many of us, covered in dust and grime, felt as twisted and tarnished inside as the gnarled metal beams and piles of debris that covered the ground in front of us.

At the same time, we had an immense, almost impossible job ahead of us, working through the grief to rebuild the department.

Listening to Father Judge's words the day before, I had never imagined how prophetic they might be. It already seemed as if we now lived in a different world. Suddenly life was stranger, and sadder, than anything we had been prepared for.

I was numb much of the time during the long days and weeks afterward, often moving through meetings, funerals, and interviews like a robot. I kept reminding myself that I had a job to do, and didn't have the time to indulge myself or my feelings when there was so much work. We had to do the best we could for the families who lost loved ones, and at the same time rebuild the city and the department. More disasters—anthrax, a major plane crash—were ahead of us.

But every day, too, there were reminders I couldn't avoid. I kept thinking back on Father Judge and Bill and Pete and the many others who were gone. I'd run into old friends at the Trade Center site and learn that their sons were missing, or open the mail and find a letter from a widow, and I'd feel a fresh stab of pain.

And suddenly I'd be on the verge again. I'd have to excuse myself, shut the door for a minute, sit back, put my head down, and wipe my eyes.

This book grew out of those days, and that grief.

I've always pushed the firefighters to review major incidents and see if there's anything to learn from them. As the weeks passed and I found myself flooded with memories, I decided to do the same thing myself. I'd sporadically kept notebooks and journals over the years. After September 11, I found myself thinking back on my whole life in the department and jotting down as much as I could remember. I'd write in the helicopter on the way to a funeral or in the car on the way home late at night.

I started out chronicling my experiences for myself. It was a way to help my overloaded memory keep track of all that was happening. But reflecting on our great department, how much of its history I'd seen, how many great men I'd known, and how much had been lost, made me want to share the story with the public. The department would go on, without many of those men and without me, and they had left their marks and would be remembered. But it would be an utterly changed place from the one where I had worked and spent my career.

So I hope this book explains more about who I am, all that I'd been through before September 11, how I came to be in an unusual and unwelcome spotlight after the attacks, what happened behind the scenes in those days, and why we did what we did. But I hope, too, that in some small way it serves as a testament to some of the men I knew and loved; that it reveals a sense of the firefighter's life, warts and all; and that it provides some insight into the life of our department, which I've been privileged to see from so many perspectives. And I hope it shows why firefighters, as a group, are the bravest, funniest, most generous people in the world, and why I love them so much, more than many of them know.

What this book can't do is help us to make sense or find meaning in the horror of September 11. Nothing can. I have never believed that any of the deaths I saw in the fire department could be explained, and I never found anything comforting or good in any tragedy.

PART ONE
THIS IS WAR

1

CAN YOU TALK
ABOUT THE LOSS?

"Commissioner Von Essen, can you talk about the loss to the fire department?"

I didn't know. I was a wreck, twisted inside, dirty outside, my hair mussed, my tie crooked, my clothes coated with dust, my brain scrambled, my whole self, like everyone else, suddenly lost in a horrible, surreal new world.

It had been maybe twelve hours since two hijacked jetliners had slammed into the twin towers of the World Trade Center, igniting massive fires that brought them crashing to earth a short time later. Thousands of people were missing and presumed dead. Rubble was scattered across the southern tip of Manhattan. All day long, people in shock had been streaming uptown, away from the disaster, marching across the bridges from Manhattan by the thousands in an eerie mass exodus. The entire city was shut down, the whole country grieving and angry from the suddenness and brazenness of such an attack on the world's most powerful nation.

I was standing behind Mayor Rudolph W. Giuliani, my boss of five and a half years, in the auditorium of the city's Police Academy, as he spoke to dozens of reporters packed together in front of us. Lights shone down, cameras snapped and whirred. But unlike the usual mania of a news conference, the atmosphere was subdued and sorrowful.

Until a minute before, I had been marveling at the coolness the boss was displaying under such immense pressure, though I had seen similar demonstrations many times in the past.

I had also been hoping no one would ask me to speak. I didn't want to have to say anything.

The loss to the department? For starters, more than three hundred firefighters were missing, most of them feared dead. I always took the death of a firefighter, any firefighter, hard. In this case, the victims included dozens of men I had counted as close personal friends. All day long, people had been whispering their names into my ear, each one feeling like a punch to my gut.

Bill Feehan, seventy-one years old, our first deputy commissioner, the number two man in the department, who had first become a firefighter in 1959 and gone on to hold every rank during his career, even, briefly, mine.

Pete Ganci, fifty-four, the tough bulldog with a chest full of medals who as chief of department was our highest-ranking man in uniform, the one who oversaw all the firefighters.

Ray Downey, sixty-three, a sharp and seasoned chief who as head of our special operations had become an internationally known expert in disaster recovery and building collapse, skills we had never needed more than now.

Father Mychal Judge, sixty-eight, the Franciscan priest and chaplain who in many ways embodied the soul of all that we were.

And there was much more than just the names and numbers, as horrible as they were. Our command structure itself had been severely crippled. We had lost hundreds of years of experience, knowledge, and wisdom.

Death had reached into dozens of firehouses in the cruelest, most sudden way imaginable and left voids that might never be filled. At that very moment, hundreds of weary and anguished men were desperately clawing through the mountainous piles of rubble that were strewn across several acres, seeking any signs of life they could find. We nurtured hopes that there were survivors in the rubble, and horrible doubts that no one was alive. Thousands of other current and former firefighters, not to mention the parents, spouses, and children of our people, were reeling from psychic wounds that cut deep and would certainly last years, if not a lifetime. All were asking, "Why?" and none had an answer.

How would they all get through this? At that moment, after a long day of tears, work, worries, and just putting one foot in front of the other, I wasn't sure if or how *I* would endure the hours and months to come, let alone everyone else.

The loss to the department? How could anyone begin to calculate it? In a matter of minutes, we had been devastated beyond belief, more than any training or planning had prepared us for, far beyond anything any of us could have imagined in even our worst nightmares.

"We've got over three hundred people that are missing, that we can't account for," I said, fumbling a little to get the words, any words, out—and keep the tears back. "We believe that many of—many of them are—are gone. We don't—we'll keep looking. We have hundreds of people over there now, trying to find as many possible locations that they might be, in—in some way, in a void or whatever and, you know, still able to breathe and—and still alive. But we believe that most of these people, I think, are—we are not going to be able to pull out, so we'll just keep working on it."

Then another reporter asked the inevitable follow-up question: "How does that make you feel?"

How do I feel? HOW DO I FEEL? I glared at the reporter who had asked the question, one I had known, and generally liked, for a long time. *How the hell do you think I feel about it? I am the fire commissioner, and I feel as if we were talking about my own children. It's my duty to protect every firefighter. I couldn't. How would YOU feel?*

Just then, I felt as if I wanted to rip her throat out. The mayor put his hand on my shoulder, gripping it hard, as if to restrain me from leaping forward.

"I don't know what to say. I—we lost people that have given over forty years.

"Commissioner Feehan had held every rank in the department, probably the most valuable people—person in the department. When I got this job, the mayor and Commissioner Safir said, 'Make sure you keep Bill Feehan.' I haven't regretted that one day. He's given his whole life to this department.

"Chief Ganci, the same thing, chief of the department, thirty-three years, thirty-four years.

"Ray Downey, we just honored him with a dinner, almost forty years of service, world-renowned for situations like this, telling me how dangerous it was when we first got there, all the possibilities, everything he was trying to do to, you know, to get the people out.

"Father Judge, I don't know if you know Father

Judge, one of the nicest men you could possibly find in the whole world.

"We haven't found other people yet, either, and I don't even want to mention their names. Some of the best people in this department. I can't find anybody from five rescues and seven squads, and it's just—it's a devastating thing.

"I—I don't know—well, the fire department will—will recover. But I don't know how."

2

IS THAT A CLOUD?

It had started as a warm, clear, sunny morning, one of those last lazy-feeling days of late summer just before the first hints of cool weather start to appear. At the fire department, and elsewhere in city government, things were winding down as the Giuliani administration entered its final season.

I had slept a little late, telling my driver that day, John McLaughlin, that he didn't need to pick me up till about eight-thirty for the ride to headquarters in downtown Brooklyn. The morning was set aside for a meeting.

I was in a great mood as we drove south along the FDR Drive, on the edge of Manhattan's east side. My thoughts were flooded with warm memories of all the old friends I had seen the day before at the rededication of Ladder Company 42, my former firehouse in the South Bronx—guys like Werner Van Elsing, the now-retired elephant who had been one of the first guys I met there, and Tom Kelly, once a new firefighter and friend in the company, now a captain. The men there had been my first mentors, colleagues, and friends when I came on the job as a young firefighter thirty-one years before.

As we neared the Brooklyn Bridge, though, I gazed idly out the window and saw something in the sky.

"Is that a cloud?" I asked.

John took a look. "No, that's a job," he said.

Buildings blocked a clear line of sight. I kept peering west, trying to see where the black plume of smoke was coming from.

Suddenly the view opened up and we could see the hole, the fire shooting out into the sky.

"Holy shit! It looks like a plane crashed into the Trade Center."

John turned up the fire department radio. There was a lot of chatter about an explosion at the north tower of the World Trade Center.

Looking at the dark smoke belching forth, I felt a chill. "We're going to lose a thousand people," I said, meaning the workers in the tower.

Minutes earlier, at 8:46 A.M., American Airlines Flight 11, with ninety-two people aboard, had crashed into tower one of the World Trade Center. It was the northernmost of the two 110-story towers that had graced the city's skyline for most of my adult life. The Boeing 767 had been hijacked soon after takeoff from Boston's Logan Airport, en route to Los Angeles.

John flipped on the siren, turned off the FDR Drive, and careened through the crowded, narrow streets of downtown. My pulse began to race, just as it had at every emergency scene I'd headed to for thirty-one years.

Through the window, I could see hordes of people already on the sidewalks, some looking up in the direction of the towers, many more walking away from them.

Most of my attention, though, was focused on the radio, which was going crazy, with all kinds of voices screaming out different alarms and directions. Units were pouring to the scene from everywhere.

At the least, I knew we had a big bad fire to put out and a major rescue to mount. I wondered if some pilot had suffered a heart attack and crashed his plane.

The dispatcher on the radio said that the command post was in the lobby of the tower, which fronted the West Side Highway. That was where I was headed. John pulled up to the curb, right by the Marriott Hotel. I grabbed my coat and white commissioner's helmet from the back and hopped out while he drove off to park the car. I knew that rescue vehicles would be coming this way in a minute and didn't want to block their access.

Pete Ganci had pulled up just in front of us. Before we could exchange a greeting, though, he turned away from the building and strode rapidly across the street. He planned to establish a staging area there, where firefighters and ambulances could gather and be directed. Seeing Pete was another indicator to me of how serious the job before us was. At his level, in a job that required more administrative duties than active firefighting, Pete only came to run the biggest emergency scenes.

I walked in the other direction, toward the building.

Overhead, I saw, a long plume of black and gray smoke shot out from the tower's upper reaches. All around me, people trapped up there by the fire were already jumping, or falling, to the pavement. Bodies and body parts and pools of blood and shards of glass lay all over the sidewalk. Screams and sirens whirled all around.

Gruesome as it all was, I tried not to dwell on it. I kept

my eyes on the door ahead of me. Like all firefighters, I'd learned over many years to look directly at the most horrible things and keep them at arm's length. If you don't do that, you can't get your job done.

At that moment, all I was thinking was, *We've got a big problem and we're going to have heavy losses of civilians*. I wasn't thinking that this was terrorism, I wasn't thinking that this was a fire we couldn't beat, I wasn't thinking that the building was going to fall down.

But some of our fire chiefs, I later learned, already suspected those things. As they'd ridden over from headquarters together, Daniel Nigro, our chief of operations, had looked up in the sky and told Pete Ganci, "We are not going to put that fire out."

I walked through the glass revolving door and entered the lobby. Inside, more glass and chunks of marble and tiles from the wall littered the floor. People were running everywhere, especially one level up, on the balcony, where security guards and cops were steering people toward the exits. Down in the lobby, where the firefighters were gathering, it was relatively calm, the usual mix of control and chaos that is typical of a fire scene.

Already, around the building, firefighters were making their way up the narrow stairwells toward the fire, while the businesspeople and government workers inside streamed down. Most were being sent in response to distress calls from the upper floors, from people trapped in elevators, people burned in different parts of the building, and people needing wheelchairs. In the lobby, men continued to charge in, wearing their black turnout coats and helmets, and they gathered in small groups in the corner.

By 9 A.M., some two hundred firefighters had already reached the World Trade Center.

The emergency command post was a large, marble-topped desk in the corner. A number of department chiefs were there, along with various aides and assistants, as well as staff from the Port Authority, barking out commands and orders and trying to get a handle on the situation.

When I joined them, they included Joe Pfeifer, the thin, mustachioed chief of Battalion 1, who had been the first chief to arrive and call in the 10-60, the signal for a major disaster; Peter Hayden, who as chief of the first division was Pfeifer's immediate supervisor; and Joseph Callan, who as citywide tour commander was the highest-ranking field chief on duty that morning. He took charge of the scene.

Everyone knew that the scope of the problem was larger than almost anything we had encountered before, but in those first minutes, it was a relatively normal and businesslike discussion of strategies and tactics. Adrenaline was running high, but things were under control, not panicky. The mind-set was that there was a lot to do, it was a huge problem, but it would get done. The chiefs and firefighters who were gathering there included some of the most experienced men in the world, who had been to thousands of fire scenes in the past and knew how to take control of a crisis and make critical life-and-death decisions quickly and with only limited information.

But all of us in that lobby knew less about what was happening than the people watching the fire on TV around the world. Anyone watching at home or work could see how deep the gash in the side of the building was, and could see the thick column of black smoke that

poured out as if from a chimney. Those of us underneath
it didn't have that perspective.

Indeed, the chiefs and their aides were desperate for
information, frantically working their phones behind
the command desk and their own radios in search of
someone upstairs who could tell us how bad things
were. Port Authority operations managers and fire
safety directors were calling tenants on the upper floors
and dialing the elevator phones, but they weren't having
much luck getting a response.

I stuck close to the chiefs, but as commissioner, I was
for the most part an observer rather than a participant.
Though I had been a firefighter myself and had answered
thousands of emergency calls in the course of my career,
a commissioner has no technical decision-making role at
a disaster scene. It's a civilian post, normally held by
men with little or no background in the field. Because I
knew so much about the department and had deep firefighting experience, I was often able to offer assistance
and insight to the uniformed chiefs in charge. But I had
long ago learned that the authority at scenes was vested
in them and that I needed to stand back and let them do
their job as quickly and efficiently as possible, while
making myself available to help if they asked. This was a
battlefield, where chain of command was critical.

My primary role at a scene was to gather information
for the mayor and the media and act as a liaison to the
other city agencies to help with resources or other needs
our chiefs might have. I had gone to scenes regularly as
commissioner, both to observe our guys and to make sure
I had a detailed understanding of every major situation.

My normal practice had been to quickly get as close to
the action as I could. But in the lobby that morning, as

wave after wave of firefighters rushed in and headed for the staircases, I found myself wondering, *How the hell am I going to get up there? I can't walk up seventy-eight floors.* It had been a long time since I'd been in the prime physical shape I'd been in as a firefighter. Even if I could have done it, it takes a long time to walk up so many floors.

Just after 9 A.M., the chiefs formed a huddle for a briefing, and I stuck my head in. Many of the upper floors were wiped out. Our focus was on clearing the buildings out and answering distress calls. "We're not even attempting to put this thing out," Chief Hayden told me. "This is strictly search and rescue."

All of a sudden we heard a high-pitched whine followed by an overpoweringly loud thud. It sounded like a bomb or maybe an elevator falling.

I heard someone say, "Another plane just hit." It was 9:03 A.M., and another hijacked jet, United Airlines Flight 175, with fifty-six passengers and crew aboard, had just slammed into floors 78 to 87 of tower two next door, spilling jet parts and debris and people all over Liberty Street. The Boeing 767 had left Logan bound for Los Angeles at 7:58 A.M.

Then someone near me said, "This is war, this is terrorism. It's certainly not an accident."

3

THESE BUILDINGS CAN COLLAPSE

Now the situation was beginning to escalate out of control, and all of us could feel it happening.

With the second attack, even more units were flooding the scene, many going up, some getting confused over which was tower one and which was tower two, some heading inside without checking in at the command posts. Off-duty firefighters, who had been looking out their windows or watching TV at home, began to arrive to help, and some of them went up, too.

Where I was, in the north tower, the telephone system was completely out. Chief Hayden would later report that the only communications available to the firefighters were their handie-talkie radios, which can have problems in high-rise buildings.

More chiefs and supervisors were crowding into the lobby. Among them was a contingent of my aides. When the first plane hit, my assistant, Captain Ray Goldbach, was already at his desk in downtown Brooklyn and could look out his window and see the smoke pouring forth. He had summoned First Deputy Commissioner Bill Feehan and Tommy Fitzpatrick, the gregarious and scholarly deputy commissioner for administration, and together they had headed toward the Trade Center in Bill's car.

I passed another deputy commissioner, Lynn Tierney, who headed intergovernmental affairs and was one of my closest confidantes. She was dressed in a business suit, and I remembered that she had told me the day before that she had a job interview with the Port Authority scheduled for later that morning on the 67th floor of the tower. Like all of us, Lynn had started thinking about her post-Giuliani future in recent weeks.

"Well, there goes the interview," I said with a weak smile, looking as always for the joke that could lighten things up just a little.

She just said, "Can you believe this?"

Across a crowd of firefighters I caught the eye of Father Judge, and we exchanged a look of disbelief. He seemed unusually anxious. I could see he was moving his lips, probably muttering quiet prayers. It was too crazy for me to go over and talk to him, though.

I also passed Ray Downey, who was utterly calm and under control as always. He turned to me and matter-of-factly said, "You know, these buildings can collapse."

That was one of many terrifying sentences I heard in the lobby. As more people arrived, the whole vast space was filled with a rising, nervous buzz generated by the babble of dozens of anxious conversations bouncing off the high ceiling and melding together. Every once in a while a sentence would detach itself from some discussion and float through the air into my ear: "The Pentagon has been hit." "They hit the Mall of America in Minnesota." "There are two more planes up there." "The Sears Tower in Chicago got hit."

The problem, as always, was that I wasn't sure what

to believe. We commonly receive inaccurate information at an unfolding disaster scene. But it was growing clear that the magnitude of this thing was far beyond anything we'd ever been through.

From outside, meanwhile, came the regular, piercing sound of crashing glass, like gunshots. It was made by bodies falling through a glass canopy over the drive on West Street.

Eventually the chiefs decided to evacuate the lobby and started talking about the need for a new command post farther away. This one seemed too exposed. The building could be hit again, and indeed, at one point someone in a uniform ran through the lobby screaming that he had confirmation a third plane was coming in. Beyond that, there was concern that jet fuel would leak down the elevator shafts and the fire would spread downstairs and explode into the lobby.

I corralled Bill, Fitz, and Lynn and told them, "We have to help these guys." We started kicking around possible locations for a new command post.

As we conferred, I found myself looking at Bill affectionately and thinking, *This is no place for a seventy-one-year-old man. He shouldn't be here.* Bill was being active and helpful, as always. No one in our department had more experience than he did, and he had once been chief of department. But he now held an administrative and advisory post, not a field one. I didn't want anything to happen to him.

I noticed that Fitz wasn't wearing his helmet. He told me he had left it in the car. So I asked Bill to hand his helmet to Fitz and to head over to the city's Emergency Operations Center at 7 World Trade Center, across the plaza. We would need to move there to coordinate the rescue operation soon, and I figured that would be a clever way to get Bill out of harm's way.

Of course Bill, as I should have known, was not the sort of guy who was ever going to give up his helmet and retreat from a scene. Instead he brushed the suggestion off and went with Fitz and Lynn to find a location for a new command post. He wasn't going to leave this scene unless he had to.

The three of them crossed the pedestrian bridge that connected the tower with the World Financial Center across West Street and entered the Winter Garden. Fitz saw that wide open space, directly across the street from the towers, as a possible command post, but a security guard told him it would take a while to set up communications. "Oh well," Bill told Lynn, "probably not a good idea to stand under all this glass anyway."

Then they went out to West Street, to the staging area set up by Pete, to take a look at the scene. The staging area was at the top of a driveway that led down to two underground garages, right across the street from the burning north tower.

I hadn't gone with them. Just as they headed off across the bridge, my driver, John McLaughlin, came in from the staging area and told me that the mayor had been there looking for me. Giuliani wanted a full report.

Goddamnit, I thought, *what a pain in the neck*.

All during my tenure as commissioner, the mayor had made a habit of racing to disaster scenes, and it had become standard procedure that I drop everything to brief him. It was my job—one I normally didn't mind doing—but I didn't want to leave the lobby when so many firefighters were heading into an inferno.

With John and my other aide Ray Goldbach following, I made for the exit, walking through a wide window opening at the front that had lost all its glass.

As a firefighter, I had been trained to check above me whenever I was outside a high-rise fire. In the lobby, bosses had been warning firefighters left and right to be careful and look up when they went outside.

Yet I was so preoccupied that I didn't even think about it.

I had taken only a few steps when suddenly, and frighteningly, a jumper whooshed by me, the body a blur that splattered on the cement maybe fifteen feet away, just on the other side of a planter. It made a sickening thud, a sound I'll never forget, like a melon or a sack of wet flour being thrown on the sidewalk. I was jolted, my heart racing. *That was too close,* I thought, *and dangerous. How could the fire commissioner be so damn stupid as to not even look up?*

It was agonizing to see people jump and be unable to do anything about it. I couldn't stop, though, to think of the horror of what those people faced that day—certain death by fire or by jumping. Later I would be haunted by some of the images and thoughts of what they went through. At the time, I had to keep moving. I needed to do my job.

As I crossed the street, John briefed me on what had occurred. He had been at the staging area with Pete and Ray Downey when the second plane hit. They hadn't been able to see what happened because of their angle of vision, but Ray had thought it was a bomb. So Pete sent John around the corner to find out what was going on. He had seen airplane-engine parts and what looked like a hundred bodies scattered all over Liberty Street. The plane had swooped right over that area and cut a wide swath into the building, creating an enormous fireball.

We reached the staging area across the street, and again I saw Bill, Lynn, and Fitz. Pete was there, too. "Where's the mayor?" I asked, and someone said he had already taken off. *Great.* Not wanting to chase him down, I decided to wait there until I got another directive on his location.

While there, the mayor had talked to Pete about the situation, and Pete had told him, "I think we can save everybody below the fire." As the mayor left, he grabbed Pete's hand and told him, "Good luck. God bless you."

From outside, I got a chance to take in the whole scene, and everything seemed much scarier. Eerie sirens wailed from every direction. Rigs and ambulances and cars zoomed by in an unending parade. There were people everywhere, many of them panicky, running up and down West Street. There was a strong sense of desperation in the air. Platoons of firefighters were lined up, looking up with trepidation at the top of the buildings. I followed their eyes and saw, for the first time, how big the hole in the north tower was, the bright-orange flames, the bodies and debris falling.

It all made me feel helpless. We had two insane, roaring fires going in two of the tallest buildings in the world. *How the hell are we going to handle this?* I kept wondering.

After about ten minutes I saw the deputy director of the Office of Emergency Management, John Odematt, walking toward me. I knew why he was coming, but I couldn't escape.

"The mayor wants you," he said. "He's at Park Place and Broadway. They're going to do a press briefing. He wants to get on the air as soon as possible."

"I don't want to do press. I need to be here." The mayor was blocks away, while my guys were busy right in front of me.

"He wants to be briefed *now*," Odematt said.

Annoyed, I started following him north, with my aides Ray and John in tow.

By the time we reached Park Place, though, the mayor had moved on again. We were growing frustrated. Someone suggested he might be at the Office of Emergency Management's operations center inside 7 World Trade Center, so we turned back to try there. But as soon as we entered the building, a guard in the lobby ordered us back out.

"This building has been evacuated," he said.

"Even the command center?" I asked. "We're looking for the mayor. Isn't he up there?"

"OEM, the mayor, they're all gone."

How ridiculous, I thought. *We've got a thirteen-million-dollar command center and we can't even use it.* The decision to evacuate the building turned out to be smart, but at the moment it just seemed silly to be walking around in circles looking for the mayor while two blocks away hundreds of firemen were running into these colossal buildings in the biggest disaster of my lifetime. I wanted to be with my guys.

"What, are we gonna walk around all day?" I blurted out in frustration.

We had just decided to go up toward City Hall and see if he was there when we heard a massive crack, followed by a vibrating rumble. Within seconds it grew louder and louder and louder until it seemed to swallow every other sound.

Then we saw a black cloud rolling toward us like a heavy blanket.

4

THE WHOLE TOWER CAME DOWN

I didn't know that the 110-story south tower of the mighty World Trade Center had folded in on itself and plummeted to earth. I wasn't even capable of imagining such a thing.

All I knew at that instant was that an enormous ball of dust and grit and blackness was heading right for us. It was 9:59 A.M., little more than an hour since the first plane hit.

Instinctively I ran through a doorway on my left and found myself in the lobby of an unfamiliar office building. Ray and John had run to the right, into a building across the street.

Through the revolving doors, I saw the cloud move down the street like a living thing that had no regard for what it encountered. It engulfed the building, hitting with an all-encompassing whoosh that enveloped us like a sandstorm. Whirling chunks of debris flew by, reminding me of the heavy volcanic dust I had once seen pouring off Mount Saint Helens on the news. It was as black as night out there.

I brushed myself off and found I was among a group of strangers who were looking in horror at the doorway

I'd come through. The cloud just kept coming and coming, stuff just billowing by the door.

I felt lost. In this lobby, blocks from the scene, with no colleagues around, I knew in an instant that whatever had happened, we had just lost a lot of firefighters, and probably hundreds of civilians, too. But I couldn't guess how many. All I knew for certain was that the situation was now wildly out of control, like nothing I'd ever known or seen before, and that suddenly there were no limits to how bad this could get.

Even at the worst fires or disasters, firefighters are accustomed to taking control of a scene, sometimes after a fierce battle, to be sure, but setting its boundaries, containing the damages and injuries, finding a way to corner our enemy. This one, though, was mutating and multiplying and outrunning us. A heavy, sickly feeling welled up in my chest, the same one I had experienced before whenever we had lost men.

Then someone said, "The whole tower came down."

I didn't, or couldn't, quite believe it. Maybe I couldn't get my mind around the possibility that one of those enormous, powerful, giant icons punctuating the sky could be destroyed just like that. Maybe I just didn't want to accept that our losses could be so high.

Whatever the reason, I didn't have time to dwell on it. As soon as the cloud seemed to have passed, I forced myself back outside, and through the murky darkness heard Ray and John calling for me. "I'm over here," I shouted, and like children playing blind man's bluff we kept calling until we found each other.

Both men were as dust-covered and filthy as I was. John looked especially shell-shocked. I told him what I'd heard, and he said he wanted to go back to the scene to see what had happened. We said good-bye and I wished him luck and asked him to stay in radio contact. Ray and I went on to find the mayor and figure out what the hell was happening.

Trudging slowly north, we found ourselves moving through a surreal, postapocalyptic landscape. Ash and dust coated everything in sight. Papers and debris fluttered down around us as quietly as snowflakes. The street seemed absolutely dead. As we walked on, though, crust-covered people started crawling out from underneath cars and walking out of doorways, like mole people coming to the surface of the earth in a science-fiction movie.

Ray frantically worked the radio and cell phone, trying to rouse somebody but having no luck. We didn't know it then, but the collapses had disrupted phone traffic, even cell phones, in the immediate area, and nothing was coming up on the radio. All our communications systems, which connected firefighters like arteries and veins, would be disrupted for days, splintering us into isolated pockets.

Finally we saw someone from the mayor's security detail approaching us, a big guy who told us to come around the corner. It turned out we hadn't been too far from the mayor when the cloud hit. There he was, with a clutch of aides—Chief of Staff Tony Carbonetti, Police Commissioner Bernie Kerik, Deputy Mayor Joe Lhota, spokeswoman Sunny Mindel. They seemed shaken but okay. They had ducked into another building nearby when the cloud came and spent a few frantic minutes thinking they were trapped and trying to find a way out. A couple of people had wrapped masks around their mouths and faces to help them breathe.

The boss started talking to me just as if we were having a quick briefing in the hallway at City Hall.

"How many guys were in there?" he asked.

"I'm not sure," I said. "Dozens, maybe hundreds."

"How bad do you think it is?" he asked me.

"Well, it's really bad if the whole tower came down. It's really bad." I didn't know what else to say, and at the moment there wasn't anything else, really. We knew so little. It all still seemed impossible, a nightmare. I kept shoving aside the big knot of emotion that was trying to seize control of my body.

The mayor, though, tried to take charge of the situation. "Come on!" he called out to all of us. "We need to find an operations center." The question was where to go. City Hall was out; its phones were down, and Bernie was saying it might be a target anyway. We knew we had to move north, away from the disaster. So as we debated where to go, the mayor started leading us up Church Street, like the Pied Piper.

All along Church Street, hundreds of people were making the same trek north, on the sidewalks and in the street. It was an unbelievable scene. Light had returned, but gritty dust hung in the air. Many people held handkerchiefs and scarves over their mouths or wrapped their jackets around their heads. Some were covered in dust and crust. A lot of them seemed like zombies, but some recognized the mayor, and called out encouraging words like "Go get 'em, Giuliani!" The mayor, looking a little pained, would call out, "Keep going! Go north!" He literally grabbed a couple of upset people we encountered, put his arms around them, and said, "Careful, take it easy, just keep walking!" Every now and then he would talk to the half-dozen reporters that had found us and attached themselves to our group, advising everyone in the area to head north, and everyone else in the city to stay home.

The mayor had already spoken to the White House and knew that this was, indeed, terrorism. At 9:41 A.M., eighteen minutes before the south tower came down, a third hijacked plane, American Airlines Flight 77, had struck the Pentagon. At 10 A.M., just as we were starting our march, another one, United Airlines Flight 93, had crashed in a field in Shanksville, Pennsylvania. More planes were still unaccounted for.

We had entered uncharted territory. I think now I must have been in shock, or at least in a daze. I was functioning, answering questions, and giving advice. But I was a little out of it, too, focused only on our little group.

At 10:28, as I was talking to the mayor, there was another rumble, this time farther behind us, and Ray grabbed me. "The north tower just came down," he said.

"What the hell are you talking about?"

"The tower just fell. I saw it."

I looked back, and all I saw was another huge cloud of debris. "What are you talking about?" I repeated.

At that moment, I couldn't quite process what Ray had just said.

My top priority, really my only one, was to get somewhere and find a phone and get the precise facts as soon as possible. During those terrible minutes, it never once occurred to me to call my wife, Rita, or any of my four kids, or anyone else. It never even occurred to me that they might wonder if I was inside the towers. I'm shocked now by how inconsiderate that was. But I was just so focused on the crisis at hand, maybe willfully blocking out as much emotion as possible, that all I was thinking, over and over, was *This is bad,* and I wanted to know how bad.

Bill Feehan and Fitz had been at the command center, at the top of the driveway, when the south tower had come down. Three or four dozen other people were there, too, including Pete Ganci.

According to Steve Mosiello, a fire marshal who was Pete's assistant and best friend, Pete looked up just as the tower started to rumble, as glass started to sprinkle down from the top like tinsel, and said, "What the hell's this?" Then, in a flash, everyone on the driveway ran down into the two garages below, followed by a blast of air and choking dust. A mad scramble began among everyone in there to find a back way out, through dust that stung their eyes and was hard to breathe and made them disoriented.

Fitz got separated from Bill in the havoc. But Steve said he emerged from a staircase in a garage on West Street, a little farther north, and he saw Pete and Bill there, among others. Bill was limping a little, and Steve went up and grabbed his right elbow to help him along.

"I don't need any help, Steve," Bill said, pulling it away. "Thank you anyway."

Pete ordered the command post and staging area moved farther north, away from the towers. All the firefighters were to go that way, too.

Then he and Bill turned to walk south, back toward the towers.

"Chief, where are you going?" Steve asked.

"Steve, I'm going to take a walk down there," Pete said.

Steve headed north to find the companies. A short time later, he received a radio call from Pete, telling him, "Steve, I want two of my best trucks." He must have seen something, maybe some injured people, that required special attention. He also described where he and Bill were waiting, south of the parking garage, near the corner of West and Liberty Streets.

"Okay, chief, I have the trucks coming," Steve told him. "I'll be there in a couple of minutes."

Then the north tower came down.

On Church Street, it was taking us a while to find a base of operations. We stopped first at the Tribeca Grand Hotel, but it had a soaring glass roof that would be hazardous if it were attacked, and besides, it seemed too public a setting. Finally, as we kept going north, I realized we were nearing Engine Company 24, the firehouse at Houston Street and Sixth Avenue. I told the mayor we could use the office there, set up desks on the apparatus floor where the rigs were normally parked, and bring in phone lines. He agreed, and we made our way in that direction.

My aide Ray Goldbach had to jimmy the door; the guys, of course, were out. We went straight to the office off the apparatus floor, usually occupied by the house watch, a firefighter who monitors incoming calls. The TV was on, replaying the scenes of disaster over and over. Everybody started grabbing phones to call family and colleagues.

The hard lines were working, but connections were still spotty. Everyone in the southern tip of Manhattan must have been calling everybody else at that moment. All our pagers started beeping, our cell phones chirruping, and cryptic snatches of frantic conversations were audible everywhere. Everyone was asking, "What happened?" "Who's alive?" Information from the scene, though, was very sketchy. Cell phones weren't working down there, Nextel phones were erratic, and we weren't getting anything on the handie-talkies. At that moment, the people in charge of the city knew as little as anyone.

After a few minutes it became clear to everyone that we didn't have enough space in the small office. The mayor took Bernie Kerik's suggestion that we go to the Police Academy, a former high school on East 20th Street that had been turned into a training center. The mayor made a few remarks to reporters in front of the firehouse, repeating his admonition to go north and get away from southern Manhattan; then we hopped into cars and drove to our new headquarters in a caravan. I got a ride from another of my drivers, Danny Lynch, who had been off duty that day but had come in to help, going first to the site, where he ran into John, then up to me.

The academy was ringed by police officers from the Emergency Services Unit, holding machine guns in a threatening stance.

Inside, we went to a huge conference room for an emergency meeting on what we knew and what we could do about it. The atmosphere was somber. By now, of course, we all knew that the towers had come completely down and that the scene was absolute chaos.

With single-mindedness the mayor immediately launched into a discussion. He seemed not too different from the man for whom I had worked for more than five years—driven, intense, wanting answers now. I could see a little extra strain on his face, and occasionally the hint of a tear in the corner of his eye, but from the first minutes there he mostly just calmly but forcefully kept pushing everyone around him for information and peppering us with questions. He seemed determined to impose some order on the situation.

We had more questions than answers at that point, starting with how many people were gone and leading on to when the National Guard should come in, what the likelihood of other attacks was, how stable the buildings around the Trade Center were, and how many trucks and men we needed for the rescue. We assumed there were hundreds, maybe thousands, trapped. Fires raged all around the site. We were talking to Washington, the state offices, and federal agencies and looking for anyone who was or had been down at the scene.

As for me, I needed help. The fire department normally took pride in its own expertise and capabilities and hated to accept resources or assistance from other agencies. But as offers poured in, from the military, from the Federal Emergency Management Agency, from other departments, I said yes to every one.

I hated to do it, but at that moment we were in complete disarray. Scattered reports and rumors of the destruction were ricocheting around the department, and I was having trouble pinning them down. When I called headquarters in downtown Brooklyn, I could hear people screaming in the background. The secretaries were hysterical, crying as they told me they hadn't heard from any of the officials who had gone down there. So many of our top people had rushed to the scene that simply tracking down who had actually responded to the alarms would end up taking hours. Wives and off-duty firefighters and reporters were barraging the offices with calls.

As word got around that we were at the academy, aides started to make their way to us to help. During one early meeting, I looked up and saw Lynn Tierney coming through the doorway toward me. Like everyone, she was covered with ash and flustered looking, having made her way from the site to the academy.

"You been down there?" I whispered.

"Yeah."

"What do you know?"

Lynn knelt down next to me. She'd briefed me many times this same way. "I have to talk to you," she said. "It's bad."

Instantly I could see in her face that I didn't want to hear what she had to say. "What is it?"

She sighed. "Father Judge is dead," she whispered into my ear. "They recovered his body."

The words cut me right to my core. For the first time that day, tears welled up in my eyes. One of my closest friends, a man I had come to love as much as any I knew, whom I had just seen across the lobby of a mighty building that no longer stood, was quite suddenly gone. We were up against something we'd never seen, something that just got worse and worse.

There was more, she said. Pete Ganci and Bill Feehan were missing.

I bent over for a minute and rubbed my eyes. Bill *and* Pete missing? The top guys in the department? How could it be? How were we going to handle this? How bad would it get?

"Are you sure about all this?"

"Yes."

I waited, in a daze, for the meeting to finish.

When the room had mostly emptied out, I went over to the mayor and knelt down, just as Lynn had with me.

"Boss," I said in a low voice, "we lost Father Judge. They've found his body."

The mayor reeled back in his seat as if he'd been dealt a body blow. He closed his eyes.

The tears came back to my eyes, and again I put my head down in my hand for a minute. Then I told the mayor the rest.

5

FROM BOX CUTTERS
TO ALL THIS

It was horrible, all of it, not just the feelings but the demands of the task we now faced.

Normally, the death of Father Judge alone would have brought everything to a screeching halt, and should have. We would have cried, and made an announcement on the fire department radio, and started to plan a funeral, and thought to ourselves, *How can we go on today without Father Judge?*

Now, though, it was just one tiny part of this enormous catastrophe. We couldn't think too much about any one aspect of it, because the whole was so great.

Throughout my thirty-one-year career, I had gotten used to the idea that my enemy, fire, was tenacious and impossible to kill but could be beaten. But this, this was something new. Once I knew the towers really had fallen, once I started hearing names like Father Judge and Bill Feehan, I began to feel in a way I never had before: *It's over. We had a battle, and we lost. We never really got a chance to fight.* Everything that happened afterward seemed like a different day.

Nothing better epitomized the new situation we were

in than the reports we started getting about 7 World Trade Center, the 44-story building that stood across the plaza from the two towers and that had housed the Emergency Operations Center. It had been set afire by the collapses, and a raging fire had quickly developed, leaving several floors fully engulfed. Looking at our TV sets, we could see orange flames shooting out of its sides through the spaces that once had been windows.

Yet *no one was going near it*. The chiefs who had taken charge at the site had determined immediately that given the damage caused by the collapses, it was just too dangerous in that unstable area and that the odds of it collapsing and killing more men were too great on a day when we couldn't bear to lose anyone else. So they had ordered the men to keep back and let it burn.

They were right to do that. It was the only safe course. But a 44-story building? We were letting a 44-story building burn down without lifting a finger to stop it? Things like that just didn't happen in New York City. In London during the war, maybe, or Berlin. But not in New York. It couldn't happen here.

Thoughts of all these things, the sorrow and the failure and the frustration, blipped across my brain all day, but I tried not to give them free rein. There were moments when I wanted to fall apart, but the mayor spurred us on, and things kept happening and events swept us along.

Just two minutes after I'd talked to the mayor about Father Judge and Bill and Pete, for instance, Joe Hoffman, the head of operations for the Metropolitan Transit Authority, walked in with a grave expression and said he had reports that the Rector Street subway station had collapsed. The mayor just shook his head, taking it in and going on to the next thing.

At some point, too, in those early hours, we heard from the White House that all this had started when the terrorists hijacked the planes with simple box cutters. When I heard that, I thought, *God, how horrifyingly simple. From box cutters to all this.*

In between our staff meetings, I was able during those first hours to put together a small makeshift staff of assistants, who were critical to our efforts since I had to stay with the mayor. Besides Lynn, Ray Goldbach, John, and Danny, more people appeared, from the office and from their homes, to help. Another of my drivers, Sal Losciuto, came. So did my younger brother Roddy and my older son, Marc, both of whom are firefighters. Roddy was also one of my regular drivers, while Marc was on medical leave with a fractured elbow, so I knew neither was likely to be at the towers. Still, I was relieved to see them and glad to see for myself that they were all right. It was a day when every personal assurance helped.

Between meetings, in rushed corridor conversations, I asked them for computers and phone lines and radios. I sent some down to the site to deliver messages and gather information. I threw questions at them: "How many lost?" "Have you heard from Pete?" "What do they need?" "Who was working?"

And repeatedly, "Did anyone find Bill?"

Information was so poor that I frequently lost my temper and unloaded on them. "What the hell are you guys doing?" I'd demand. "Why can't I get this info?" I didn't quite understand why cell phones weren't working, why the radios were so bad. Hours were passing by and information was still sketchy and it was all so damn frustrating.

For some time, we couldn't even figure out how many men we had lost. Some fire marshals at headquarters had started calling firehouses, and a roll call was being attempted down at the site, but compiling a list would take some time. Still, we needed to try to get a handle on it for identification purposes and the briefings we were giving the press.

We all knew the tally would be high, but I was certain it would be beyond even the numbers being bandied about. The planes had struck just as the shift changed, which meant more guys would be at the firehouses, drinking coffee, talking about fires. Our guys loved what they did so much that I knew many would have climbed aboard the trucks and gone along, even though they were off duty. They wouldn't have wanted to miss a job this big.

At one point the mayor asked me from across the table, "What do you think the number is? A hundred?"

I stuck my thumb up and pointed, indicating he was too low.

"One fifty?"

I kept pointing.

"You don't think it's two hundred?"

I shook my head. "More."

"Over two hundred?"

"Over two fifty, probably closer to three hundred. Could be higher than that."

"It can't be that high. It can't be." He shook his head. No one else believed me either.

We settled on "more than two hundred" for the first press briefing. We knew that number couldn't be too high. But I knew it was still way too low.

Even as we tried to nail it down, we found ourselves surrounded with painful reminders that this was about much more than just the numbers.

Early in the afternoon, after a trip down to the site, one of my drivers brought Steve Mosiello back to the academy. He had asked to see me. Steve was an absolute mess, caked in ash and very distraught.

"I think Pete's dead," he said.

"You're thinking the worst, Steve," I said. "Maybe he's okay."

"I'm pretty sure," he said, his eyes filling with tears. He kept saying that we needed to search, that it would be dark soon and we had to have lights down there so we could keep looking. I told him we were working on getting lights and heavy equipment in and starting a rescue.

He just looked straight ahead. "Commissioner," he said, "I cannot go home without his body."

Even harder for me was seeing Beth Petrone, the pretty, spirited, and funny brunette who was a personal assistant to the mayor. Beth was married to one of our finest young captains, Terry Hatton, a ramrod-straight leader of the elite Rescue 1. I knew Terry well, had known him since he was a kid, since his family lived only two doors down from mine in Rockville Centre.

The first time I saw Beth in the hallway at the academy, I asked, "Was Terry working?"

"Yes," she said, with deep sadness. "He's gone."

"You don't know that," I said, not quite believing it. "You know Terry. He's fine."

"He's gone," she repeated, and my heart just fell.

Beth told me later that she had been standing outside City Hall during the evacuation, when the first tower fell. She said later that at that instant she felt a connection inside her sever, and she fell to the ground, clutching at the dirt, certain in an instant that Terry had been killed and was now part of the same dust running through her fingers.

Upset as she was, though, she had refused to go home. She had made her way to the academy to help the mayor, had kept going, somehow, like everyone else.

As the hours passed, Beth still hadn't heard from him. When people who had been down to the site came to brief me, she begged to sit in, saying she wanted to know what was happening down there and promising that she wouldn't show any reaction.

But she didn't have to. When I bumped into her in the hallway, or looked at her across the conference table, I saw grief etching itself on her face. Every time, the sight nearly made me break down.

6

THIS IS THE
TASTE OF DEATH

It wasn't until midafternoon, around 2:30 P.M., that I finally had the chance to return to what had been the World Trade Center.

With my brother Roddy and son Marc, I hopped into my car and made my way south through the now abandoned area of lower Manhattan. It was a city utterly transformed. The usually bustling streets were almost ghostly. Paper and debris were spread about for blocks. We could drive only as far south as City Hall Park, still a few blocks away, where a staging area had been set up; the rest of the area was blocked off to all but emergency vehicles.

As soon as I stepped out of my car, two fire marshals walked up to me and said, "Commissioner, you need protection. We're assigned to you." I had never had security in my life.

"Okay. Come on." They fell in behind me, walking toward the site.

We had gone only a short way down Murray Street, tromping through ankle-deep paper and ash, when my cell phone rang. The noise startled us. We had thought all cell phones in the area were out.

On the other end was Ray Goldbach. He was down at the scene.

His voice sounded a little shaky. "Tom, they found Bill," he said. "They think Pete is right next to him." The two were lying beneath rubble near the corner of Liberty and West Streets, where Pete had radioed Steve Mosiello to meet them.

The news was expected, but still devastating. Without responding to Ray, I handed the phone to Roddy. "Confirm that," I told him, choking a little as I spoke. He lingered behind me, speaking to Ray, while I wandered away. I stood alone for a minute on the empty street and put my head down. *Bill and Pete are really gone.* Other than Roddy's voice, it was absolutely silent around us, as if we were walking through a city that had just been buried in a volcano.

After a minute or two, I was ready to go on. I told Roddy to call Lynn, who was with the mayor, and tell her what had happened so she could let him know. Then I started walking.

With Pete gone, Dan Nigro was our acting chief of department. He had taken charge of the site, assisted by Frank Cruthers and Frank Fellini, two able chiefs who had been off duty and come in from their homes to help out. When Chief Cruthers arrived, Chief Nigro and Chief Albert J. Turi told him, "Frank, you're going to have to take charge of this. I don't think either of us is in any condition to do things right now."

Chiefs Cruthers and Fellini were able to help bring some order to the scene. But it had been chaotic at first. So many leaders were lost that fire companies arriving at the site had a hard time in the first minutes finding senior commanders to direct them. The debris had created barriers, too, that impeded the search.

One of the first things Chief Nigro had done was establish a new command post at Stuyvesant High School, a few blocks north of the towers, where men and trucks were being told to gather. That was where we headed.

After we reached the high school, we turned and started walking south, toward where the towers had been. We made our way through a crowd of several hundred restless firefighters, fresh men who had arrived to help with the rescue. With 7 World Trade Center burning, the chiefs were holding the men back for their own safety, and many were grumbling about it. "Can you believe this?" I heard someone say. And: "It could take days for that building to come down." "Why won't they let us in there?"

Suddenly, as we made our way through the men, there we were, at the edge of disaster. Nothing could have prepared me for what I saw.

We were standing on West Street looking south toward the area where the towers had stood. It was an alien landscape. Looking up in the expectation of seeing the towers, I completely lost my bearings for a minute.

From where we stood, I could only see partway south. The pedestrian walkway that had once crossed West Street, connecting the north tower to the World Financial Center, had fallen, blocking the road and our view of some of the worst damage. The walkway was to prove the biggest impediment in those first days, preventing us from rolling any cranes or trucks or other large vehicles into the heart of the site as long as it blocked the way.

But what I could see on this side of the bridge was horrifying and incomprehensible enough. Mountains of rubble seemed to be everywhere, some of them eighty feet high. Two-ton beams and massive pieces of twisted steel were scattered about. In the distance, I could see the tall, skeletal spires that had once stood over the doorway of the south tower framed starkly against the sky, like a tree stripped of all its leaves. Up and down West Street were crushed rigs and ambulances. Streams of smoke rose from the ruins, creating a gray, nasty fog that hovered over the site.

A pungent, acrid taste filled the air, and I thought, *This is the taste of death*.

Around the periphery, cars were burning everywhere, their alarms screeching, their tires occasionally popping. It was the only loud noise in an eerily quiet landscape.

The debris dwarfed, practically consumed, all the people in the area. It seemed so still, so dead, that it took a minute for my eyes to adjust and pick out the tiny people moving against that backdrop. The only things I had seen to compare with these piles were pictures of Berlin in 1945.

There weren't that many men in this area, which was close to the still burning 7 World Trade Center. Those who were there were dust-covered and seemed dazed. Many had been right there when the buildings came down, had dived under trucks and covered civilians with their bodies and choked as the cloud overtook them and imagined that they were about to die. Some had rescued colleagues who were trapped by rubble or inside burning cars in the minutes immediately after the collapses.

We had taken only a few steps when one emerged and started walking toward us. I saw that it was Steve Mosiello. After seeing me, he had returned to the site to help dig for Pete and Bill.

As he neared us, I could see he was crying and holding out a crumpled helmet that I recognized as Pete Ganci's. He had just come from the area where they had found the bodies.

"This is all that's left of him," he said, his face twisted in grief. I started crying as we fell into each other's arms. "It's just not right," he said. "He's my best friend."

"I know," I said. "I know."

After a minute Steve pulled back abruptly. "I have to go. I have to go out and tell his family." He walked off sadly, clutching the helmet tightly.

As we went on I recognized a few other familiar faces in the crowd massed along the outskirts, waiting for the okay to come in to begin digging. Roddy pointed out an older, almost bald man with a sad face, who was waving us over. I recognized him as Jimmy Boyle, the former president of the firefighters' union and one of my first mentors when I went to work for the union in 1983, beginning a long involvement that laid the groundwork for my current post as commissioner.

I loved Jimmy, but I didn't want to talk to him just then. There was more to see, more information to get. I thought that Jimmy, who like any good union man always had ideas about how things should be done, would distract me from the task at hand.

So, a little dismissively, I muttered, "I don't want to see him."

Then Roddy said, "His son is missing."

I couldn't believe it. Jimmy wasn't there to question. He was just waiting to look for his boy. *His boy.*

I walked over to Jimmy and threw my arms around him. "I'm so sorry," I said. Until that moment it hadn't yet occurred to me that beyond all the names I recog-

nized immediately, there would be so many men who
had lost sons and brothers and fathers. For days afterward I would be running into old friends like Jimmy
who would say, "My son is in there," or "I'm looking
for my brother," and each time it would feel like *my* son,
my brother in there.

A little farther south I met Chief Cruthers, and he
rounded out the details of what I had already heard.
Many of the chiefs who had been there that morning
were missing. Among them was Ray Downey, the head
of our special operations. His deputy and heir, Charlie
Kasper, was also unaccounted for. No one could find
Donald Burns, one of our most knowledgeable and experienced chiefs, either. He had been sent to take charge
of the operation at the south tower after it had been
struck, and hadn't been heard from since it went down.

The chiefs expected 7 World Trade Center to fall im-
minently, but couldn't predict when. They weren't too
worried about the other fires burning on the periphery.
So far, the rescue workers still functioning hadn't found
too many wounded—some burn victims and gashes, but
not as many as had been expected. They hoped that once
7 World Trade collapsed we could get a major search effort going and find the wounded inside.

After the briefing, I told Roddy I wanted to see what
lay on the other side of that pedestrian bridge. To get
there, we had to walk back north, then west to the Hudson River and south around the World Financial Center.
We would reemerge on West Street, but much farther
south, on the other side of the bridge, and could walk
back up to Liberty Street, to the corner closest to both
towers. It was a good ten-minute hike.

When we reached Liberty, again I got hit by the scale

of the disaster as if by a sledgehammer. Things looked even worse there, if that was possible. I had thought I was prepared. But being in the wreckage on that first day was like walking to the edge of the Grand Canyon for the first time, as I had on a family vacation once. I was stunned by just how broad and deep that massive gouge Nature had made in the earth was, even though I had seen it on TV many times.

Where we stood, the piles of wreckage dwarfed everything in sight. Thirteen hundred feet of tower had been reduced to compact mounds of destruction eighty feet high. Some people had gotten to work down there, though there wasn't much they could do but forage around in the rubble. Some had formed the first "bucket brigade," a long line of people sprawled across one of the piles, scooping debris out with five-gallon buckets and passing them along to be dumped on the periphery. Most of them wore catatonic expressions and moved robotically. They looked like ants next to all that steel and rubble, their effort seeming futile in that vast wasteland. I thought of old movies I had seen depicting ancient slaves building the pyramids in Egypt.

As I walked the area, I thought of other building collapses I had seen in my career, and I noticed something weird that made the scene even more chilling to me: Perverse as it seemed, I realized there was *less* wreckage than there should have been. There were no phones, no chairs, no computers, no desks, none of the implements and decorations that I knew must have filled all the offices and lives up there. The more I looked around, the more I saw that there was almost nothing but steel and plaster and other building materials.

It was as if all traces of the people who had arrived for

work there just a few hours before had vanished from the earth entirely.

Not everything I saw was so spirit-crushing. At one point I looked up on the pile and saw another face I recognized: that of a chief with whom I had had a few run-ins in the past, some of them real shouting matches. I knew he had always thought I was a dictator, and I had always thought he was a lousy manager who couldn't make tough decisions.

But I saw that, even though he had been on medical leave, not even working when the towers fell that morning, he had put on his uniform and come in and climbed on the pile and started directing men and lifting debris and doing his damnedest to try and help his brothers. *Look at that guy,* I thought to myself. *Just look at him. This is what our job is all about.*

7

COULD ANYONE REALLY
BE ALIVE IN THERE?

I returned to the academy feeling even more drained. The weight of this thing was growing by the minute. At times, as we headed into late afternoon, and the depth of our losses became clearer, I doubted whether I could keep going.

I hid my doubts from everyone else. But at one point I stole away from the conference room and ducked, alone, into an isolated cubicle. For five minutes, I let myself go and cried.

I had to stay focused, though. Whenever I looked at the mayor, or passed Beth in the hallway, or thought of Jimmy Boyle and the other men who were waiting to look for their loved ones, who were counting on me and the rest of the department and the city to help them, I found the strength to keep going. I shook off my tears and returned to my desk.

By then, early drafts of a list of the missing were making the rounds, the names scrawled on a yellow legal pad. It was still an incomplete jumble, giving only whatever details were known, sometimes just listing the units that had been working. We couldn't yet account for the many off-duty firefighters who had simply raced to the scene after watching it all on TV.

But it was heartbreaking enough as it was. Scanning it, I saw name after name I knew: friends, sons of friends, guys I had helped place in a house, guys I had known in the union, at my old firehouse, from virtually every stage of my career. Every house on the list connoted something different to me. As commissioner, for instance, I had created five squads, elite units comprised of some of our most aggressive and highly trained firefighters. They were designed to back up firefighters with less training and experience. The list told me that they had been absolutely decimated.

It is the nature of our fire department, of our longstanding philosophy of aggressively attacking fires, that many of our leaders and many of the best, most able firefighters were the ones who were going to be lost. The fire department is the only place I know where the higher up a man moves, the greater the chance that he will place himself at risk. The best, most enthusiastic firefighters willingly expose themselves to the highest level of danger.

But I still kept thinking they shouldn't all have been down there.

I knew that there was probably no procedural change that could have kept many of our men from going to the scene. That's how dedicated they were. They stood ready to put everything on the line for the city and their brothers.

But it was unbelievably frustrating and maddening to see evidence start to pour in of what we had lost and feel unable to stop or at least contain it somehow. "What are we gonna do?" I kept asking the people around me, not expecting an answer.

I still harbored hopes that at least some men on that list would be found alive. Miraculously, rescuers had already pulled a group of six firefighters and one woman they had been trying to help from a collapsed stairwell. Though they were inside the towers, somehow they had survived the disaster, and I was sure others had, too.

Yet it was impossible not to be haunted by the devastation I had seen down there. I didn't want to believe it, but I privately wondered, *Could anyone really be alive in there?*

At about 4:30 P.M., my son Marc pulled me aside and thrust a phone into my hand. He had called my wife, Rita, for me. We hadn't spoken yet that day, though Ray Goldbach and Marc had talked to her several times to reassure her I was all right.

Rita had gone out to Rockville Centre to stay with Marc's wife, Lorette, who was eight months pregnant. They live in our old house, which we had left when I became commissioner and we moved into a Manhattan apartment. Ray had called her soon after the attacks to tell her I was safe, but even out in Rockville Centre she had been dealing with the ripple effects of the attacks. Outside on the sidewalk she had run into Terry Hatton's mother, Grace, as she left her house two doors away. Grace said she was going to Saint Agnes Church to pray, and that her husband, Kenny, a retired deputy fire chief, was inside going crazy. She kept saying, "Terry's gone, Terry's gone." A short time later, the nephew of Marc's best friend had come by the house to alert the family that his father, a broker at Cantor Fitzgerald, was missing. He wanted to know if Marc might have any information.

When I put the phone to my ear, I heard Rita say hello and ask me how I was. Then it all started pouring out.

"We lost Father Judge, we lost Feehan, we lost Ganci," I said. "You are not going to believe it. We lost Terry."

"What? What?" Rita thought I meant that they were lost, not dead. She couldn't imagine that all those people were dead.

"We lost Ray Downey. We lost Donald Burns." I kept listing names, not even sure of what I was saying.

"How are you?" she said.

"I don't know. I'm okay."

"I'm not sure I can get home tonight, into the city," she said. "All the bridges are shut down. The city is emptying out."

"Don't come home," I said. "Stay there. I don't even know when I'll be going home."

Then Marc told me I was needed, and it was time to go. Rita and I said good-bye and I hung up, without even thinking to tell her how much I love her.

A little later I got a call from Ray Goldbach, who was still at the scene with Roddy, waiting as the rescuers unearthed Bill's and Pete's bodies. It had taken them several hours to dig down, but Ray said they were now close. Two ambulances were waiting outside the World Financial Center to carry them to the morgue.

"Put them on the same ambulance," I told Ray. Bill and Pete had been good friends, as well as the best that the New York City Fire Department had to offer. I was awed by the courage they had shown, sending everyone north, away from the towers, while they went south, into the heart of danger.

Now, I thought, they deserved to take their last ride together.

* * *

Around 5:30 P.M., just as the sun started to drop below the horizon, 7 World Trade Center finally crashed to earth. The destruction of a 44-story building was now only the third-worst collapse in recent memory, and a mere footnote to the disaster.

But it enabled us to begin the rescue in earnest. Once the dust cleared a little, the chiefs allowed the hundreds of impatient firefighters gathered north of the site to go at the pile.

Without heavy equipment, and with our over-whelmed chiefs only beginning to organize some structure, firefighters and dozens of volunteers simply swarmed over the wreckage. Many joined the lines removing debris bucket by bucket. Others scrambled in and around the rubble, diving into old elevator shafts and balancing precariously on beams, sometimes taking huge risks as they searched for signs of life. The air was thick and hard to breathe. We were short of phones, radios, respirators, shovels—virtually any piece of equipment you could name.

At the Police Academy, we were gathering records on the buildings and trying to assess what we were likely to face down there. The news wasn't good. We had no way of knowing yet how bad the damage was underneath all that rubble. But right under the towers, seven stories deep, was embedded a huge manmade structure called "the bathtub" that was the foundation of the towers and designed to prevent the Hudson River from rushing in and flooding the area. The engineers worried that one long retaining wall might have been cracked, even badly damaged. Beyond that there were other questions, like what would happen if the giant tanks of freon gas, used for air conditioning, that sat underneath the towers were pierced. Some engineers thought they could release poisonous gas.

But we didn't know what else we could do but keep digging as we worked on our plans. Even now, the men down there wanted to put themselves on the line to save lives.

As dusk settled down on this changed world, and one meeting blended into another, and we heard more and more bad news, that pile, and those men, became the focus of my life. I paid little attention to reports of what was happening elsewhere, of the attack on the Pentagon, of the plane crash in Pennsylvania, or the sorrow and rage being registered across the country, or the talk of an organization called Al Qaeda and a man named Osama bin Laden. It meant nothing to me. There was no room inside.

I was simply consumed with the desire to get inside that pile.

8

WILL DETERMINATION BE ENOUGH?

Late that night, after one last press conference, the one where I was asked how I felt about all this, I returned to the site and walked among the men for several hours.

It seemed even bleaker in the dark, a ghostly wasteland of death. FBI and ATF (Alcohol, Tobacco, and Firearms) agents, wearing goggles and helmets, stalked about everywhere, toting machine guns and wearing respirators, like some futuristic soldiers.

We had gotten a few klieg lights trucked in, but not nearly enough. In some areas the only light came from the moon overhead and the orange fires that still burned in the buildings and cars on the periphery. They cast a haunting, primitive glow on the smoky ruins, intersecting the plumes of smoke that snaked up from the depths.

There were many more men down there than when I had first visited, but a lot were frustrated and grieving and angry that they couldn't do more, that there didn't seem to be more to do. Many just scuttled in and out of the piles, looking for a sign of someone they could help.

But already the chiefs were starting to get some work organized. Trucks rolled around on the outskirts, accepting the first piles of rubble from the bucket brigade and rolling off to the Dumpster. Their rumbling engines made the area sound like a construction site. Ironworkers had come and started to attack the first of the thick, heavy steel beams that were everywhere.

Like a slap, I noticed a couple of bins where workers were collecting the helmets and equipment of fallen firefighters.

Still, against the whole scarred and jagged landscape, we seemed to be making only the smallest of inroads. It was hard not to feel that the immense job ahead of us, not to mention the pain that would come with it, would be almost too much to bear.

"Are you all right?" I asked people as I roamed around. "How are you doing?" A few men came up and asked me the same, or gave me a hug. Like me, many of the men remained sooty and shabby from the collapses more than sixteen hours before.

At one part of the pile, I glanced down and saw a young captain I knew well, a short, dark, strong man in good shape and with a serious face. It was Joe Downey, one of Ray Downey's sons.

As I saw Joe searching, I realized that, although the mayor had named Ray at the news conference as one of the men who were gone, we still had not recovered his body. There was a chance, however small, that he was alive.

I went up to Joe and shook his hand. "I'm sorry, Joe," I said. "We don't have your father. We haven't found him. I feel terrible that we mentioned him."

I could see Joe was angry—not at me specifically, just angry. He had the look of a son who was certain his dad was okay.

"My father might be alive," he said. "Why would someone say he was dead? You got bad information."

"I don't know why. I don't know how. We have not confirmed that he's dead." I desperately wanted to believe that at any minute someone would dig a hole in the right place, see a glimpse of light, and suddenly, there they'd be, fifty or a hundred firefighters, hurt, scared, but alive, just waiting for their brothers to find them, and that Joe's father would be at the head of them.

"We're gonna find him," he said, determinedly.

"I know. I know." I shook his hand again. "You take care, Joe."

Everywhere I looked, I saw more men like him, grim-faced, determined, anguished, many of them familiar. As a longtime commissioner, former president of the fire-fighters' union, and firefighter before that, I figured I knew about as many people down there as anyone.

I tried to appear hopeful. But as I walked the perimeter of that site and saw just how big it was, how far the rubble stretched, I kept asking myself questions that I didn't know how to answer. *How long will this take us? Can we pull this off?*

In some ways it began to feel to me as if what had died that day was the entire fire department, the organization I had worked for and loved for thirty-one years. It was clear that this was not going to be something we ever would, or could, quite put behind us.

Somehow, of course, we would keep going. The strong and dedicated men around me, hurting though they were, were proof of that. I could see and feel their determination.

Standing at the edge of despair, though, I truly wondered, in those dark moments, whether determination was going to be enough. The road before us seemed long and impassable. Just then, I couldn't see the end of it. Everywhere I turned there was just too much death.

Over and over, I asked myself: *How in hell are we ever going to get through this?*

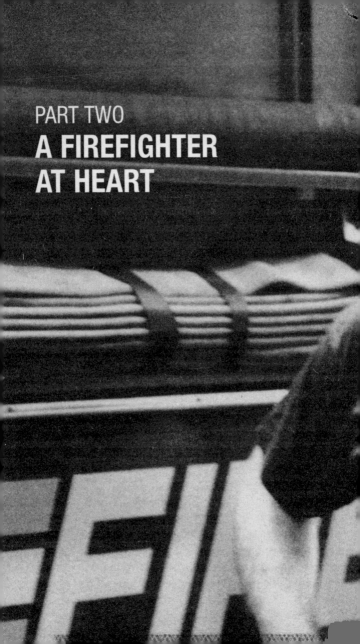

PART TWO
A FIREFIGHTER
AT HEART

9

TO THE FIREHOUSE DOOR

For me, it had all started on a sweltering summer day in early July of 1970, when I knocked politely on the front door of Ladder Company 42 in the South Bronx. A lean, strong, and largely clueless young man of twenty-four, I was reporting for duty as a probationary firefighter for the city of New York.

A tall, muscular brick of a man, clean-shaven and with a short haircut, came to the door. "Yeah?"

"Hi, Tom Von Essen," I said a little nervously, extending a hand. "I'm starting here today."

"Oh, Tom, hi," he said, growing more friendly. "Come on in. I'm Joe Daly. Lemme show you around."

Joe took me through a passage and up two flights of stairs to a room filled with lockers. "That one will be yours. You can dump your stuff there." Then we went to the back of the house and into a large, pine-paneled lounge. A handful of men sat drinking coffee and jabbering. A couple of them, I noticed, were enormous.

They quieted down as we walked in, though, and all eyes turned toward me.

"Guys, meet Tom Von Essen," Joe said. "Our new proby."

"The new guy, huh?" one said.

"Yeah." I tried to smile and stuck out my hand. "How you doing?"

They offered me some coffee and a seat in a raggedy old chair. They seemed friendly enough. But I was acutely self-conscious. My proby status was all too apparent. I had come dressed in my clean, pressed full-regulation uniform, after spending a long time fussing over my appearance in the mirror before I left that morning. But most of them wore dungarees with holes and tears, and work shirts spotted with dirt and oil stains. I just knew I looked like an idiot.

For a few minutes we made very awkward, polite conversation. I told them I was from Ozone Park, married. They told me their names, and I tried to memorize them.

Then I opened up slightly. "I feel a little silly," I admitted. "I'm all decked out here."

"Don't worry," someone said. "That won't last."

And suddenly the alarm sounded, and my unlikely career was under way.

Fire fighting had been far from my first career choice. It was just the job I ended up in after nearly screwing the rest of my life up.

Born in December 1945, just four months after the end of World War II, I grew up in Ozone Park, a working-class Queens neighborhood of compact wood-frame houses, narrow lawns, and middle-class aspirations.

We weren't an especially emotional family, but I knew I was loved by the attention my parents paid me and the structure they surrounded me with. My dad, Frederick, was a cop in the 79th Precinct, a clerk for the captain. He hammered into my head the importance of being absolutely honest, and he made clear his faith in higher education. A talented high school pitcher, he had been sent to St. John's University on a scholarship by the Brooklyn Dodgers, but had interrupted his studies to enlist in the army. When he came home and got married, he'd had to find a job, and never finished his studies. I think he'd always regretted that. My mom, Catherine, like all moms in our neighborhood, stayed home. Each day she made sure my homework was done, that I had clean clothes, and that she knew where I went after school.

Every Sunday we went to Nativity of the Blessed Virgin Mary Catholic Church, where the priests preached of the need to do my duty for God. I loved church as a child—the pageantry, the air of mystery, the sense of purpose and values. I attended mass every First Friday, joined the choir, and kept careful track of how many plenary indulgences I accumulated—hopefully enough to skip Purgatory and go straight to Heaven.

During the week, I went back to Nativity for school, where the nuns deeply impressed me with their self-discipline and devotion to the children and the poor. I got smacked with a few rulers, but most of them amazed me with their sense of calling and commitment.

At an early age I had already formulated an image of the kind of man I wanted to be: as self-sacrificing and committed as the nuns, and as honest as my father. I lay down strict standards for myself, in school and elsewhere. I aimed for, and usually got, straight As. I never smoked or got into any trouble. In my grammar school yearbook, I boldly wrote as my personal motto, "No steps backward."

From the time I was twelve or thirteen, I worked hard. First I had two paper routes and cut lawns. Then I became a delivery boy at a butcher shop. When I got older, I worked as a waiter and bartender in the neighborhood tavern, Tutie's.

At the playground, I threw myself into baseball and basketball, spending hours alone at the hoop honing my jump shot. I wasn't a natural athlete, and I lacked the killer instinct, but I worked hard and enjoyed the camaraderie of team sports. I loved the way team sports let you test yourself against others and against your own past performances. If you won, you got a great reward, but if not, it wasn't the end of the world—and you still got to push yourself.

For inspiration, I looked to stars like the Yankees' Mickey Mantle and Willis Reed of the Knicks. But more than their stats, what I admired was the fact that they played so well when *hurt*. That seemed like the height of manhood to me.

And I found role models in my own neighborhood, too. I played on baseball and basketball teams coached by Eddie Egan, the police detective who was the model for Popeye Doyle in *The French Connection*. While physically unimpressive, with a sloping potbelly and a tight, curly band of hair, Egan told incredible stories of sitting in dark basements for two days waiting to collar bad guys, and of fistfights in dingy dives. On his days off he went to bad neighborhoods and looked for trouble. Once he even showed up at a basketball game with some guy he'd just arrested. He cuffed him to the stands, came over to the bench to coach, and kept him there till the game was over.

Up through eighth grade, I did a great job of meeting my own standards. I finished as one of the top three students at Nativity. Under the Catholic school system, that qualified me to attend a scholarship school, Bishop Loughlin, where tuition was just $100, a fourth of the price of other Catholic high schools.

Loughlin was just the sort of place I had hoped to attend, as the next logical step in my upward progression. A tall, imposing edifice of gray stone in downtown Brooklyn, founded by the Christian Brothers a century earlier, it was a crown jewel in the Catholic school system. An impressive roster of past and future civic leaders had passed through its doors—including, a couple of classes ahead of me, a serious young man, a member of the Opera Club, named Rudy Giuliani. Our paths never crossed there.

It was also, unfortunately for me, much more demanding academically than anything I'd encountered before. The students there were the best the city had to offer, and were much more competitive than I had been used to at my little neighborhood school. The teachers assigned hours of homework in a range of subjects that were new to me, from Latin to geometry.

It wasn't long before I felt overwhelmed and frustrated and began to get my first Cs and Ds. In response, I cut back on my studying. The worse I did, the easier it got to make excuses instead of sitting down to engage the material. As the rotten grades piled up, I lied to myself about what was happening, footnoting my high standards with vows to do better on the *next* test and promises that *tomorrow* I'd get back to that term paper.

My parents seemed helpless, or unable, to intervene. Our family had grown, and I now had younger brothers and sisters. They absorbed all my mother's time and attention. My dad was away from home more, taking part-time jobs to pay the bills. I was out a lot, too, at games and work, and generally avoided them when I was home.

By the end of sophomore year, my grades were so bad that the school warned me there was no chance I'd finish in four years, though I could stay for a fifth if I wanted. But that wasn't for me. Two years away from college, and freedom, I wasn't going to take on a new burden. Of course, I was also privately embarrassed and chastened to be floundering after all the years of being told how smart I was.

Instead, I transferred to the public high school in my neighborhood, John Adams, figuring the workload would be easier and that everything would fall neatly into place. But that didn't happen. I couldn't pull it together. My future college career seemed suddenly in doubt. I was getting angry and frustrated with myself, but still I just wouldn't *study*.

One day I was sitting at a high school basketball game with my dad when he spotted a friend across the room and waved. We started walking over to greet him.

On the way, Dad leaned over and whispered, "Don't say anything about leaving Loughlin."

In an instant, I realized that he was so embarrassed about my flameout that he hadn't told any of his friends about it.

I didn't want to let him know it, but I felt crushed.

To be sure, there was one other *big* reason my grades plummeted when I reached high school. Her name was Rita.

Rita Scelza was a pretty, tomboyish brunette who lived only two and a half blocks away from me in a red-brick fortress. One of my two best friends, Lefty, lived right across the street from her.

I didn't get to know her, though, until we reached the eighth grade, and the girls' and boys' classes were combined into one. She made an immediate impression. The chemistry between us was instant, strong, and mutual.

Before long I was finding all sorts of reasons to be over at Lefty's house or, more specifically, outside his house, where I might have a chance to talk to his neighbor. Soon she and I were hanging out a fair amount, along with Lefty and my friend Mikey, who had a small crush on her himself. One warm summer night, Mikey and I even fell into a debate on her front porch over who should date her, and ended up flipping a coin for the rights. Standing on the line between childhood and adolescence, it was all childish fun, something we treated as just a game. But when I won, I was relieved and happy in a way I'd never known.

It became very serious very fast. I wanted to be with Rita all the time. Not just because I was a fourteen-year-old with raging hormones, an experimental nature, and a pretty girlfriend. We could spend hours fooling around, but we could also have fun just sitting and talking. Rita was a good listener and much more open than my folks.

We'd walk all around the neighborhood, past the hairdresser and the dentist and Donelson's Hardware Store and Tom's Drugstore on the main drag, Liberty Avenue. We'd go to the Liberty Bakery, where Rita was sent every day to buy buns, or to the fruit store to get lemon ices. We'd visit the bocce court where the older men of the neighborhood liked to gather, or walk over to the dairy farm that stood on Balsam Field. We'd go to a 25-cent movie or take the train into Manhattan to catch a show. With my job as a delivery boy and her large extended family, we ran into people we knew everywhere, and soon became fixed as a couple in their minds.

Neither of our families approved. My parents blamed Rita for my academic troubles. My mother looked down on her as an Italian from a less educated family. Rita's parents didn't like my German background and seemed to suspect that maybe I wasn't such a good kid.

Late one night, I went to Rita's house hoping to lure her outside for a conversation, and started tossing pebbles at her window. She slept right through it, but the noise woke her parents. They called the police to report a disturbance in their yard.

The next thing I knew, whirling sirens and blinking lights were coming down the street and I was scrambling across the roofs of the garages along the alley, making a run for it. I hadn't gotten far before a cop drew his gun and barked out, "Stop!"

I put my hands up and waited for him to drag me back in disgrace to Rita's front door. Now she was up, along with the rest of her family. All of them were huddled expectantly at the bottom of the stairs.

"Do you know this kid?" the cop asked her mom.

"Yeah," she said slowly, glaring at me. "We know him."

The daggers in her eyes told me precisely where I stood.

But by far the biggest problem in my relationship with Rita was me.

As deep as my feelings ran, I was scared of getting too close. All during high school, we rode a roller coaster.

We'd be going hot and heavy, things would be great, and then I'd start to worry that maybe we were getting too serious, or the little Catholic voice inside me would condemn us for all the fooling around we were doing. I'd sit her down and coldly explain that it was all too much, that I was taking advantage of her, that maybe we shouldn't see each other anymore.

A few weeks later I'd start hanging around again and begging for another chance.

Rita thought I was nuts. "You're doing it anyway," she'd say about the sex. "Why don't you stop driving yourself crazy about it, for God's sake?" But she was also much more mature than I was. She had been raised to expect marriage at a young age, and already knew that I was the man she wanted to be with.

I, on the other hand, was torn between what I saw as a great, certain thing and the alluring possibility that something else was out there. For years I bounced back and forth while she patiently put up with me.

After I sputtered to the end of high school, I enrolled at St. Francis College in downtown Brooklyn, hoping for a fresh start. I majored in accounting, thinking it would give me a solid base for law school.

But could any subject be duller? I had never been good at math, and it wasn't long before I slacked off studying again. I dropped out after a year, worked a while, then returned, all the while continuing to compile uninspiring grades.

My on-and-off relationship with Rita became more agonizing as we left our teens and I realized that the theoretical marriage we had talked about so casually was suddenly looming in front of me. Half our friends were settling down, and Rita, who was working as a secretary in Manhattan, had started dropping hints.

During one particularly rough stretch at college, the dean ordered me to see a school psychologist to discuss the reasons for my poor grades. The discussion quickly veered off into my relationship.

"I'm going with this girl and I'm having sex with her," I explained.

"Well, do you love her?"

"I do. But I really don't want to get married."

He pondered that for a minute. "So, you don't like her?"

"No, I do. I do like her. I love her."

It went on like this for forty-five minutes. Finally, the guy concluded, "So, you want to stay with her, but you don't want to stay with her."

"Exactly!" He was a genius.

While I tried to keep living my life as always, I knew it couldn't last. One day, during a period when Rita and I had broken up, I was walking home from my Sunday baseball league, in my uniform, when I saw Rita going into her house with her date—a tall, good-looking guy in a uniform, who I knew was a pilot serving in Vietnam.

I looked down at myself, standing there in my uniform like a six-year-old, and I felt like a moron. *When are you going to grow up?* I asked myself.

Eventually I managed to propel myself forward enough to buy a ring with most of my savings. One spring day, I called Rita from a phone booth near her office and asked her to come down and meet me. When she appeared, I slipped the ring on her finger. She was thrilled.

Then I immediately took off for a trip to California with a friend.

Over the next weeks and months, I managed to put off discussing our wedding plans. By winter, though, I could tell Rita was getting wary. She started pressing me to set a firm date.

I finally called her up at work one day and told her I had some bad news. I think she knew what was coming. I said I just wasn't ready to get married. I told her she could keep the ring. I suggested we wait before doing anything about the joint savings account where we had socked away $2,600.

In the past, Rita had always been placid about our breakups. This, though, was much more serious. She started bawling at her desk, and was still crying when she got home that night. Her mother told her, "He can't hurt you anymore like this. It's been too many years. I'll do anything for you, but you have to promise me that you are never going to go back to him."

Teary-eyed, Rita agreed.

Five long months passed, during which Rita and I never talked or socialized. I dropped out of college again and went back to working in the city. Sometimes I'd spy her on the subway platform, and found it hard not to stare. But to make sure she didn't see me, I'd hide behind a post.

I finally broke down and started calling to plead for one more chance. Rita refused. I recruited my friends Mikey and Richie to help, and they convinced her to meet us for lunch. Yet even there she hung tough. She wasn't going home to tell her mother we were back together, she said, unless she had a definite, unchangeable, absolutely-in-stone date. So we set one, and this time it stuck.

Rita and I were married in January 1968 at Nativity. Most of our friends, not to mention the people in the neighborhood who had watched our rocky relationship develop through the years, were thrilled. Our parents were not.

For my part, I didn't really feel like celebrating with either one of our families. Moreover, we were sitting on a secret: a few weeks before the wedding, Rita had learned she was pregnant.

Rita said I could choose the song for our first dance as man and wife at our reception. I chose "Born Free"— one more example of how nuts I am, and what she has had to put up with.

Marriage, and fatherhood, finally forced me to grow up.

In August, Rita gave birth to a beautiful baby girl whom we named Pamela. Holding her in my arms, feeling a new kind of overpowering love, I realized that now there was a small human life depending on me to live up to those standards I had laid down so many years before.

As if to emphasize my new responsibility, it was only a few weeks later that I had to leave home. During my last spell at college, I'd signed up for a naval reserve submarine officers program that had sounded like a good way to fulfill my military commitment, agreeing to serve on active duty once I'd graduated. But under the terms of the program, I had to enlist immediately if I dropped out of college. As a result, when Pam was just a few weeks old, I left for submarine school, then an eighteen-month stint on a diesel submarine.

With my $2,400 salary, we had moved into the only

affordable place we could find: a one-room basement apartment with a large boiler sticking out from one wall. It cost sixty dollars a month. Rita and Pam lived there while I was away.

The only furnishings we had were a chair, a TV, a crib, a Castro convertible sofa that doubled as our bed, and the one nice thing we owned, a maple-wood kitchen table from Ethan Allen that Rita's parents had bought us—which we still have.

By the time I got out of the navy in the spring of 1970, I was determined to do better for my family and get serious about a career. I wanted to go back to college and finish this time—and maybe, then, go on to law school.

In the meantime, I needed to find a job.

As it happened, when I was in college in 1966, my dad had suggested I take the fire and police department qualifying tests as a safeguard. Shortly before my discharge from the navy, I was notified that my name had come up on the FDNY waiting list.

I knew nothing about the job. But the salary was $9,499, a lot better than I had been doing. Moreover, the work schedule of two days and two nights a week would give me time to be with my family and to attend classes. So I signed on.

It sure wasn't my dream job. But I figured it would only be for a few years, just long enough to get my degree and launch my *real* career. Then, finally, my life would be on track.

10

THE SOURCE OF THE FIRE

I've remembered the feeling dozens, maybe hundreds, of times over the years:

I crawl haltingly forward on my hands and knees, the floorboards creaking under me, my heart pounding in my chest, my pulse throbbing in my forehead.

Keeping my mouth close to the floor, I can only take in shallow breaths through my nose.

With every bit that I inch forward, it grows noticeably hotter. I'm already wearing thirty pounds of clothes— thick dungarees, a T-shirt, and a work shirt, the work shoes we call chukkers, a heavy canvas coat and bent leather helmet. All are as stained and torn now as the clothes I saw on the other men in my company on my first day.

The heat in a burning hallway is especially unbearable on hot summer days. But in the winter, when I know I stand a good chance of being outside in the freezing cold for several hours, it can be even worse. On those days, I'm usually wearing long johns and a heavy sweater, which only increase the saunalike feeling.

Adding to the strain, I lug a heavy fire extinguisher with me, clanking it on the floor every time I lay my

*heavily gloved hand down. In my pockets, I carry pliers
and a screwdriver, a piece of rope, and a flashlight.*

*Sweat pours down my brow, trickles down my back,
squishes in my shoes. Even before I reached this hot hallway, I was sweating from all the running—from my
warm cot to the truck, from the truck to the front of the
building, then up four flights of stairs.*

Speed is everything in the fire department.

*All I can see ahead of me is thick black smoke, billow-
ing up to the ceiling and darkening the hallway.*

In a few seconds, I will be diving into it.

After I became a firefighter in 1970, I spent most of the
next sixteen years working in Ladder 42. There, I had a
total immersion course in firefighting.

Starting in the mid-1960s, New York had been swept
by crime, racial unrest, drugs, civil disobedience, and ri-
ots, which together spurred an epidemic of fires. Eventually the late sixties and early seventies would be known
as the War Years.

Just a decade before I joined, in the year 1960, the department had received 94,135 total alarms. Of those,
1,630 had been considered serious fires, that is, those re-
quiring extra alarms.

In 1970 there were nearly three times as many alarms,
for a total of 263,659. The number of serious fires more
than doubled, to 3,508, and the number of lives lost rose
from 207 to 310. New York firefighters were responding
to an average of 350 calls a *day*.

In the South Bronx, we were right on the front lines of
the battle. Our house received twenty or thirty calls a
night, sometimes even more. The first alarm would usually come in just as the shift started, and they'd keep

coming right to the end. They'd come when we'd just sat down to eat and when we'd just fallen asleep in the middle of the night. They'd ring when we were on the way back from another fire, soaking wet. Sometimes when we were on our way to one fire, we'd pass another.

A lot of alarms would be false, or from car fires, or food left on a stove. But a tremendous number were real fires, too—especially during the long night shift, which ran from 6 P.M. to 9 A.M. I don't ever remember a night when we didn't go out again and again and again.

Riding around on the rig, we could see why. Every societal trend and social statistic that we read about was being dramatized right outside our firehouse door. Like Harlem, East New York, and the city's other poor neighborhoods, the South Bronx was rapidly falling apart. The stable, mostly Jewish families that had once dominated the area were fleeing in droves. Taking their place were poorer immigrants, primarily from Puerto Rico, many of them with large families. They crowded into the neighborhood's century-old wooden tenements. As the population shifted, landlords let these buildings deteriorate, allowing electrical wires to fray and garbage to pile up in the hallways, creating fire hazards.

Plenty of longtime welfare recipients wanted out, too, but they were unable by law to move except in the event of a fire. Often they would clear out their few valuables and torch what was left.

The more the neighborhood spiraled downhill, the greater a magnet it became for junkies, homeless people, and bored kids. Congregating on street corners, in empty apartments and abandoned buildings, they'd set fires by accident or out of boredom. People came from across the city to dump cars for one reason or another, parking them in our streets and setting fire to them.

In my first year alone, I fought more fires than most men today do in ten. I battled fires in residential apartments and industrial buildings. I helped rescue families. I learned which projects seemed to have fires in the garbage chute every Sunday night, when the janitors were off duty.

And fires weren't the only risk we faced. Bouncing through the streets, clinging to the back of the open-air trucks we rode in those days, we were an inviting target for kids hurling rocks and cans. Once in a while we'd get to a fire to be greeted by garbage cans thrown off the roofs or fusillades of bottles and glass.

By the end of a shift I'd be exhausted and filthy, with black streaks coating my clothes. I'd be coughing up smoke-blackened snot. The sooty smell in my hair and on my skin wouldn't fade for several days.

It was thrilling and terrifying, and it was absolutely the best place in which to be forged. The South Bronx taught me what being a tough, hardened firefighter was all about.

As I continue toward the apartment, I look to my left and see Joe Daly, the man I met on my first day at work. He has become one of my closest friends and mentors here, someone I've come to know as a savvy firefighter and a deeply religious, methodical straight arrow. I feel a lot safer when he's at my side.

Joe carries an ax and a halligan tool, a long crowbar with a sort of claw at the end. Both are used to open doors or to punch holes in walls if necessary. If they don't work, Joe will slam into doors with his shoulders, and given his tremendous strength I know those doors will come down one way or another.

As the guy handling the fire extinguisher tonight, I'm called the "can man." While Joe pounds our way in, my job will be to stand ready to spray the fire as soon as we get close enough.

It's the job usually given to the youngest, least experienced guy, the one who's likely to need other firefighters around him. But it's my favorite assignment because it puts me right in the action. I love seeing life-and-death decisions played out right in front of my eyes, regardless of whether I'm involved in the actual decision. I like knowing how things work, what causes fires, and how they get beaten.

Other members of our company are outside, performing their jobs. The outside vent man is big Werner Van Elsing, who stands about six-foot-two, weighs about 290 pounds, and is strong as an ox. His job is to run up the fire escape, opening windows and, if necessary, chopping holes in the walls to allow smoke out and draw the fire away from the door where we will be entering. He's one of our canniest veterans and another of my mentors.

Up on the roof is Mike McLaughlin, a quieter guy but really dependable, one who never criticizes but leads by example. His job is to open the roof door or vent it with his ax if the fire heads upward. It's a critical but lonely job that leaves the man assigned to it either out of the main action or right in the very dangerous center of it. It's usually reserved for the best, most experienced firefighters.

Our crew isn't the only one here. Though I'll get first

crack at the fire with my extinguisher, we'll almost certainly need the engine guys to put it out. Our primary job in the ladder company is search and rescue. The engine companies are the ones with the heavy canvas hoses that can deliver great volumes of water.

Right now a group of guys from Engine 73, the house right next door to ours, is coming up the stairs dragging a thick line, ready to attack the fire as soon as we lay a path to it and the pump operator in the street begins sending water all the way up here.

As I move, I can hear Marty Henry, our tough, wiry captain, breathing right behind me. He's right up my ass, as we say in the firehouse.

"Come on, come on," he says, in a low, steady voice that perfectly mixes coolness and urgency. "A little bit more. A little bit more."

Nothing could make me stop right now, but knowing Captain Henry is behind me really makes me want to go on. I know he'd pull me back if he thought it was necessary. He's as smart as any veteran firefighter I've met. I respect him for other reasons too: he has a big family—six kids—and is an academic, with a degree in English, as well as a good, religious person.

In his quiet, insistent way, he's a true leader who has the respect and admiration of most of our guys. It's lucky I trust him to look out for me—since in this situation, I have no real choice anyway.

The closer we get to the fire, the more my adrenaline pumps. We are only ten feet from the door now, and we have no idea what lies behind it. It could be quick and easy. It could be a roaring inferno. It could be one of those hard-to-find fires, hidden behind burned couches *and around dangerous corners, one that will be found only after we've crawled around some more. We could even stumble across the body of some lonely old man unable to get out in time, or a relative who was left behind and forgotten.*

Whatever it is, we have to move fast. Fire spreads quickly in these old wooden buildings.

Most people would probably think I'm crazy to be here. I know that some of my neighbors out in the suburbs do. They always say that I should give up the job for something a little safer.

Not too long ago, I would have thought the same thing. Even now, it's sometimes hard to believe I'm here. The sense of danger is strong. I've developed a real awareness of death, how quickly and unexpectedly it comes in and changes everything for someone, for a whole family, in a minute. I've seen guys get burned, and a few who've even gotten really messed up. I know that one wrong step and the chaplain and someone from the firehouse will be driving out to see my wife. She'll be crying, my kids will have no father, and thousands of firefighters will pull out their dress blues and stand at attention while my casket rolls by.

Yet I feel more alive right now than I can even explain.

I was surprised at how much—and how quickly—I came to love being a firefighter.

Today I can understand why. Firefighting was a culmination of many things I'd already enjoyed in my life. Like the sports teams I'd played on, it allowed me to test myself every day, pushing myself physically in difficult situations and sharpening my senses. I loved showing what I was made of, not just to Captain Henry and the other guys, but to myself.

I also loved being part of a unit, knowing we all had to do our job in order for the team to be safe. In the darkness of those hallways, we could often only communicate via touch or sound. There was no way to put out a fire on your own. You needed to pay attention to every detail, so that you could be there when the next guy turned to you for help, and you had to trust that he would be there for you in return.

Facing those dangers linked us together in some unspoken bond, and made me feel a part of something larger than myself in a truly profound way.

Firefighting was also rewarding work mentally. Every fire offered a different challenge. Figuring out how to put each one out as quickly and safely as possible, which tools to use and how best to corner the flames, was like solving a puzzle. Only it wasn't an academic exercise, like the math tests I had hated studying for. You had to make instantaneous calculations in the heat of the moment.

Most important, it was fun—the most fun I'd ever had. I wasn't stuck behind a desk somewhere. I wasn't in a 9-to-5 rut, riding the train to work and back and spending my days indoors. I wasn't stuck at some desk waiting ten years for a promotion.

I was a soldier having adventures every day.

We reach the door, and Joe gingerly extends his arm toward the handle. If it's hot, that means the fire is right on the other side.

"Come on, come on," Captain Henry says insistently.

"How is it?" I ask.

"Not bad," Joe says. We won't face a fire immediately, but will have to find it instead.

He turns the knob slowly. As the door opens, smoke pours out, and we plunge in.

As one of the senior guys in our house, Frank Pampalone, likes to joke on the rig en route to a scene: "Out the windows and up the shaft, here's a chance to show your craft."

For a minute, it's too dark to see anything. Staying low, we start scurrying around like mice, Joe going toward the kitchen while I look into the hallway that leads to the back bedroom.

Inside, I'm almost desperate now to find the source of the fire. But outwardly, I move slowly, methodically. I can't see more than about three feet ahead. All my senses are going wild.

I'm more cautious than some of the risk-takers at my house. I have a very healthy fear of the power of fire. Up close, the orange and yellow flames are deceptively beautiful. You can't forget the choking smoke and nearly unbearable heat, of course. But you can get mesmerized, almost relaxed, as you watch fire rise up into the air, licking the timbers, kissing the ceiling above, rolling in waves, like the ocean. The fire can fool you, can almost make you feel safe.

Suddenly I turn a corner and see it, shooting up from the charred heap that was a bed. I spray my can on the blackened mess and call for the others. It doesn't have much effect. Captain Henry has been watching me, though, and has the engine guys right there with their line, almost ready to blast the flames with lots of water.

They are always quick to remind us that fires have been extinguished without a hook, but not many are put out without water.

Once they get at it, the fire is fairly easy. It had already blown out the windows, allowing heat and smoke to escape. That happens often in these old buildings.

As bad as it was in that hallway, without that venting the fire would have been far worse as it doubled back on us, the heat so intense that it would make crawling up the hallway seem like a day at the ice rink. Those are the moments when you really have to prove your toughness. New kids always back off instinctively. But we have a lot of old veterans in our house who are tough as nails and have leather lungs, who stay there until the skin on their faces looks like it's melting.

Some of those guys are so dedicated that all I can do at times is watch them in awe, wondering if I have it in me to dig down like that. I don't think the respect and affection I hold for them will ever leave me.

Fortunately, this particular fire is much more the norm for us, and hardly that serious. A lot of smoke pours up as the fire dies, but it's anticlimactic. The fire is being defeated. Heat lifts almost instantly, and the air starts to clear. I can feel my adrenaline draining away, my heart slowing down.

As the smoke clears, I get a look around the apartment. It's only a three-room place, but I notice that the sofa bed in the living room is open, that there's a crib nearby, and there are three more cots in the back. At least five people must be crammed in here.

And now they have lost their home.

* * *

For a somewhat sheltered white kid from Ozone Park, the South Bronx revealed a whole new world, a look into the dark side of society that I've never forgotten.

At fire scenes, we'd often pass people on the front stoops and in the hallways wearing the vacant stare that told us they were high. The tenement stairways invariably reeked of urine, even in the cleaner buildings.

I'd enter an apartment and find stuff piled everywhere, always more than the people living there had room for. Often there would be a big, ugly, growling animal for protection. The moldings would have fifty coats of paint on them. Cockroaches would be crawling around the kitchen walls and floors, seemingly impervious to the smoke. Sometimes they were so thick that when I left, I'd have to shake my clothes out so I wouldn't carry them back to the firehouse.

Most fire victims seemed to be elderly couples who'd lived in the area for decades and couldn't afford to move or young single mothers with too many kids. I'd stand in these apartments thinking, *They didn't plan this right. They can't afford these kids, but they've got them anyway.*

Like all the guys, I developed a tough hide that kept me from getting too worked up over the sad situations I saw. Part of the toughness required of firefighters is learning to function and do your job with a clear head even when you are seeing horrible things. Unlike cops, moreover, firefighters are there just long enough to get a glimpse before it's time to go back to the firehouse.

One day, though, we had put out a small fire in an apartment with only a couple of rooms. It had been a typical good job; we had gotten in quickly, knocked the fire down, and saved the building. The damage was lim-

ited to that apartment, but much of the living room and
kitchen had been destroyed.

It was a hot summer day and we were tired. We sat
down to rest for a minute on the remnants of the couch,
now torn and smoky but fit for our purposes. Without
thinking about it, one of the guys went into the refrigerator and grabbed a few beers. As always after a fire, we
started joking and laughing to unwind.

Suddenly the guy who lived there appeared in the
doorway, looking at us as if we were the worst men in
the world.

I'll never forget the mix of shock and horror on his
face. Instantly I imagined how the scene appeared to
him, and I understood: you've walked into your apartment, you've just lost a lot, and you see these callous
white guys sitting on your couch, drinking your beer,
and laughing. *This poor guy's got to deal with this
tragedy,* I thought, *and here we are, making it all into a
big joke.*

That wasn't what it was about for us. We didn't want
to hurt that man. We wanted to save his apartment, and
we did the very best we could. We didn't think there was
anything wrong in having a beer. But of course there was.

I went up and apologized profusely, but he just turned
and walked away.

That encounter always bothered me. I thought of myself as a good guy and hated to be viewed as a jerk. But I
was, that day. Ever since, I've tried to remember the importance of seeing the situation through someone else's
eyes.

What I hated most of all was seeing deprived children.
I'd always loved kids, and had been planning since my

teenage days to have a large family of my own. After Pam, Rita and I had three more kids in rapid succession: Erica, Marc, and Tom.

My firefighting schedule let me be the kind of active, involved parent I'd wanted my own folks to be when I was young. Many days I saw the kids off to school in the morning or managed to be there when they came home in the afternoon. I had time to help with homework, shoot hoops in the driveway, and attend volleyball games and school plays.

Every day in the ghetto, though, I saw kids whose parents were distant and uninvolved. Often there was only one parent, and sometimes just a boyfriend or a relative, to look after a kid. In our neighborhood of well-kept lawns and shade trees, we could send our kids over to the municipal playground to play. In the South Bronx, the best a mother could do was a vacant lot.

Seeing families torn apart by poverty regularly reinforced my love for my family, by giving me strength to draw from in difficult times. My days of cavalier selfishness were long over. Now, to come home to my family after a long, tough shift was an unbelievable joy.

Sometimes we arrived at a fire too late to save a child. Often there'd be an aunt or uncle or friend that had been staying in the apartment and had run out without taking the baby along. After a fire like that, I'd want to go out and choke the relatives, or start the fire again and throw them in it. We all felt that way.

Once, I found myself crawling through a smoky tenement with a younger firefighter named Tom Kelly. Tom was the can man that day, while I lugged an ax and halligan. Following the usual procedures, staying low to the ground as we headed down a long hallway, we felt around

STRONG OF HEART   97

with our hands, like blind people, to make sure we didn't come across any victims.

In one back room, I felt the legs of what seemed to be a crib. I stood up and patted it down inside. There was nothing there.

But after we got the fire out, we went back for our final search. That was when I saw it: the lifeless form of an infant. He had been burned to death.

It was horrible. I understood instantly that I had mistaken the baby for a pillow or a doll. Maybe, if I hadn't made that mistake, he would be alive.

The guys tried to reassure me. The heat was too intense, they said. There was no way the baby was alive when we got there. We would have felt him wriggling around, or heard him cry.

I knew they were right. But my heart wanted to deny what my head knew. For days afterward I was haunted by the memory of that fragile little form, and wracked by a terrible guilt.

Driving home from work that night, my eyes became clouded by tears. All the way home, they streamed down my face.

I duck into the hallway to catch my breath while the engine guys finish the fire off.

"Good work," Captain Henry says. I just nod appreciatively. In a minute we'll go back and search the place again, to make sure there's no one inside.

Once again, we made it through, managed to find the fire with no serious injuries. We didn't need the crazy risk-taking that comes when a woman is standing downstairs screaming, "My baby's in there," a declaration that sends guys plunging inside in an almost foolhardy way to save a life, and that brings them out with charred coats, cut knees, burns on their arms, gashes on their heads. We didn't even need backup rigs.

But none of that diminishes the real pleasure of beating the enemy. It seems almost impossible that our streak of good luck will continue, but we've won once again. The department always wins its battles with fire.

With the hard work done, it's time now for the usual process of cleaning up and waiting for the police to come and secure the apartments that are damaged. It will probably take no more than thirty minutes.

But I can't wait to get back to the firehouse. I'm sore and damp. I desperately want to change my shirt. At the very least, I hope we'll have time for a cup of coffee before we get our next call.

I check my watch. It's only two in the morning. Still seven hours to go on our shift.

Plenty of time for more insanity.

11

LA CASA DEL ELEFANTE

As much as I loved fighting fires, some of the best times came in between calls.

After knocking down a fire, we'd pack the rig up and roll through the dark streets back to the warmth of our spacious three-story red-brick firehouse.

Ladder 42 stood right in the heart of the crumbling neighborhood, at the corner of Prospect Avenue and 152nd Street. Yankee Stadium wasn't too far away. Across the street was the Flamingo, a seedy bar with neon-streaked windows that stayed open until four in the morning. We called it the "Flaming O." Occasionally, if we were lucky, entertaining bar fights spilled onto the street in front of us.

Our chauffeur, Patty Gilchrist, would back the truck into the bay of the silent house, and we'd start to bring it back to life. I'd head for the tiny kitchen behind the bay and scoop some coffee grounds and water into one of the slightly damaged Farberware pots we'd been given by workers at the company plant a half-mile up the road.

While the coffee percolated, its aroma drifting

through the house, we'd prepare for the next call. Captain Henry would go upstairs to his office to finish the paperwork on the last one. Mike McLaughlin would check his roof rope and other equipment. Patty, whose job was to drive us to the scene and if necessary climb the ladder to provide backup, would go over the rig. I'd refill the can.

Only when we finished could we sit down in our pine-paneled lounge, relax, talk, and wait. Van would magisterially sit down and prepare to hold court. He had opinions about everything.

For me, the firehouse was a big part of what made the job so special. Crossing through those doors, you entered a protected enclave that was part locker room, part fraternity—an oasis from the pressures of fighting fires and the decaying world outside. It was a place to be with your best friends, blow off steam, learn from your elders, complain about everything, and laugh your head off—all with the same guys with whom you shared dangers, the only people who fully understood the unique pressures of your job.

Van would crack a few jokes, and Patty would roll his eyes. After a while Captain Henry would come downstairs and in his low-key, friendly manner get us talking about the fire. "Tom, did you have to break any windows before the engine line was ready?" he'd ask. "What about you, Pat? Did you have a good shot at the window with the ladder, or was it blocked by the power lines in front?" Mike would talk about his journey up to the roof, how he'd actually had to run up the staircase of the next building over, crack open its locked steel door at the top, then jump over from that building to the roof of the one where the fire was. Van would explain which windows he'd taken out, and why.

All of it was batted about informally, without too much criticism or too much praise. Captain Henry wasn't one to fawn over a man, or put him up for a medal, just for doing his job. But he also wouldn't jump down your throat if you'd honestly made the wrong decision in the heat of the moment. If you had screwed up, he wanted to make sure you understood what you had done wrong, and why. If you'd done everything right, well, excellence and dedication were simply what was expected.

All of us in the house absorbed those attitudes from him, and I was to carry them with me when I became a boss. In a life-and-death job like ours, the margin for error was small. It seemed reasonable to expect that you'd fall within that margin or go find another job.

Around that table, there was a modest but deep, workmanlike pride. We were craftsmen talking about technique. The older firefighters always had little tricks to share, or stories of past fires. There was always something for a young firefighter to learn.

Fortunately, Ladder 42 wasn't known only for the prowess of its firefighters. As much I liked the work, I never would have stayed in the job as long as I did without all the humor and craziness.

We were known as the Elephant House, or "La Casa del Elefante," as it was painted on our truck. The nickname was in honor of five or six tall, beefy veteran firefighters who dominated our ranks, guys like Van Elsing.

I'm about six feet tall and was in pretty good shape

then. But I felt dwarfed by the elephants. Each stood at least six-foot-two and weighed at least 250 pounds. Some were deceptively big-bellied, but all were incredibly strong, like football linemen.

With their strength and experience, the elephants were a tremendously comforting presence at fires. There was nothing as reassuring when you were making your way into the heat and smoke as seeing one of those huge beasts come barreling down a smoky hallway, ready to break down a door or tear down a ceiling. They seemed able to endure more heat and pain than most of us, while always keeping an eye out for the younger and smaller firefighters around them.

They were funny as hell, too. They had embraced their collective identity, and decorated the walls with pictures of elephants. Someone had swiped a sign from the Bronx Zoo reading "Don't Feed the Elephants," which for a while was displayed out front. A few of the guys had even made an elephant's butt out of plywood, painted it pink, and screwed it to the back of the truck.

Just about everyone in the house had been assigned an appropriate nickname. There's an art to nicknaming among firefighters, one that mixes irony, mockery, and affection all at once. Van Elsing, for instance, with his sloping gut and double chin, was invariably referred to as "Big Van" or "Mrs. Elsing's Little Boy."

Many of the best nicknames came from Bobby Blair, a particularly mountainous elephant who seemed to sit in the lounge all day, making remarks that no one else could have gotten away with. It hadn't taken Blair long to find out that I was studying for a college degree in my spare time, and had plans to go on to graduate school. From then on, I was known as "Doctor."

At fires, I was always at risk of someone asking me, "What do you think we should do, Dr. Von Essen?" If I said something especially stupid, someone was certain to ask, "What do you expect from a college man?"

All you could do, of course, was laugh and go along. If you showed any sign of resistance, the joking would increase tenfold. But I genuinely thought it was funny, given all the grand ambitions I harbored for myself.

When I found out that another guy in the house, Joe Curry, had also been targeted for his college background, I even extended the joke. Soon Joe and I had a routine for those times when we found ourselves at a scene performing some particularly disgusting, menial, degrading chore that made all our educational pretensions seem especially ridiculous.

"Dr. Curry," I'd say, with a slight trace of an English accent, "please remove that urine-stained, roach-infested mattress."

"Right away, Dr. Von Essen," he'd respond high-mindedly.

Beyond the running jokes, you were subject to relentless teasing about your ethnic background, your utter stupidity, your complete lack of sexual prowess, your female relatives' incredible sexual prowess and their generosity with it, your likely homosexual proclivity, your total ignorance, big gut, skinniness, huge nose, ugly skin blemishes, lousy cooking skills, hideous wardrobe, premature baldness, and unnatural hairiness. Twenty years before any of us had heard the phrase "political correctness," we were joking as far beyond its boundaries as possible.

A good deal of firehouse humor doesn't translate well to the outside world. But inside those doors, it was a necessary release valve for a group of tough, hard-edged men who were regularly risking their lives. It kept everything from getting too heavy. Ever since, I've always found it easier to make a wisecrack at stressful moments than to stop and open myself up.

And the humor wasn't just verbal. In our house, water fights, even food fights, could break out at any time.

One of my closest friends, Jim Ginty, a skinny little guy who was half the size of the elephants but as tough and brave as any of them, owned a "laughing box," a small handheld object that emitted guttural laughs at the press of a button. He would carry it along to fire scenes and transmit the laughs over our handheld radios. We'd be out in the middle of a freezing night, having just knocked down a tough fire, trying to catch our breath, when suddenly the shrill, hyena-like sounds would pour out of the radios, hurting our ears but making us smile. We'd just look at each other and mutter, "Ginty."

Sometimes the craziness found truly bizarre outlets. One day one of the guys brought in a pet alligator he'd gotten somewhere. Somehow a second one showed up. We built a huge plastic tank in the bay to house them, and guys started regularly bringing them mice and chunks of meat. On one particularly disgusting occasion, the gators consumed a live chicken, scattering blood and feathers everywhere.

The presence of the alligators became widely known in the department, and soon firemen were coming from all over the city to see them. They grew to be seven feet long, so big that most of us were afraid to go near them. Eventually, only one maniac was willing to feed them and clean their tank. We finally had to give them to the Bronx Zoo, where, for all I know, they still are.

We were always willing to spread the fun around, too. One of Ginty's favorite things to do when he arrived for the six o'clock shift was to call one of the nearby houses and spread a couple of false rumors. "You guys hear that the contract was signed?" he'd ask. Or "I heard three engine companies are being closed."

Through the rest of the night, the rumors would spread through the battalion like wildfire, getting embellished in each retelling. Firefighters are among the biggest gossips on earth. Around midnight, Ginty would go back to the phones to see what his rumors had morphed into. Then he'd saunter into the kitchen, chuckling, with his report: "Word now is that *eight* houses are being closed."

We maintained a running feud with Engine 41, which was located not far up the block. One night while we were out at a multiple-alarm fire, they removed the pink wooden elephant butt from the back of our truck. In retaliation, while they were out on a run a few nights later, we raided their house and stole all their mattresses.

After some hostile communications, a truce was arranged and a meeting set at their house for a contraband swap. We unloaded the mattresses from our truck and stacked them on the floor. Very solemnly, one of their guys produced a large burlap bag, opened it—and slowly poured a stream of pink-colored sawdust into a pile on the floor.

It was only after a few minutes of outrage and curses from us that they admitted it was just another joke.

Along with the laughter, the firehouse was the scene of debates, arguments, diatribes, and sometimes serious talks.

The TV in the lounge was always on, usually tuned to news or sports, and it inspired all sorts of discussions. We talked about the war in Vietnam, the city's financial woes, the spate of hijackings, and the disasters afflicting the Yankees. Anyone who was unfortunate enough to appear on screen was fair game for abuse.

Sometimes the conversations turned quite deep, especially when we got to talking about the social breakdown we were seeing firsthand. Everyone was angry that neighborhoods like the South Bronx were being allowed to die.

Some firefighters put the blame on the residents themselves. Others blamed the feckless city administration of Mayor John V. Lindsay, which had been swept in on high hopes of a generous new liberalism, yet had proved utterly unable to handle the city's decline.

I usually took the contrarian position, pointing out all the ways I thought the city let people down, forcing them into lousy jobs or making them send their kids to bad schools. As a kid, I had been a Kennedy idealist who believed in the possibility that government could improve things.

Naturally, I was branded the house liberal. Most of the others were deeply conservative, reflecting their backgrounds. They were real blue-collar men who had been forced by circumstances to go to work in their late teens. Some had fought in Korea or Vietnam. Few of them had been to college. A lot had big families that they had to work hard to support. Ginty, for instance, had no interest in moving up the ranks to become an officer, but to pay the bills for six kids on a fireman's salary, he had to spend all his days off washing windows. Somehow he also found time to learn to play the bagpipes so he could volunteer for the department's bagpipe band—something he still does today.

We had our limitations, of course. If the crowd in the lounge got too large, the odds increased that at least one wise guy would make bonehead comments about how he could do a better job than anyone else at any task, no matter how little he actually knew about it. If we were watching, say, a documentary on microsurgery, that guy could be counted on to yell out, "I know a better way of doing that!" and explain that he knew of a better procedure that the city wouldn't pay for, which he'd read about recently in a medical journal that his brother-in-law (who was a med student at Columbia) had brought home, and that's why that patient on TV was going to die.

We were also rather insular. As a group, the fire department is disproportionately white, male, middle-class, and Catholic. The kitchen was not the place to hear a wide range of opinions or experiences.

Even as a young firefighter, I thought we had too much of a bunker mentality. Most of the men seemed to view the administration as a distant and essentially irrelevant entity, a place that existed solely to issue onerous regulations and threaten budget cuts and layoffs, not to do anything positive for us.

But even our shortcomings never detracted from the common feeling we shared of belonging to a secret men's club that no one on the outside, even our families, was privy to.

As a group, we did everything for ourselves. We had committees to handle housecleaning and buy coffee and plates and other supplies, a union delegate to field our concerns and bring back news about contracts and other union business, and a rotation for making meals.

The kitchen wasn't much, but some of the guys, I was surprised to learn, were quite good cooks. Every night we sat down to dinners of steak, pasta, roasts, or chicken, often meticulously prepared with spices and sauces.

Pete Ganci, whom I didn't know then but who was starting his own career in Brooklyn, used to advise young firefighters that whenever their wives asked what they ate at the firehouse they should say, "Hot dogs." The reality that you were often eating better food there than at home, he said, would be too hard on them. Ginty joked that he regularly told his wife he'd eaten bologna for dinner.

If there was a downside, it was that we ate too much heavy German and Italian food, reflecting the dominant ethnic makeup of our house. Even if a meal was good, it wasn't much fun to be assigned to the roof at a tenement fire and have to run up six flights after a heavy dinner of pot roast and potatoes.

We always seemed to have one or two Irish guys, too, who thought they could mix three cans of tomato sauce with two cans of tomato paste and call it spaghetti sauce. Even I was a little better than that, though my only "real" meal consisted of roast beef, baked potatoes, a boiled vegetable, and the hope that someone could put a gravy together.

The men worked hard to keep the place clean, and even to make it something of a showplace. Their pride was reflected in that large, pine-paneled lounge I had seen on my first day, which jutted off from the kitchen. It had once been a courtyard, but a few years earlier the guys had gone out and bought the paneling and other materials to build the room themselves. The kitchen was a tight space, and they'd needed a place to sit.

To furnish it, someone would periodically bring in an old couch or chairs that he was planning to throw out. But the furniture never managed to last much more than six months. We'd sit in there in our dirty clothes, and eat all our meals, spilling sauce and crumbs all over it. Soon we'd start picking up mites and lice from it, or imagine that we did, and someone would have to drag the stuff out to the curb. Finally we came up with the idea of chipping in to buy custom-made benches with heavy-duty vinyl upholstery, which we could simply wipe down.

We were so well known for tidiness that it became something of a burden to the engine company next door. Though connected to us through a hole in the wall of the bay, the men of Engine 73 and Squad 2 had their own separate house, a cramped two-story building that they barely fit into.

They were smart, tough, and dedicated firefighters over there, but they were incredible slobs. While we took pride in our spacious quarters, our custom-made lounge, and our alligator tank, they let their quarters go to hell; they even seemed to revel in making it as messy as possible.

Eventually they won a nickname of their own: "La Casa Caca." Visiting chiefs would ask, "Why don't you guys fix up your quarters like the men next door did?"

One night, an officer from another house who was covering at the engine company found out how strongly the men felt about questions like that. When he sat down to dinner, they served him his food directly on the table—without a plate.

I can remember driving to the firehouse one evening during my first year on the job. I had just left Rita and the baby, reluctantly, for the drive in heavy traffic from Ozone Park. It was a Saturday night, and while I was going to work, everyone else in the city was getting ready to go out.

I crossed the Triborough Bridge and entered the Bronx just as the sun was starting to go down. All along Prospect Avenue people were hanging out on their stoops, some dancing, a few wearing glassy-eyed expressions. Children were running around naked. Music was blaring from all directions. All the fire hydrants were open for blocks and blocks. A torrent of water was pouring downhill, under the wheels of my car.

For a moment I felt as if I were heading up a river in some distant land. *What the hell am I doing here?* I thought. *This is crazy. Maybe I've made a mistake.*

But when I walked into the firehouse, suddenly it was like coming home. The guys from the day shift were still there, hanging around the lounge and greeting me warmly. Shift change was my favorite time of day because it was when we traded gossip, and you got to hear everything you had missed over the last few days. With ten guys at work instead of five, the banter was always faster and funnier.

I got some coffee and went into the lounge. Van and Gilchrist, already there, cleared some space for me on the couch. "What's up, Doctor?" Blair asked me. Looking around, I suddenly felt really happy to see them.

I didn't understand this then, but I realize now that I

was already beginning to feel that firefighting might not only be a temporary thing for me. After starting one family with Rita, I had somehow stumbled into a second one at the Elephant House.

12

THE UNION POLITICS
WERE A KILLER

I was sitting in the lounge one day in 1981, just starting to slurp a cup of coffee, when Big Van walked up. Towering over me, he pointed and said, "You're our new union delegate."

Van, who had been our delegate as long as I could remember, had first raised the idea a few days earlier. I was skeptical. I'd never been too interested in the department's two firefighter unions—the Uniformed Firefighters Association, which represents roughly 8,700 firefighters, and the Uniformed Fire Officers Association, which represents 2,400 officers.

But Van, sitting down and putting his enormous arm around my shoulder, convinced me it would be a fun, even valuable, experience for me, and a good way to help the house. The delegates represented firefighters at union meetings, helped them with counseling and other services, and kept them informed of department business. It would be good, he said, to have a younger firefighter in that role.

So I agreed. Without a clue, I'd just begun a fifteen-year involvement with the UFA that would carry me, improbably, from the firehouse to the union presidency and then to the commissioner's office.

The union came into my life just as I needed a new challenge. Now thirty-five, I still loved firefighting, but the job had become less exciting as the city rebounded and the number of fires dropped. The older elephants were moving to slower houses or retiring.

I had little desire to be an officer—which was fortunate because, though I'd taken the lieutenant's test twice, I'd put no effort into studying the thousands of pages of rules and procedures one needed to master, and I'd flunked. But I'd lost interest in another career.

In 1972 I'd conquered a lot of demons by graduating, finally, from St. Francis, with a degree in economics. I'd made a lot of time for my studies, even squirreling myself away in a small closet at the firehouse, and had landed on the Dean's List. I'd gone on to seek a graduate degree in education at the C. W. Post Campus of Long Island University, thinking that with my love of kids I might make a good teacher. When I graduated in 1982, I was thrilled. I was finally certifiably educated.

Teaching, though, turned out to be somewhat unsatisfying. As part of my studies, I'd enjoyed a six-month assignment with a social studies class at Elmont Memorial High School on Long Island. But after graduation, when I started working as a substitute in South Ozone Park on my off days, I didn't like it much. I spent most of my time chasing kids around and trying to establish some order. Besides, the schoolroom lacked the fun, the humor, and the drama of the firehouse.

* * *

So in 1983, when the UFA treasurer, Tom Reilly, a friend of mine from Engine 73, asked me if I wanted to run for Bronx trustee, I was open to the idea. It would be a big change: a two-year, full-time job in an office downtown, a union car, a raise and expenses, one of ten seats on the UFA board. It would also give me a chance to learn more about the department and help out the firefighters.

The Bronx trustee served sixty companies, about 1,700 firefighters, helping with medical benefits, equipment shortages, and personal problems. For me, the job deepened considerably my view of the firefighters. I never lost my strong admiration for most of the tough, strong men I worked with. But as I became privy to the personal side of their lives, and all the things we never talked about in the kitchen, I learned that they were as human as the rest of society, and prone to the same problems.

I helped men get counseling for drinking problems or rocky marriages. I found financial advisers for men with money problems, and lawyers for those in legal trouble. More than once I answered my phone at 2 A.M. and found myself speaking to a firefighter who had been arrested out in New Jersey and needed bail money. If he was a good guy who had just made a stupid mistake, as most of them were, I might end up tapping my department connections to help him avoid disciplinary action. I spent a lot of time making such "contracts," as we call them.

Sometimes I found myself sitting in my office, with the door closed, as some firefighter poured his heart out. At those times, my job was just to listen and console.

*   *   *

In the union boardroom, I became an unwilling student of union politics. They weren't pretty.

The UFA president, Jimmy Boyle, was a veteran of Engine 217, with a reputation as a good firefighter. He was also a gentle, thoughtful man who exuded affection for people. I was impressed by the way he soothed the widows of firefighters killed in the line of duty. He spoke forcefully of his desire to improve working conditions and win better contract terms from the city.

But the board was hard to manage. Some members were his declared enemies, seeking ways to upstage Jimmy and boost their own chances in the next election. Most of his friends were well-meaning but clueless. One guy especially was a font of stupidity. When the department instituted pregnancy leave for female firefighters, he suggested we demand that male firefighters be granted "sexual leave," if necessary, to build their sperm counts.

I learned a lot about budgets and contracts, made a lot of friends in the department, and found much of the inner workings of government fascinating. But the politics were a killer. The board meetings dragged on like a root canal without the Novocain. As the next election approached in the summer of 1985, I considered quitting.

Nick Mancuso changed my mind. A tough-minded Bronx firefighter, he ran against Jimmy as UFA president, a job he had already held once. Nick seemed like the right man at the time.

I decided to run for secretary. The job would let me help formulate policy while running the day-to-day operations at the union office. I won that year, and again in 1987 for a three-year term.

Among other duties, Nick put me in charge of the safety committee. Safety had been a big concern for me since my early days on the job. I was convinced we often sent too many guys into fires. Too many men suffered severe burns, tar in their eyes, knee and back injuries. Too many overweight guys suffered heart attacks outside burning buildings. At any given moment, hundreds of firefighters were out on medical leave. I wanted the union to fight for more stringent standards, procedures, and training that would make the job safer. We pushed for equipment like bunker gear, clothing that would protect the men from severe burns, especially on their unprotected upper thighs. Safety was to be my pet cause for the rest of my career.

The department wasn't much help. Though some people there were sympathetic, they were perennially short of money. The appointed commissioner always had a tough time pushing the staff chiefs who ran the department. They were protected by tenure and promoted by passing tests, not through merit. Some were creative and thoughtful. But none had been trained as managers, and none were accountable to the commissioner, or anyone, really. When a chief was unmotivated, little got done.

The unions had long complained, for instance, about the soot and diesel fumes that rigs belched out into the firehouses. None of our firehouses had ventilation systems to funnel the gunk out. It built up on ceilings, walls, and tables. It hung in the air. Firefighters couldn't help but breathe it all in.

After we'd complained enough, the department finally

took action. They started painting all the firehouse ceilings black, so no one would notice the soot.

In the ensuing battle, I made as close, and unlikely, a friend as I ever had in the department. The UFA's new sergeant-at-arms, Danny DeFranco, was a longtime veteran of Engine 17 on the Lower East Side. A short thick guy, he had a big head, thinning gray hair, and large strong hands from his longtime second profession as a licensed plumber.

As a UFA delegate for his house, Danny was often a showboat at our monthly union meetings. He regularly seized the microphone and hectored the board over what he saw as its willingness to make concessions to the city and its lack of interest in safety. His solution to every problem was to rally the men for a protest march. We called him "Rent-a-Riot." Nick was so suspicious of him he asked me to chair the safety committee partly to keep Danny under control.

But Danny turned out to be more resourceful than any of us thought. He spent weeks researching exhaust systems across the country until he tracked down a small midwestern company that manufactured one, called the Niederman, that would alleviate the problem. He persuaded us to support the union's financing for installation of a Niederman in his house, then demonstrated its effectiveness to the assistant commissioner. After several years of union lobbying, the department finally agreed to install one in every firehouse.

It was a valuable lesson for me both in the dangers of underestimating someone and in the importance of knowing a subject cold.

* * *

Working late nights, Danny and I grew close. I realized his over-the-top fanaticism concealed a large, generous heart that had endured much pain. His son, a diver and rescue firefighter, had been killed in an accident, and Danny could never finish a sentence about him without a tear in his eye. Danny's safety crusade, I saw, stemmed from his grief and his need to fill the void in his life.

He was incredibly loyal. My love for the firefighters was often tempered by doubts about their wisdom on some issues. I had a strong sense of right and wrong, and little sympathy for reprobates and rule-breakers. My inclination was to work with the department where we could. But Danny loved every firefighter unquestioningly, even when they were gaming the system. He always wanted to fight the department, no matter what the issue was. It was hard not to be moved by his devotion.

He also brought ingenuity to the job. He often rummaged in the Dumpster at headquarters in search of documents or letters that might be of interest to us—and invariably found some. He thought the department was dragging its heels on cleaning up the asbestos in firehouses. So when a house was scheduled to be tested, he made sure it would register a level that would require a cleanup. He started carrying some asbestos around in a briefcase, and before a test he would sprinkle it around.

For years we argued the benefits of confrontation versus accommodation. Years later, when I became union president, Danny would always encourage me toward a showdown on some issue.

"Tommy, you can't agree with the department," he'd say, wagging a thick finger in my face. "We're labor, and they're management."

"But what if they're right?" I'd ask. "Shouldn't we support them if they're right? Isn't that the rational thing to do?"

"Tommy, you're not supposed to be rational. You're not supposed to be reasonable. You're not supposed to be fair. You're the UFA president."

During my years as secretary, the UFA fell into a feud with Mayor Ed Koch. Since the droll and charming former congressman had won election in 1978, the city had rebounded from the budget and crime woes of the 1970s. Exuding optimism and humor, Koch had become a popular political figure.

But early in his third term, he angered firefighters when he ruled that the police would be in charge at all major disaster scenes. It was a slap in the face to us. The two departments had long jockeyed over such control, and sought some clarification. The police-run dispatch system tended to notify the police first and firefighters last on major calls. It gave the police steady opportunities for glory and a way to help justify their budget.

The mayor's decision cemented that control. And more than ego was at stake. Firefighters responded to scenes faster. Bumping them to second-class status, we believed, could cost lives.

Soon we antagonized the mayor, by opposing his plan to require uniformed city employees to live in the city or contiguous counties. We had guys living in some of the areas in question. With the support of upstate politicians, we got a grandfather clause passed that allowed many of them to stay.

Koch *really* hurt himself with the way he started closing firehouses. He had good reason to do it; the number of fires had dropped since the War Years, and the city budget was getting squeezed. But it was always a political hot potato. Firefighters, naturally, always flipped. Community activists and council members whipped up community residents. A mayor had to proceed carefully. Unfortunately, Koch didn't.

On Super Bowl Sunday 1988, Engine 232 in Brownsville received an alarm and raced across Brooklyn. When they reached their destination, they learned it was a false alarm. So they rolled back to their headquarters—a Quonset hut, set up as a temporary firehouse two decades earlier, known as the "Tin House."

They found fire department cars blocking the driveway and department big shots walking around out front. The chief of operations, Homer Bishop, waved them off the truck and told them the house was being shut down.

The guys were livid, stunned that their own department would stage a false alarm to engineer the closing. The mayor salted the wound when he bragged that it was a "brilliant" way to avoid a showdown with activists.

This time we had a legitimate need for "Rent-a-Riot." On a warm Thursday in February, during morning rush hour, five thousand firefighters marched across the Brooklyn Bridge, halting traffic and chanting obscenities. Soon a mysteriously high number of firefighters were calling in sick.

The next year, after he'd shut down Engine 41 in the Bronx, the mayor got on stage at the Medal Day ceremony, a hallowed annual event where the department pays tribute to heroes from the previous year, and was roundly booed before he could speak. "I want you to listen to this! I want you to listen to this!" he stammered.

"The only reason I am here is to honor you!" Finally he just stormed off, furious.

The tension spilled into our talks on a new contract, where the city took a hard line on pay raises. They also pushed to trim the crews on all engine companies to four men from five, plus an officer. At the time, 138 of the city's 210 engines had five. Cutting them back would result in dozens of reassignments, add to the workload in engine companies, and substantially reduce overtime. The men would have less backup at fire scenes, which would potentially put them at greater risk.

In negotiations, we got the proposed manning cut killed, and a better raise and more benefits than the police, in exchange for an increase of fifty-four hours a year in every firefighter's work schedule. The compromise would allow the city to save money on overtime while we preserved our manning. The board overwhelmingly approved it. We felt it was a credit to our hard work, and especially to Nick, that we had gotten so much out of so little.

But when we brought it to the next delegate meeting, the men exploded.

The meetings had always been slightly raucous affairs. They were held in hotel ballrooms, with three hundred or more firefighters in attendance. A lot of delegates saw meeting night as a time to catch up with friends and have a few drinks. Others liked to stand before the microphones and yell at the board.

From the stage, Nick tried to explain how far we had come from the city's opening offer. But one speaker after another told us to reject the contract and bring the issues to an arbitrator. Nick pointed out that, historically, arbitrators ruled against the unions. None of the speakers cared.

The opposition was so heated and widespread that we felt we had no choice but to go along. So instead of voting on the contract, we went to arbitration. And as Nick had warned, we got creamed. Handed down in the middle of 1989, the ruling from the arbitrator cut all our engine crews back to four men, just as the city had originally wanted.

Though the board had advised against arbitration, the decision only fueled the anger against us. At every meeting, the delegates denounced us as traitors and incompetents and anything else they could think of.

One month, a fire marshal we called "Mr. Fiduciary" because he was always dropping that word into sentences to make himself sound smart, worked himself into a frenzy as he stood at the microphone attacking Nick. Veins popped out on his neck and his face turned beet red as he pointed at Nick and screamed, "Fuck you! Fuck you!"

Up on stage, Nick, who had been taking a pounding for months, finally lost it. "Fuck *me?*" he yelled, angrily pointing his meaty paw at the guy in the audience who faced him. "FUCK YOU!" He gave the bird to the whole crowd. They started booing him and screaming curses.

Nick just got madder. Pushing the lectern aside, he shouted, "Come on, mothers!" In an instant, two guys rushed the stage. More goons followed from the side. Right where I sat, taking the meeting notes, asses and elbows started flying as shoving matches broke out all around me. In the audience, delegates cheered and laughed. Then chairs and tables started getting overturned—including mine. My notes went everywhere.

Watching from the side, my brother Roddy saw me go down and was sure I'd been slugged. He jumped onstage and made his way toward me, shoving bodies aside to get to where I was. When I looked up, he was breathing hard and red-faced. His fists were clenched, and he looked ready to start swinging.

All I could do was laugh. I hadn't been punched. I had just gotten down on the floor to collect my notes. Water pitchers had been sitting on some of the overturned tables, and I was afraid the notes would be ruined.

A little relieved, Roddy got down to help. As we crawled around, bodies rammed into us from all sides. The audience roared as if at a football game.

Suddenly it struck me how ridiculous this all was. "Can you believe these guys?" I asked him. "Look at this mess." In the middle of all those fights, I started laughing hysterically.

The next election wasn't until the summer of 1990, but we all knew months in advance that we were going to get bounced. It was virtually a clean sweep. Jimmy Boyle was voted back in as UFA president.

When it happened, though, it still hurt. I had been in the union full-time for seven years. Now my career there was stalled, and maybe even over. I wondered whether my career as a firefighter might be, too.

13

A GAMBLE PAYS OFF

The next few months were difficult for me.

I was back in the firehouse after seven years in the union, but I was forty-four and feeling it. My skills were rusty, and the thrill of knocking down fires was gone. So were most of my old friends and mentors, who had retired or been promoted elsewhere.

The sting of getting booted by the firefighters lasted a long time. At fires, I'd sometimes catch guys from other houses glaring at me. One night someone called the firehouse and accused me and the other board members of embezzling money. To someone who prizes honesty, a false accusation like that really rankles.

For months, I brooded, remembering all the smart guys I'd known who had done things the right way, studying to be lieutenants and moving up. I was still a fireman, just as I'd been two decades earlier, with the salary and status to prove it.

I thought seriously of quitting. After twenty years, I was eligible for a retirement pension equal to half my salary. Rita and my kids urged me to put the pain behind and start fresh.

To give it a try, I went on leave early in 1991 and took

a job that had been offered by a friend of mine who worked in real estate. For six months I was an assistant manager for Mendik Company, collecting rents and fielding tenant concerns in an office building at 2 Park Avenue South, between 32nd and 33rd Streets.

The work was okay, but as the months passed and the pain of losing ebbed, I really missed the department. One day I was showing a prospective tenant around a suite. As he fired technical questions at me, I faltered for answers, and I realized how little I knew about what I was doing. I felt sure he thought I was an idiot.

The moment crystallized the reality for me that, despite my recent disappointments, I was a *firefighter*. My heart lay with the troops. Whatever abilities and knowledge I had concerned firefighting. Whatever expertise I possessed had to do with knocking down fires or the inner workings of the union. I felt I still had a lot to contribute in areas like safety and training. After seven years in the union, I knew as much about the department as anyone, and appreciated the troops more than ever.

Before that point, my career had been one of seizing opportunities that came my way, more than consciously taking steps forward. I'd never made my youthful dreams of law school and professional success come true.

Now, realizing what I really wanted, I decided to take a risk.

In the fall of 1991, I returned to Ladder 42. The next union election would be in the summer of 1993. I intended to run for the job of UFA president.

Running for president was a huge undertaking that consumed most of my spare time for the next eighteen months. For help, I called my brother Roddy and asked him to be my campaign manager.

Roddy is fourteen years my junior and very different from me. I'm light-haired and fair-skinned; he has tight curly dark hair and a moustache. I'm intense and overly self-critical; he's light-hearted, easygoing, and sociable.

When Roddy was little, I always made time to take him out for ice cream, to the beach, or over to the playground to shoot hoops. As a teenager, he'd drifted, quitting high school, working in a restaurant, and partying too much. I pushed him to get his equivalency degree, and after he had, prodded him to take the firefighters' test. Firefighting is a great job for someone like Roddy was then, a good guy who works hard and loves camaraderie but lacks discipline and direction. He'd joined the department in 1982, and I'd tapped a connection I had with a department official named Bill Feehan to get him into a good house, Engine 332 in East New York. Roddy had thrived there, becoming popular in the house and winning a reputation as a tough nozzleman.

Our close relationship, his willingness to work hard, and his easy rapport with the troops made him a perfect manager and companion for the grueling days of campaigning. In the weeks before the election, we spent long days together visiting firehouses and working in the campaign office we'd set up in an old butcher shop in Glendale. Roddy was always there to help write pamphlets, address mail, work our phone bank, or sound firefighters out about their views on the candidates.

I'd gotten a few breaks during the election. Under Jimmy, the UFA had been beset by internal quarrels and a poor relationship with Mayor David Dinkins, who was making a lot of noise about closing more firehouses.

Frustrated, Jimmy had decided not to run again, and was telling people he planned to endorse me. His setbacks, meanwhile, had mostly erased the memory of the manning issue that had gotten me thrown out of office a few years earlier. They also enabled me to run on my record as a straightforward union leader who was committed to safety, could work with city officials to get things done, and would be honest with firefighters.

The election was close, but I won in a squeaker. It was the happiest, and most relieved, I'd felt in years. When I got the official word, Rita hugged me, and friends and colleagues started calling with congratulations almost immediately. That night we had a huge party at our house in Rockville Centre to celebrate.

I became UFA president on August 1, 1993, two years after I'd made the decision to stay with the department. I'd taken a big gamble with my life, and it had paid off.

Being UFA president was the most rewarding job yet in my career. Under my watch, the UFA brought the members a new, more comprehensive life insurance plan and worked with the UFOA to win passage of a bill in the state legislature that provided a disability pension to active firefighters with certain types of cancers.

We restored our relationship with the international firefighters' union, which had been severed years earlier. We hoped that would boost our clout in contract negotiations and give us more resources to tap.

We provided support for one firefighter's campaign to add the names of the troops to the national bone-marrow registry, and in the following years we helped sign up thousands of the brothers. In the years since, more than three dozen of them have contributed their marrow to people in need.

I threw myself into the job, arriving at the office by eight-thirty every morning, staying till well past dark, lunching at firehouses, and attending department functions several nights a week. As a manager, I tried to deploy all I'd learned by watching Jimmy and Nick: planning out meetings, sticking to our agenda, working with, and sometimes cajoling, the other board members to minimize disagreements and get things done.

It was satisfying and fun. I got to know firehouses in every borough and politicians across the city and state. I enjoyed the pressure of delegate meetings and having to answer for all I did, and became a better speaker and promoter of my policies. Just as when I was a young firefighter, I found something new in the job every day.

A critical factor in my success was the strong working relationship I was able to build with the administration of Mayor Rudolph W. Giuliani, which took office only a few months after I did.

I didn't really know Giuliani too well. I first met him a few weeks before my election, on a hot summer Sunday morning. That day, I'd gotten up early, put on my suit, and gone down to a senior citizen's center in lower Manhattan where he was speaking.

A former federal prosecutor who had made a name for himself by prosecuting Wall Street figures during the financial scandals of the 1980s, Giuliani was a smart, charismatic, and sometimes abrasive man who was challenging Mayor Dinkins in the 1993 election. Giuliani had been the Republican nominee in 1989, too, and lost, but he had come remarkably close for a Republican in a city that was 80 percent Democratic. Now, with Mayor Dinkins faltering amid economic problems and several ugly racial incidents in the city, Giuliani was winning traction with his forceful manner and ideas for aggressively containing petty street crime and luring small businesses into the city.

I'd gone down to meet him at the advice of Tom Regan, a former firefighter who was now advising Giuliani. Tom had suggested that a photo op might benefit both of us in our respective campaigns—me because the candidate was popular with firefighters, and him because he needed union support.

When he finished his speech, I went back outside and planted myself on the sidewalk, where, as arranged, I would intercept him as he went to his car. When he emerged into the hot sun, I shook his hand while a photographer snapped a few pictures.

Giuliani smiled at my greeting and asked how I was doing. But he seemed a little distant. "I love the firefighters," he told me.

"Well, they're pretty unhappy with Dinkins," I told him. "I think they'd certainly support you if I win my election. But I can't make you any promises until then."

Giuliani said he appreciated that, said good-bye, and ducked into his car. The whole encounter had lasted three, maybe four minutes. He seemed wary of looking as if he was close to some guy who could well turn out to be a loser.

After I won, I rallied the union behind Rudy Giuliani. We publicly endorsed him and were the only municipal union to do so. We set up phone banks of firefighters to call voters on his behalf every night. We sent men out on

Election Day to accompany sick and elderly voters to the polls. Mayor Dinkins was so mad he accused us of intimidating voters and choosing sides for racial reasons.

I just thought Giuliani was the best man for the city. Mayor Dinkins had had his shot, and it hadn't done much for New York or for the firefighters. Giuliani seemed committed to bringing a new philosophy to city government.

On Election Night 1993, I was mingling at Giuliani's campaign party and standing not far away from him when it was announced that he'd eked out a close victory. A throng of people made its way toward him, and I joined in. When I offered him my congratulations, he hugged me and said, "Your guys were unbelievable. They were everywhere."

I felt the force of the new Giuliani philosophy almost immediately. A couple of weeks into his term, he invited the city's labor leaders to a morning meeting at Gracie Mansion. While we waited around a conference table, some of my peers teased me for being the only one smart enough to have endorsed the new mayor.

After a few minutes a door opened, and then the mayor strode in, his face all business. He sat down at the head of the table and got right to the point. The city, he said, was in a financial crisis. Revenues were falling short. There was a budget deficit. He could fix it, he was certain, but it would take a few years.

In the meantime, he wouldn't be able to give much to any city employees. That included raises.

In the months ahead, the city negotiated a series of tough contracts with all the labor unions, which would have a longer duration than normal in exchange for no raises during the first two years. With such unappealing terms on the table, talks between the UFA and the city negotiators dragged on, and weren't resolved until after I became commissioner in early 1996. As with every other union, the final five-year deal gave the firefighters no raises in the first two years.

From then on, in the eyes of some firefighters, neither the mayor nor I could ever do right. Some men even accused us of arranging a quid pro quo, with me endorsing the mayor and signing off on the contract in exchange for being named commissioner.

In fact, we barely got to know each other during my whole term as UFA president. I'd shake his hand at firefighter funerals and see him at the occasional award ceremony. He'd always be pleasant. But we never talked in any depth.

Once, I was invited to sit with him at a Yankees game, and I thought I'd have a chance to raise a few issues with him. The mayor is renowned for his love of baseball, and I figured he would be at his most relaxed and approachable in the ballpark.

But he turned out to be such a huge baseball fan that we didn't talk at all. He was totally consumed by the game. He just leaned forward in his seat, counting pitches, and seemed to know the lifetime stats of every player off the top of his head. I spent most of the afternoon staring at his shoulderblade.

He did manage to acknowledge me, every second or third inning. His eyes still locked on the action, he'd tilt his head in my direction and say things like, "Can you believe that pitch?"

Soon after the mayor's election, I was working in my office one day when a tall, lean guy with stiff posture and a grim expression appeared in the doorway. It was Howard Safir, the mayor's new fire commissioner.

A former U.S. Marine and head of the U.S. Marshals, whom the mayor had met while working at the Justice Department, Safir was a total outsider who knew nothing about our department. But the mayor had called him the best manager he ever knew. And it was a big gesture for him to venture over to our offices and sit down with me.

In private, Safir said he wanted to build a constructive relationship with us. "I know we won't always agree," he said. "But I promise never to bullshit you if you'll promise the same."

I realized I was very lucky. His straightforward, direct approach was very similar to the style I tried to use, and fit with my preference for compromising where we could. If he wanted to work together, we'd have a chance to get more things done. Outside the contract, the only real power I had as UFA president was my ability to influence the department. As I'd seen firsthand, it was rare that commissioners and union leaders could truly collaborate.

Howard lived up to his word. Though we didn't always agree, we talked on the phone several times a week and met regularly. He always took my calls and listened to my concerns about issues like bunker gear, the protective clothing that had finally been approved by the city but for which we hadn't yet gotten the funds. For such a forbidding-looking man, he even took it well when I nicknamed him "Rommel" because of his stiff demeanor and asked him, "Have you ever thought of wearing leather boots and getting a couple of guard dogs to walk around with?"

Together we were able to restore five-man crews in sixty busy engine companies, a victory for safety and the men and a partial negation of the costly 1989 arbitration.

Early in his administration, the mayor himself demonstrated his commitment to the department. On March 28, 1994, three firefighters responding to a call at a three-story red-brick building in Soho were hit by an enormous fireball on the floor above the fire. One of them, James Young, thirty-one, was killed, while two others, Charles Seidenburg, twenty-five, and Captain John Drennan, forty-nine, were taken to the burn center at New York Hospital–Cornell Medical Center, with painful burns over more than half their bodies. Seidenburg would die the next day, while Drennan would hang on for more than five painful weeks and eight operations.

In my capacity as UFA president, I went to the emergency room to offer my help and moral support to their families. It was a terrible scene. Both injured men lay on gurneys, writhing in pain. Jimmy Young's body was nearby. I got choked up at the sight. I had worked with Jimmy's father, Harry, in the South Bronx, and known him to be an outstanding battalion chief. Then, as now, personal connections made such horrors even worse.

The mayor swept in with Howard in tow. As they looked down on the burned men, I heard Howard tell him, "If these guys had had bunker gear, this might not have happened."

"What do you mean?" the mayor asked.

Howard explained that bunker gear had been approved but held up. The mayor seemed incredulous. "What are you talking about?" he demanded of Howard. "Look at these guys. They need it now." Then he added, "I'll fix this right now." He walked over to the phone and called someone.

A short time later, Abe Lackman, the head of management and budget, hurried into the hospital. He went to meet the mayor and Howard in a private room with a glass door. I was standing outside.

As soon as Lackman entered, the mayor started yelling. "What's all this about bunker gear?" he asked. "What's the holdup?" Defensively, the budget director tried to get a few words in, but the mayor just waved him off. "I don't care," he said. "You find the money tomorrow, you put the money aside, and you buy this gear."

The clothing finally started arriving in firehouses in May.

I soon learned that the mayor had some ideas of his own for the department.

Howard told me it was a top priority for the mayor to have more firefighters answering medical calls. Under Mayor Dinkins, the department had already taken on some medical calls. It was standard practice in many departments, but it was a major structural change for ours, which expanded the job well beyond the scope of fires. In the course of their normal duties, firefighters had handled some medical emergencies over the years. Under the mayor's proposal, we would become true first responders.

The mayor had learned firsthand how slow and poorly staffed the city's existing ambulance service was. One day before his election, his next-door neighbor had suffered a heart attack. The mayor had called 911, but waited more than an hour before an ambulance showed up. In the meantime, he had called the fire department and talked to a lieutenant who gave him a special number that he could call to get a fire truck instead. The mayor was dumbfounded that such a service wasn't available to everyone. (His neighbor, by the way, survived.)

Eventually the mayor wanted to fold the ambulance service completely into the fire department.

I told Howard I thought both were great ideas and gave him my full support. I firmly believed the firefighters would benefit from medical training. The city would gain, too, since fire engines responded to calls much faster than ambulances. By adding to the firefighters' duties and workload, moreover, we'd be able to protect their jobs and preserve firehouses in future budget-cutting rounds.

I thought Emergency Medical Services, the agency that handled medical calls, was often overlooked. Some of its 3,000 paramedics and emergency medical technicians were ill-trained and poorly qualified and could only improve as part of a larger department where most employees were well equipped, trained, and experienced at responding to calls quickly.

A lot of firefighters hated both ideas. At union meetings, they complained that they had joined the department to fight fires, not resuscitate asthma patients. At one house, a guy built like a Coke machine walked up to me, put his face two inches from mine, and screamed, "I ain't doin' it!" I thought he was going to pop me.

Implementing both programs would take years. It was time-consuming work that wouldn't be finished until well after I became commissioner in the spring of 1996. But in the end, both succeeded. Our firefighters received better training and more money. Ambulances shaved several minutes off their response times. And the improved quality of EMS gave city residents vastly improved service.

Early one morning in March 1996, I was home shaving when the phone rang. I raced from the bathroom to my little home office, my face half-coated with shaving cream, so I could grab it before it woke Rita up.

"Tom, this is Howard," said the voice on the other end.

"You SOB!" I said. "You *did* get the job!" He started laughing.

Rumors had been flying for weeks that Police Commissioner William Bratton, who hadn't been getting along with the mayor, was about to leave and be replaced by Howard Safir. I hadn't believed them, but had teased Howard a fair amount about it.

"Congratulations. I know you're a cop at heart. You've been great for us, and you're going to be terrific."

"There's another part to this," he said. "We want you to be fire commissioner."

"What? Get the hell out of here. You guys are crazy."

I really thought he was joking around, and warned him not to put my name out there. I had a union election coming up that summer and had already been criticized for being too supportive of the administration. If word got out that I had been considered for the job, even jokingly, I'd be in trouble.

"No, there isn't anybody else but you," Howard assured me. "It's yours if you want it."

"You've got to be kidding me. You guys are nuts. Why would you do something like that?"

"It's simple. I told the mayor I think you're the best

guy in the department, and the mayor said, 'Find out if he's interested, and if he is I'll call him.' So, are you interested?"

I was beginning to believe him.

"Absolutely."

"Okay, he'll call you in a few minutes."

A little stunned, I walked slowly back into my bedroom. My wife was still lying in bed. "What happened?" she asked drowsily.

"You're not going to believe this. They want me to be fire commissioner."

She sat up, instantly awake and looking shocked. "What do you mean?"

Then the phone rang again.

14

THE CITY'S THIRTIETH
FIRE COMMISSIONER

I was sure a mistake had been made. The men who became fire commissioner were lawyers, judges, political appointees—or fire chiefs. No mere union president had ever been offered the job. Nor had grunts who didn't pass the lieutenant's test.

When the mayor introduced me as the city's thirtieth fire commissioner at a press conference the next afternoon, a reporter asked me how it all felt.

"This is weird, really weird," I said.

The mayor never told me why he offered me the job. I am sure Howard Safir's recommendation made the difference. The mayor knew I liked his ideas and was receptive to change. He might have seen my appointment as throwing a bone to the unions.

In some ways I felt I was well prepared. Though I hadn't passed any officers' tests, I had gotten a great practical education in the intricacies of the department. I knew what it felt like to crawl down a burning hallway and what it felt like to sit through a budget meeting. I had been to every firehouse in the city, built friendships throughout the department, and immersed myself in safety issues, medical training, and the absorption of the ambulance service.

In other ways, I was nervous as hell. As commissioner, I'd be operating in a new political realm where I'd be under much greater scrutiny. I'd seen previous commissioners lose support from their mayors and go down in flames—and Rudy Giuliani was well known to be a demanding boss. I had a bad feeling I'd be called into his office one day and told, "This isn't working."

Some of the troops were happy that a firefighter who they knew cared about them was leading the FDNY. Others, though, accused me of going over to the enemy.

I really felt, however, that the commissioner's basic responsibility was not too different from the UFA president's: to improve the safety and efficiency of the firefighters, thereby making it safer for the citizens we are sworn to protect. The main difference was that the commissioner could effect change proactively rather than reactively.

It still seemed unreal at my swearing-in ceremony in late April. The mayor had a grandstand installed on the steps of City Hall, hung with big American flags and red-white-and-blue bunting. Dignitaries and bagpipers were invited. My four kids were there, seated next to Rita and me. Having them there to see that moment, after all the struggles I'd been through in my career, made me prouder than anything else that day.

Happy as I was, though, I felt a real absence. A few months earlier, I had noticed that Danny DeFranco was having chronic trouble breathing. He didn't want to see a doctor, though, so I asked him to meet me at department headquarters one Sunday to discuss a firefighter's medical-coverage problem—and when he arrived I'd taken him to the department lung specialist, Dr. David Prezant, and told him, "Dr. Prezant's going to examine you now." It was the only way I could think of to make him get a checkup.

The diagnosis was worse than I had feared: terminal asbestosis in his lungs, with only a few months to live, at most. Despite his crusade against asbestos, he'd been exposed to it often as a young plumber, before its dangers were understood. A few days before Christmas 1995, Dr. Prezant and I drove out to Danny's home on Staten Island to break the news to him and his wife, Pat.

Danny entered the hospital soon after Christmas, and died several weeks later, at the age of sixty-one.

I was devastated to lose such a vital force in my life. In my speech, I swore in Danny's honor that safety would be my number one commitment as commissioner. In my office, I hung a huge picture of him. In the next six years I found myself looking at it often for inspiration.

The next day, I went to give testimony at my first City Council hearing. I was to learn that my new role required more diplomacy than being a union official ever had.

For some time, the mayor had been pushing a plan to eliminate the city's 16,000 fire-alarm boxes. They had stood on many street corners for more than a century, and had once been a vital connection between the citizens and the department. Now, in an era when everyone had three phones at home and a cell phone in their pocket, they were used far less and were just too outdated to justify the expense of maintaining the system. But eliminating the familiar boxes was an emotional issue in many neighborhoods, and the mayor had taken some heat for his proposal.

I walked into the hearing carrying a compromise plan he'd given me to defuse the situation. It called for cutting about half the boxes.

But Sheldon Leffler, a Queens city councilman who had little use for the mayor or his team, questioned whether even the compromise plan was too much. "What if an older person has to call in an alarm and the alarm box is two blocks away instead of one?" he asked late in the day.

By this point in the hearing, I had been fielding questions and challenges for some time. I thought the challenges were getting ridiculous. "How crazy do you want to make these scenarios?" I asked. "Now we have elderly people who have to walk another block to report a fire? Come on. I mean, how many elderly people do *you* think are running to alarm boxes to report fires?"

It was the truth. Unfortunately, I had opened my big mouth while a group of eighty senior citizens, brought to City Hall to attend the hearing, were sitting in the balcony. As soon as I finished speaking, I heard a roar of boos from the gallery.

When I walked outside, a reporter from the *New York Post,* Dan Janison, was waiting for me. "Boy," Dan said, "it's going to be fun covering you!"

After years of watching and working with the department, I had a laundry list of ideas for reform. Whether I was removed by the mayor in a month or lasted a long time, I wanted to fight for the things I believed in—especially safety.

From my first day, I sought to make sure we constantly upgraded our equipment. A host of new products were coming on the market for improving the job, from infrared cameras to higher-grade gloves and boots and fire-resistant hoods, but we weren't keeping up on all of it. I regularly prodded our officers to crack down on fire-fighters who didn't wear protective equipment like the hoods. I remembered well how much we had hated wearing all the proper gear when I was in Ladder 42, and how invulnerable we'd felt. Yet I'd learned on the safety committee how bad some injuries could be and what risks men took when they didn't follow procedures.

Another area I focused on was training. Many of our men never received formal training once they'd left the academy. But we implemented a range of mandatory programs designed to refresh their skills and introduce them to new techniques and situations, like dealing with hazardous materials. We had never held training at night, even though that was when we faced many of our worst fires; now we did.

Our proby training at the academy needed a major overhaul. It was still using virtually the same curriculum as when I was a student. The instructors handed out mimeographed sheets from 1950s textbooks.

To spearhead the revamping, I tapped a man named Eddie Geraghty.

A six-foot-three marathoner in his early forties, with a moustache and easy smile, Eddie had joined the department in 1978 and had become a strong captain in Engine 236, dedicated to safety and pushing himself hardest of all to lead by example. With another officer, he had even written his own updated safety manual.

When I asked him to take charge of the proby school,

he was thrilled. For two years, he attacked his mission almost as if it *were* a fire. By the time he left, the entire program had been revamped, made tougher and refocused on the latest technology and techniques.

There was a lot we were able to accomplish during my time as commissioner. I never would have achieved half of it without dedicated officers like him.

At least once a week I found myself outside a burning building or near a large water-main break, roaming around in my white helmet, talking to the firefighters. As commissioner, I wanted to be a visible presence in the field, so the men would feel comfortable with me and understand my ideas. In the mayor, I also had a boss who always wanted the most up-to-date, detailed information on any crisis.

Besides, getting to go to scenes was the most fun part of the job.

But going as commissioner required a big adjustment for me. Listening to the radio en route drove home for me the enormous responsibility I'd taken on. Whenever there was a report that firefighters on the floor above a fire hadn't been heard from, or that someone had been seriously hurt, I felt a heavy weight and thought, *Oh no, oh God, don't let this happen.*

At the same time, once I reached a scene I had to hold back and let the chiefs do their job, even though my every instinct told me to grab a hose or a halligan tool and help out.

On June 15, 1997, I went to a huge five-alarm fire at Saint Philip Neri Catholic Church, a towering, century-old institution with an imposing stone edifice right on the Grand Concourse in the Bronx.

With the fire contained but still raging, I went inside to take a look at the damage. Smoke filled the church. The rear ceiling, near the altar, had collapsed. The front had been roped off as a precautionary measure.

While the firefighters worked the other end of the church, I noticed that behind the ropes stood three beautiful statues of the Blessed Mother and other saints. If the fire spread up front, I saw, they would be destroyed.

I ran outside and asked a couple men from Rescue 3 to come in and help me. We went behind the ropes, hoisted one of the statues above our heads, and carried it outside.

We went back for another, but underestimated how heavy it was—at least a thousand pounds. Four of us strained to get it above our shoulders.

Just as we started moving, Deputy Chief Robert Carbo, the commander at the scene, came up to us. "What are you guys doing?" he asked angrily. "This is a collapse zone!"

"Chief, don't yell at them," I said, gasping as I stuck my head out from one corner of the statue. "I asked them to come in here."

He fixed me with a glare. "Commissioner, this is absolutely outrageous," he said. "I'm in charge here. This is an unsafe area. You're putting our men in harm's way."

"Okay," I said. "Hang on. The statue is a little heavy." He let us carry it out, but after we'd put it down, resumed chewing me out.

I felt like a fool. Chief Carbo was right. I'd undermined his authority. All of a sudden I felt like a proby again, being chewed out by my captain and thinking how much I still had to learn.

* * *

Fortunately, as commissioner, I was able to work alongside one of the best teachers I ever had.

Bill Feehan, the department's first deputy commissioner, had become a firefighter in 1959, after serving in Korea as a marine. In the intervening years, he had held every rank in the department, even the job of commissioner on an interim basis, and become its unofficial voice of reason and institutional memory. He could drive anywhere in the city and at almost every block recount details of a fire he or someone else had battled there at some point in the previous four decades.

Though technically a civilian now, Bill's proudest position had been as chief of department, the top job among firefighters. He still answered his phone, "Chief Feehan." But he had a broader range of experience by far than anyone else in the department.

I'd known Bill for years. In the union, we all thought of him as a decent and compassionate resource in the commissioner's office. His sentimentality about firefighters made him an easy mark when we needed a contract or some other help for a firefighter—teasingly, we nicknamed Bill "Commissioner Cave."

At the time of my appointment, Bill was sixty-six and had been talking of retirement for years. Three years earlier, when I'd won the UFA presidency, he'd sent me a congratulatory note in which he called himself "a very short timer." But he showed no signs of slowing down, and no one ever believed his retirement talk. He loved the job too much to step down.

Indeed, when Howard Safir had sounded me out about succeeding him, he'd told me there was one condition: "You have to keep Bill Feehan."

"That's a no-brainer," I said. "I would have done that anyway."

Once I started working alongside him, I learned that, besides being a smart fire officer, Bill was something of a character. Lean and elegant, with a warm smile, he dressed in Eisenhower-era clothes—spiffy herringbone jackets and madras ties—that made him look as if he'd stepped out of an old *Dragnet* episode.

Outside of his kids and grandchildren, the fire department seemed to be his whole life—especially after his wife, Elizabeth, died in 1995. Every morning he rose early and stopped off at the North Shore Diner in Bayside for a breakfast of rye toast, two eggs, hash browns, bacon, and coffee. He was always at his desk by seven, and usually worked at least twelve hours.

Detail-oriented and methodical at the office, Bill was so focused on work that he often lost track of his personal life. He routinely forgot to pay his bills and taxes, and was always getting his power or phone cut off. He didn't file for Social Security, and wasn't even aware he was eligible for it until I asked him about it one day. He was always telling new stories of some mishap he'd had, and invariably we teased him about them. We all knew that Bill was so absorbed by the fire department and his family that he just didn't have time for everything.

With its huge couch and open door, his office was a gathering place for members of the staff to drift into during the day for coffee and catching up, while Bill, at his desk, worked on a speech or proposal. A largely self-educated man who loved reading, especially military history, Bill was a terrific writer, and he handled many of our speeches. He was also a good public speaker, who so radiated honesty that we invariably turned to him when we needed to deliver unpalatable or potentially embarrassing news to a hostile group. Bill's unassuming and self-effacing manner was rarely questioned, and usually managed to defuse any controversy.

Late in the day, people sometimes returned, planted themselves on the couch, and poured cocktails. While they shared department gossip or debated policy, Bill would quietly keep working. Only after finishing whatever he was doing would he push his chair back and pour himself a scotch.

Sometimes it was past ten by the time he finally left. We used to tease him that we'd come to work some morning and find that he'd passed away at his desk.

Often he and I would be the only people still working late at night. We had some of our deepest talks about the department at those times, and I'd listen as Bill shared stories of the history he'd seen and some of his ideas for reform. He was essentially cautious, while I was prone to be more aggressive. But that cautiousness, matched with his historical knowledge of the department, balanced my hunger for change and understanding of firefighters in the field.

Whenever I brought Bill ideas—which I did more and more—he could tell when, if ever, they had been tried, what similar actions had been taken, how they had worked, and who would or wouldn't support them. I absorbed so much from those conversations.

Bill couldn't contain his deep feelings for firefighters. Once, he summoned a young fireman from the academy to talk about why he was getting bad grades and skipping classes. He routinely interceded with people having such problems. Before the meeting, Bill groused about the kid and warned us, "I may have to fire him!" When he heard the fireman was there for the 9 A.M. meeting, he told the secretary, "Let him wait!" He didn't bring the kid into his office until that afternoon.

For an hour, we all wondered what was happening behind Bill's closed door. We assumed Bill was hammering him. But we couldn't make out any noise but a low murmur.

Finally the door opened, and Bill came out. He had tears in his eyes.

He pulled me aside into a corner. "Tommy, we've gotta give this kid a break," he said. "He's a good kid. Let's give him a second chance." Wiping his eyes, he recited the kid's litany of woes, from his troubled childhood to his struggles as a single parent. The kid got his chance.

But Bill had no tolerance for phonies and slackers. Once, he was out at a restaurant when he overheard a firefighter at another table bragging about how he had been extending his medical leave with a phony injury. Bill recognized the guy, but didn't say anything to him that night. The next day, he simply transferred him down to headquarters for light duty.

For four or five days, the guy sat in the office, doing paperwork. Bill never acknowledged him. Finally the guy asked what was going on. Bill unloaded on him.

Bill also hadn't lost the quiet toughness of a hardened firefighter. Late one day in July 2000, we got a report of a major natural gas explosion a few blocks away from our office. Bill turned to his assistant, Henry McDonald, and said, "Let's go."

The explosion had leveled several Brooklyn brownstones, leaving behind a mound of dense rubble. As the firefighters scrambled through the pile, searching for victims, Bill roamed the sidelines with the chiefs. He ended up staying all night long and well into the next day. At 3 P.M., he and Henry went back to the office to shower. Exhausted, Henry told his boss he was going home, and Bill said he'd be right behind him. That night, after a nap, Henry turned on the TV to watch the news and saw Bill still there, standing on the podium at a news conference, talking about the collapse. When Henry came into work the next morning, Bill was already there.

When I first became commissioner, I was a little uneasy about how well Bill and I would get along. He was so much more experienced than I was that it felt a little strange to be his boss.

But Bill promised me his unconditional support on my first day in office, and it never wavered. Whatever I asked, he did, and he never held back. He sincerely believed that, instead of looking over someone's shoulder or trying to do someone else's job, you should focus on doing the best you could in the one you had. He had been shaped by the ethic in good firehouses, where every man on the rig, from the man assigned to the roof to the can man carrying the extinguisher, had an important job to do, and success depended on each doing what he should. "If you're the can man," he liked to say, "be the can man."

About a year after I started as commissioner, Bill and I were eating dinner at Forlini's in Little Italy one night when he suddenly looked at me with a very serious expression.

"You know," he said, "I was deeply hurt and highly insulted when you were named commissioner. I thought

I deserved it more. I've been around a lot longer and done a lot more than you."

I was a little taken aback and didn't know quite what to say. Was he quitting?

"After a while," he went on, "I saw why. They saw qualities in you that I didn't have. You can deal better with the politics and the unions, and you have the stomach for tough fights. I realized they absolutely made the right decision."

Coming from one of the most knowledgeable, experienced firefighters the department has ever known, that compliment meant a lot. Knowing that it came from a friend meant even more.

15

SAINTS AND SINNERS

As commissioner, I found, I was exposed to a wide range of experiences every day—some tragic, some funny, some inspiring, and some pathetic. It was one of the best parts of the job for me. I worked with wonderful people, and got to test myself in all kinds of circumstances, too. Every day there was something different to learn.

Death was one of the most painful realities.

One evening in January 1997, John Hannon, a thirty-two-year-old member of Ladder 17 in the Bronx, was driving home from work when a wheel came loose from a truck on the Major Deegan Expressway, crossed the median, and smashed through his windshield. He was brought to Lincoln Hospital in critical condition.

I rushed to the hospital as soon as I heard, as did the mayor and some members of our staff. Hannon hadn't been injured in the line of duty, an event that I dreaded, but in a freak accident that could have happened to anyone. Still, all of us felt a responsibility to help him as one of the brothers. It was rough seeing this healthy kid, a popular firefighter, a Golden Gloves boxer who had stayed at the firehouse late that night to watch tapes of boxing matches, a beloved member of a large Irish family, lying in a hospital bed hooked up to tubes. He died the next morning.

When we gathered the family together so the doctors could tell them what had happened, one of his brothers burst out, "Not my brother! Not my brother!" and ran from the room in agony.

For a second, most of us froze—except Father Mychal Judge. He immediately turned and followed John's brother. When we emerged a few minutes later, Father Judge was sitting in the corner of the hallway, holding the brother in a ball as he cried, and reassuring him in soothing tones, "It's okay, it's okay."

I'd first met the Franciscan priest a few years earlier, when he had become a chaplain in the fire department. Once I became commissioner and started seeing him at major fire scenes, performing masses at department ceremonies, and counseling people in need, we grew much closer. He always carried a pager and responded to calls throughout the city. The previous summer, when TWA Flight 800 had crashed into the Atlantic Ocean, Father Judge had gone out to Long Island to be with the families of the victims every day. I'd seen up close what peace and serenity he carried with him even in the most difficult moments, and how reassuring his caring presence could be.

One day early in my tenure, he'd appeared outside my office and asked for five minutes of my time. When I shut the door, he told me he wanted me to know that he was there for me whenever I needed him. After that he made it part of his job to reach out to me, regularly sending me encouraging cards and notes in his strong, slanted hand-

writing, and calling often to catch up. He frequently offered encouraging words at a tough moment or when a
critical story had appeared in the newspaper. "*You* are
the commissioner," he wrote after seeing me give one
speech. "You were great today. Everybody in that room
knows that *you* are the commissioner."

Gradually, I became comfortable opening up to him.
I'd always kept a lot of my feelings and frustrations inside, and hadn't even shared some of them with my wife.
But it was easy to trust in Father Judge's wisdom and
soothing presence. Knowing he was there was an enormous comfort to me during stressful days.

Rita and I had made sure all our kids were baptized. But
we had become Christmas-and-Easter churchgoers. In
our house, Sunday morning was usually a time for work
or sports. My religious life was confined largely to funerals and masses for firefighters and occasional prayers for
my kids that I'd mutter under my breath when I walked
by a church.

I still liked the basic message of the church, the idea of
doing unto others as you would have them do unto you.
But I'd fallen away from organized religion after I'd entered my twenties and gotten caught up in my career and
family. I'd grown disillusioned by some of the priests I'd
met and listened to in high school, who didn't seem very
spiritual, and I disagreed with the church's stands on
birth control and on priests getting married.

Father Judge, though, seemed to me to epitomize what
the priesthood was about. He talked easily of his love for
Jesus, but was never judgmental or unfairly critical of
anyone. His homilies, unlike so many I'd heard, used the
gospels to convey simple but beautiful messages of faith,

love, and understanding. He didn't get too caught up in doctrine. "Don't overthink God's plan," he'd say. "Recognize He has one, and don't get in the way of it."

He lived, with very few possessions, in a simple room at Saint Francis of Assisi Church on West 32nd Street in the Garment District. When given a donation or even a gift of money, he invariably gave it to someone who needed it more.

As commissioner, I saw how extensive the network of people he counseled and cared for was. He maintained contact with dozens of those he'd met over the years, some of them at tragic moments. He worked closely with firefighters who had family or alcohol problems, and he was also involved with homeless people, gays, and AIDS ministries.

Part of his empathy might have come from the fact that he was gay, and knew what it was like to be disliked for who you were. He'd come to me early on and told me about his sexual orientation, just to alert me, but I'd already known about it, and told him I didn't care. What mattered and defined him more than anything was his basic decency.

Father Judge wasn't afraid to show his human side. He could be vain about his looks, and loved showing off his snow-white hair. He groused about the bureaucracy he had to deal with in the church—which wasn't so different from the one at the department. We bonded over our mutual love of traditions and common willingness to challenge the hierarchy.

Father Judge liked to do things his own way. At memorial masses in firehouses, he regularly told firefighters, "You are doing God's work, and God wants you to receive His body and blood. He forgives you, He loves you. Everybody, bow your heads. Tell God you're sorry for your sins. Now, come and receive Our Lord." General absolution like that expressly violates church rules. Someone even reported him to the cardinal, who ordered him to stop. But Father Judge just found a more subtle way to keep doing what he thought was right, and I admired his conviction.

He fed my spiritual side in a way no religious figure had in a long time. I saw how he brought people back to a church that was driving many away. He became very close to my family. When my grandson was born on October 1, 2001, we named him Mason Judge.

Along with Father Judge and Bill Feehan, there was a whole group of incredible people I got to work with as commissioner. Michael Regan, my first press spokesman, was a terrific advocate for firefighters, while Kerry Kelly, chief of our bureau of health services, and Dr. Prezant, the assistant chief, revolutionized medical care for the firefighters. Our budget director, Steve Rush, was tireless at finding us new resources, while Roy Katz did a great job overseeing all firehouse reconstruction and renovation projects, though he had an odd habit of consistently estimating the length of time to complete any project, no matter what it was, as eighteen months.

One of my closest and most important advisers was Lynn Tierney, whom I hired away from the Port Authority to be my deputy commissioner of intergovernmental affairs. Feisty, sarcastic, knowledgeable, and dedicated, Lynn threw herself into the job, and we developed an immediate rapport. She did sometimes tedious but vitally important work, like getting us grant money for special equipment. But she didn't leave the job at the office. She was always looking to do more and to learn the nuts and bolts of firefighting. At all times of night she could be seen at third-alarm fires throughout the city, asking questions and looking to help in any way she could. Her doggedness won her respect from many of our chiefs—not always an easy thing for a woman and a civilian to do—and made her an indispensable part of my team.

One of the duties Lynn took on was the grim task of helping the families of firefighters who had been hurt or killed, gathering the details of their lives for me and the mayor, and looking to help them where she could. She brought great sensitivity to the task.

Someone else who became indispensable to me was Tom Fitzpatrick—Fitz, as we called him. I'd known him as a firefighter in the Bronx, where he had a reputation for toughness. Later he served in Rescue 1. After becoming a captain, he had served as Howard Safir's executive officer, and I asked him to stay on with me.

A big man with a shock of curly blond hair, Fitz has a wry sense of humor and an analytical mind. He was another safety fanatic, who played a vital part in helping me develop plans for the department and strategies to implement them.

A large part of the job was dealing with firefighters who got into trouble.

Two days after Labor Day in 1998, my press officer, Michael Regan, poked his head into my office, looking very anxious, and said, "We need to talk." The day before, a local TV station had aired footage of a racist float that had been part of a Labor Day parade in Broad Channel, a mostly white, working-class neighborhood in Queens. Placed on the back of a pickup truck, the float had taken as its theme "Black to the Future: Broad Channel 2098." The guys on board had worn blackface and mops as wigs. They carried boom boxes and tossed pieces of watermelon and Popeye's fried chicken to the crowd lining Cross Bay Boulevard.

One of the participants, incredibly, had tied rope around himself to reenact the recent vicious murder of James Byrne, the black man who had been tied to a truck in Jasper, Texas, that year and dragged to his death. The whole ugly display had been captured on videotape.

At first, watching the news, I'd thought the guys behind the offensive display were just a few imbeciles, and I'd forgotten about it. But Mike told me that the press had uncovered the identities of the people on the float. Two of them were off-duty firefighters, while a third was a cop. The mayor had already announced that any city employee involved in that "disgusting display of racism" would be fired. Almost immediately after the story broke, people all over the city were calling for these guys' heads. For days, news of the march dominated the TV and newspapers.

The float was bad enough in itself, of course. But the mushrooming story had wider implications that we had to take into consideration.

The mayor, of course, never liked any story that made New York look bad, and this one definitely did. He and the police were also sensitive to the constant accusations of racism made against them by community activists and political opportunists.

Only a week earlier, the mayor had been roundly criticized in the black community for sending 3,000 cops to the "Million Youth March" rally in central Harlem, in which some 6,500 people had participated. Before that, he'd strongly criticized the event because its organizer and main speaker, Khalid Muhammad, was a former Nation of Islam official who had called Jews "bloodsuckers of the black nation and the black community" and had also made inflammatory remarks about Roman Catholics, whites, and homosexuals. The mayor had first denied a permit for the march and then tried unsuccessfully to block the march in court, denouncing Muhammad as an "incendiary racist," words that infuriated some activists.

The fire department was vulnerable on the issue of race, too. We weren't institutionally racist, but we were 94 percent white, in a city that was now less than 50 percent white. We were working to recruit more minority members, but it was an effort that required time. There were firefighters with racist views. We generally got less grief on the subject than the cops, because everyone knew firefighters were color-blind when it came to rushing into a fire. But diverse, we weren't.

Soon after Mike brought me up to speed, I invited the two firefighters into my office for an off-the-record talk one afternoon. I wanted to evaluate them for myself. They were respectful enough. But I was appalled that they had been so stupid.

"What the hell were you thinking?" I asked them. They hemmed and hawed and said very little.

After the meeting, my gut feeling was that these were private citizens who had been on their own time on their day off and who had not identified themselves as firefighters. I thought they were entitled to their constitutional right to be idiots.

When I sat down with the mayor to talk about it at

City Hall, though, he quickly overruled me. He and I had by now established a relationship where we could speak more candidly to one another.

"Look, whether they meant it or not, these guys are representing the department," he said, in his emphatic voice. "They're sending a message that the department doesn't care about people having these views."

"I agree, boss. But can we really fire someone for exercising free speech? That bothers me."

"Look, of course they're entitled to say what they think. But that doesn't mean the city has to employ them. It would be a signal to all the citizens of the city that the department doesn't care."

I realized that he was right, of course—that I had been focused on the fire department while he had a more global perspective on the situation. As he said, if those guys stayed, it could hurt us for years.

Over the next few months, under an intense media spotlight, we took steps to remove the men. Their lawyer argued that their float had been satirical and intended to mock the residents of Broad Channel for their own racism. In the end, they sued the city to get their jobs back. The case is still winding its way through the courts.

In some ways, I felt bad about firing them. I didn't think they were evil, just stupid. But in the end, I felt it was the right thing for the department and the city.

It hurt my reputation with the firefighters' union, though, and in some of the ranks. In one newspaper, an unnamed firefighter called me "a vindictive SOB" and was quoted as saying, "If we all got fired for doing stupid things, there wouldn't be anyone left on the job."

*　*　*

In the fall of 1999, I threw myself into a fight I *loved*.

Engine 273–Ladder 129 in Flushing, Queens, had long been troubled. Years before I became commissioner, the ladder truck had run a red light and struck a car while responding to an alarm. Inside the car was the daughter of a fire marshal, who was killed.

Accidents are inevitable when huge trucks career through crowded city streets. An investigation showed no wrongdoing in the house. But the death haunted the men for years. Many had sought counseling for their guilt.

Then, in 1997, our new computerized 911 system had tracked a false alarm call to a pay phone in the same firehouse. The perpetrator turned out to be a member of the company. He had wanted to stage an accident on a call and use the documentation to claim a disability pension. Of course we fired him as soon as he was found guilty in a trial.

Worried about the problems in the house, I started keeping a closer eye on it. I sent a couple of good officers into command jobs there, but both came back and told me that some of the men in the house were slackers and taking both units down the toilet. With the battalion not doing its job and other officers unwilling to help take on the fight, I moved the good men out.

In the fall of 1998, a friend called to tell me that some of the men at the house were dogging medical calls. When one came in, they would wait a couple of minutes to respond, hoping an ambulance or maybe another house would pick up the call first. This was the last straw.

I started digging around, talking to people I knew who had been through the house to confirm the reports.

To make absolutely sure, I sent a couple of internal investigators to sit across the street in an unmarked car and time how long the house took to respond to calls. Their data nailed it. One of the officers, they found, would sometimes wait four minutes after an alarm before opening up the door. They were supposed to be out within one.

It was incredibly disheartening. In my firefighting days, we had gotten thirty or more calls a night and raced to every one. I couldn't believe any firefighters in our department wouldn't do the same.

By now I was convinced that the rot was deep. We tried to identify the offenders, but once again their housemates mostly clammed up for fear of seeming like squealers. Finally I concluded there was only one (admittedly drastic) way to fix the situation: move everyone out of there. In late October we announced plans to transfer fifty-four guys, which was almost the entire house. This was no time for a code of silence. I wanted them, and everyone in the department, to know that. We wanted to make it abundantly clear that we couldn't allow any slackers when it came to the protection of the citizens.

But the transfer announcement sparked an uproar. Residents of the community complained that I was destroying their local firehouse. The unions went after me, too. I received angry letters accusing me of wielding too broad a brush when most guys in the house weren't at fault.

In the end, we didn't have to go as far as we'd thought. Faced with the dismantling of the entire house, enough members there, along with union officials, spoke up and identified the offenders; we made some transfers and others shaped up.

It felt great. The actions we'd taken had an immediate impact on the house and the department, reminding everybody who we worked for and how much the city depended on us. The house today is a vastly improved place—busy, with a good group and officers that are respected. It was a big victory for the department, the good people in the house, and the neighborhood.

16

THE ATLANTIC AVENUE FIRE

Friday, June 5, 1998, was a major turning point in my career. And I spent most of it in a bad mood.

That morning the newspapers were filled with stories of a drunken brawl involving about forty firefighters, which had broken out at a midtown restaurant two days earlier. Witnesses said firefighters were smoking cigars, walking into the women's rest room, peeing openly in the park outside, and making lewd comments to female patrons on the patio—even before they started fighting. When a couple of guys started brawling, a cop had tried to break them up—only to find himself summarily thrown over a large planter.

What made it worse was that the whole thing happened only a few hours after our annual Medal Day ceremony at City Hall. The guys had come straight from the ceremony, normally the proudest day of the year, still wearing their dress-blue uniforms. Their behavior had ensured that, instead of praising our heroes, the city would be talking about us as a bunch of louts.

I interviewed firefighters all day, trying to get to the bottom of what had happened. I didn't have much luck.

Most had sudden "memory lapses." While I could understand that sort of behavior from the troops, I was furious with the officers who wouldn't talk about it. I thought they were shirking their duty.

I could tell we were in for a long, frustrating investigation. Indeed, while we eventually would end up fining eleven firefighters a total of 130 days' pay, we would never clearly know what had started the fight.

I wasn't in the mood for a party when I left the office the night of the brawl and drove out to Queens for a dinner with the Vulcan Society, an organization of black firefighters. I knew how important it was that I be there to talk to the troops and show my support, however. Increasing diversity in the department was an absolute necessity, and an area where we'd had very little success.

As I waited in line to get dinner, my driver called and said we had a serious fire brewing that we should probably check out. I left my plate and ran out to meet him.

As we sped to the scene, I listened closely to the radio. There were early reports of missing men.

The first call had come in to Engine 332 at 8:22 P.M., reporting an oil-burner fire at 2530 Atlantic Avenue. It was a shabby hundred-year-old three-story wooden row house with a luncheonette on the first floor. It was connected to four similar buildings, which stood on a dark, narrow service road just beneath an overpass. The row house next door was vacant.

Only heavy smoke was visible to the first companies, but a closer look showed that the fire had spread throughout the building. The officers in charge quickly called in more alarms. Eventually this would be a five-alarm fire, which meant that fifty-two trucks, engines, and other equipment and a total of 220 men responded to the scene.

The first firefighters to arrive encountered a woman out front who was screaming, "My mother's inside! My mother's inside!" Men from Ladder 103 and Ladder 176 raced in the front door and ran upstairs to the second-floor rear apartment, to force the door and search for the woman there. Behind them, men from Engine 332 dragged a hose.

The fire was fierce. It had consumed everything quickly, even structural supports. At some point there was a sickening crack and the floor gave way. Instantly, five men plunged into an inferno. The furniture and appliances from the apartment tumbled down after them and pinned them to the floor. They were stuck in a fire-filled pit, in what had been the luncheonette, and surrounded on all sides by flames—even underneath them.

As the survivors later described it, the next few minutes seemed like hours, days. Most of the men were screaming in agony. Lieutenant Timothy Stackpole, certain he was about to die, started screaming the "Hail Mary" at the top of his lungs.

Outside, Battalion Chief Ed Kilduff was asked by the chief in charge, Tom Galvin, to see how the rescuers inside were doing. Kilduff took several men and led them up the stairs to the rear apartment. When they reached it, all they saw was the engine company's line dangling over the edge of a hole filled with fire.

Kilduff raced back outside and started gathering people for a massive rescue effort. Word of what had happened spread quickly through the ranks. Firefighters ran to the back of the building and plunged in with hoses and hand tools.

Four of the men lay in the middle of the floor, pinned under beams and radiators. Another one was pinned against a back wall—and on fire.

The rescuers extracted him and another man quickly. It took longer to clear the debris off the other three. When the rescuers finally reached Stackpole, the lieutenant stopped praying long enough to tell them, "Go out and get the eight biggest gorillas you can find and get this radiator off of me."

It took twenty-five minutes. The rescuers cut, bruised, and burned themselves as they dug. The last man they reached, at the bottom of the pile, wasn't moving.

Outside, they learned that despite what the woman believed, there hadn't been anyone up there at all.

I went straight to Brookdale Hospital, where most of the injured had been sent. Everything was chaotic there. The emergency room was very small. Wave after wave of guys were brought in on stretchers. Everywhere I turned, there was a gurney with an injured firefighter. The doctors seemed overwhelmed.

Then the paramedics wheeled in Scott LaPiedra.

Photos I would see later showed what a handsome man Scott LaPiedra had been. He had looked younger than his forty years. Looking down now, I thought he was dead. He had severe burns over more than 70 percent of his body. His face wasn't recognizable. His skin was a slithery, blackened mess. Miraculously, he was still breathing, and had let out a small moan when the rescuers reached him. But I had never seen anyone alive look worse.

A minute later, they wheeled in the body of James Blackmore. He had been the man at the bottom of the pile. He was blue all over.

Right in front of me, a doctor checked his vitals, noted the time, and pronounced him dead.

It was hard to believe. I knew Jimmy. He was a lieutenant in my brother Roddy's house, Engine 332, and a father of four kids. He had been in the department for twenty-one years. A little later I found out that Roddy had seen him at work that evening, just as he finished his shift and Jimmy came on. Leaving the firehouse, Roddy reminded Jimmy that he had worked overtime and needed the lieutenant to finish the paperwork in order to get paid. "No fuckin' way!" Blackmore had teased him, laughing.

Standing between the stretchers, I felt overwhelmed. Losing one of our guys, one of *my* guys, in a fire was harder than I'd ever imagined. It made me feel as if I had been beaten up.

But I reminded myself of all that I could do to help. So I talked to their doctors, and checked in with the chiefs at the scene, and made sure we had sent chaplains and firefighters out to the homes of the families to give them whatever they needed. I called Roddy and broke the news to him and sent him to sit with Sue Blackmore, so she would have someone from Jimmy's house there for her.

Of all the things I've asked him to do for me over the years, this was to be the hardest for him. As he walked up to the Blackmores' house, he could see through their window that Sue and the kids were watching news of the fire on TV. That's when he rang the bell. When they looked out and saw him, they knew, and they all broke down immediately.

In the same room lay two of the other three firefighters who had been in the collapse, Terry Quinn and Brian Baiker. Both were from Engine 332. I went over to see how they were.

Terry was a good friend of my brother's, and I had known him a long time. He had serious burns on his face and head, and was crying out in pain as the doctors plugged him with tubes and needles. He was deeply disturbed too; he had been lying directly on top of Jimmy Blackmore in the pile, and had spent the whole time shaking his shoulder but never getting a response.

But Terry had the stubborn mulishness of the best firefighters, and through all his pain, he was cantankerously cursing everyone out and good-naturedly grousing about his injuries: "Hey, watch where you stick that, Doc." Seeing Terry complain, I knew he would be okay.

I didn't know Baiker at all. He was a proby who had just gone to his first fire that very afternoon with my brother. He, too, was going to be okay, though he had burns over 30 percent of his body and was very upset. When he told me he was worried that his mother would be so angry with him for getting hurt that she wouldn't let him go back to the firehouse, I saw he was more upset by the possibility that he couldn't stay a firefighter than he was about his own pain.

I had missed seeing the third man, Lieutenant Stackpole, from Ladder Company 103. He had been at Brookdale only briefly before being sent on to New York

Hospital–Cornell Medical Center in Manhattan, where there was a specialized burn center. He had suffered deep, painful burns on his leg, back, and arms. After I left Brookdale, I drove over to see him.

Timmy had been talking nonstop since being brought into Cornell, telling joke after joke and rambling on about how beautiful and overwhelming it had been to see so many firefighters rush into a crumbling building to save their brothers.

Soon after arriving at the hospital, still on a gurney in the emergency room, he had asked for a phone so he could call his wife, Tara, and tell her he had been hurt before she saw the news on TV.

But his son Kevin had answered instead. Hearing his voice, Timmy had assumed a calm tone, just as if he were still at the firehouse, hanging out. "Hi, it's me," he'd said very matter-of-factly. "Is Mommy around?"

For several minutes, Timmy had joked and chatted with his son, giving no indication that he felt any pain. Finally he'd said, "Well, just tell Mommy I am in the hospital. I got hurt."

Calmly he'd added, "And turn off the television. You can't just watch television. You have to do your home-work. . . . I know, I know. . . . Well, I will talk to you. Good-bye."

Then he'd hung up and resumed his monologue.

I arrived at the hospital burn center not long before Tara. He was still on a stretcher, talking a mile a minute as hospital attendants poured water on his legs, trying to alleviate the pain of his burns. His face and hair were coated with plaster dust and bits of glass.

Once Tara arrived, along with Timmy's mother and

other relatives, doctors moved him to a private room and tried to clear it so he could calm down a little. But then the mayor swept in with his entourage. He always came to the bedsides of seriously injured firefighters and took a deep personal interest in their recoveries.

Once Timmy saw the mayor, he started shouting about the restaurant fight that had been all over the morning papers. "Mr. Mayor, don't judge the department because of a few bad apples!" he called out. "These are the real firemen, the thirty guys who dragged us out!" His voice rising, he added, "I don't want any individual acts of bravery awarded here. This is an award for the whole department or none at all."

The mayor asked him what had happened, and Timmy started recounting the horror of each moment. As he spoke, the room hushed while nurses, doctors, and attendants drifted in to hear the story. For ten minutes Timmy held everyone spellbound as he walked us step by step through the ordeal, from their mission to rescue a woman who wasn't there to the sudden drop into the fiery pit and the bravery of the men who carried them out.

Just as it seemed he had finished, he turned to his mother and added, "Oh—and Ma, I wore clean underwear!"

The whole room burst into laughter. Smiling, the mayor turned to Tara and asked, "Is he always like this?"

It made us feel that maybe he would be all right.

The last stop of the night was Jacobi Medical Center in the Bronx. Scott LaPiedra had been air-lifted there from

Brookdale. The doctors wanted to get him into a hyperbaric chamber as soon as possible. Once he arrived, though, the doctors determined he was too unstable to be put in the chamber. Scott seemed certain to die.

When we reached the emergency room we saw that Father Judge was already there. Addie LaPiedra had arrived only a few minutes before. She was a young, pretty woman with curly blond hair, dressed in aqua overall shorts. As soon as I saw her, I thought sadly, *She looks like she should be hanging out with her friends at a record store, not preparing to bury a husband.*

I went forward and hugged her. Father Judge took her hand and started talking to her in his soothing tones. God was good, he said. He assured her we were all there for her. The mayor spoke softly as he told her how sorry we all were. Addie just seemed dazed. She didn't seem to understand how grim the situation was.

When Dr. Prezant came out, pulled us into a small private room, and told us the situation, though, everything became clearer. Scott was alive, but his outlook couldn't have been grimmer. Addie's large blue eyes widened as she absorbed what he was saying.

Even then, she resisted what she'd heard. Scott, she told us, was a marathon runner, a strong and determined man in his prime. She was sure he was going to fight the battle of his life. As she talked about their years together, I realized just how dependent she was on him.

After he finished, Dr. Prezant brought us in to see Scott. He was propped up in bed, immobile, and burned completely black. He had no hair, no lips, and no ears. His eyes looked like pieces of charcoal. Tubes and wires shot out from him in every direction.

Addie took a long hard look. Then she turned and ran out of the room. Instantly Father Judge went after her. The rest of us followed.

Addie ran up the hallway, almost in a frenzy. She didn't know where to go. She opened a door and it turned out to be a broom closet. She opened another, but by then we had caught up with her. Gingerly we guided her to a conference room that the hospital had set aside for us. She was unable to return to the burn ward that night.

For hours, the mayor, Father Judge, and I sat with Addie as she rocked back and forth. Father Judge held her hand. She said very little. But there was nothing, really, to say.

17

DON'T YOU GIVE UP

The fire on Atlantic Avenue was the most devastating event in my professional life before September 11. It was the first time we'd lost men and had such terrible injuries in the line of duty under my watch. I found myself in the middle of a crisis, trying to comfort the families, restore the firehouses, and bring the department back. As commissioner, I felt a deep responsibility for the men, as if they were my own children. The depth of that feeling surprised me.

In the days and weeks afterward, I worked hard to support the family members and victims, reaching back into my own history and knowledge of the firefighter's life for inspiration. I talked a lot with Father Judge. I was deeply moved to see how the firehouses gathered together to support the families and honor their fallen brothers.

Jimmy Blackmore was buried on June 10, five days after the fire, on a lovely and sunny early summer morning. The service was held at Saint Kilian Roman Catholic Church, out in Farmingdale. Thousands of people attended. The men from his company, wearing their dress blues, sat to the right of the altar. My brother Roddy, a pallbearer, was right up front. Many of the men were near tears the whole time.

It was always hard for me to find the right words to comfort the firefighters at times like that. Seeking ways to reassure the families and the firemen that a death had not been in vain, I turned back to the traditions I had known and my belief in what we did. On that day, I had brought a long speech honoring Jimmy.

But when I stood up and looked at the faces of the guys in the engine, and saw Sue Blackmore and her kids, I closed my manila folder. I had some things I wanted to say to them and to everyone in that room, things I felt deeply but rarely said to anyone.

I started by mentioning that several weeks earlier I had been at a funeral for a police officer. There, Howard Safir had talked about how the word *hero* is so overused these days. His words had stayed with me. I agreed, and said so.

Looking at Sue, I went on: "But I was at that fire last week, and I want you to know that word should be used for your husband. The fire officers that were with him, the chief that was outside in the street, the firefighters that got hurt, those that didn't get hurt but were just a few steps away from being seriously injured . . . they immediately became a rescue force that was just unbelievable. . . .

"I want you to know that everybody did everything they possibly could, more than was humanly imaginable. There's nobody in this room right now that tries harder to figure out ways to prevent this than me. It's all I really think about. I've been around long enough to know that we will never prevent this type of tragedy, no matter what we do. But we're fortunate enough that we'll always have people like your husband who are willing to make that sacrifice for strangers. Not for a family member, not for someone that they know or someone who is part of their life, but for someone that they have no relationship with and are not even positive is there. When they think someone's in there, they do everything possible to get them out.

"I want you to know there are eleven thousand firefighters and fire officers in this city and thousands around the country that all really respect what your husband did. You have a legacy that is with the New York City Fire Department now. Thank you all for sharing him with us for those twenty-one years."

Over the next month, we reconstituted our informal support group to help the families. It included me, Father Judge, the mayor, Bill Feehan, Lynn Tierney, my driver John McLaughlin, and Drs. Prezant and Kerry Kelly. We sat with the families for long hours. We tried to make sure they had anything they needed—drivers, help paying bills, whatever it was.

Timmy Stackpole, after his voluble performance on the night of the fire, had taken a turn for the worse and went through a rough first week. He had been put on a respirator, so he couldn't talk, and then developed pulmonary problems and double pneumonia. When he was sufficiently recovered from that, he underwent the first of what would be many skin grafts. His legs were severely burned and almost immobile.

I stopped by to see him nearly every day. The hospital was on the corner where I lived, so I often dropped in on my way to work. I felt it was important for the men to see and know the commissioner, to know there was a real face behind the department that was grateful for what they had done.

As Timmy recovered and started his long rehabilitation, we quickly became friends. He was as funny and talkative all the time as he'd been the night of the accident. With Timmy, there was no such thing as a *short* story. He was naturally happy, so upbeat that it seemed to burst from him. Before long we were bantering like guys who'd worked in the same company for years. I learned that Timmy and I shared the same attitude about teaching young firefighters. He was always talking about how he looked out for his group.

He talked so much, in fact, that often I didn't even need to say anything. He would just launch into a monologue about how lucky he was, how scared he'd been that night about dying, how he'd prayed to God to save him, and how his whole life still lay in front of him. It was all wonderful.

He was also incredibly tough. As he started to recover the use of his legs, he had to go down to the gym for regular workouts that were sometimes so painful he would pass out. After his physical therapist revived him with smelling salts, he would start again. Sometimes I'd sit with him while he rode a stationary bicycle, urging him on: "Come on, you can do better than that!"

He'd roll his eyes. "*You* try it."

From the first weeks, he vowed to return to active duty in the fire department. I had doubts. His legs were really badly burned. "You just focus on getting better," I'd tell him. "Don't worry about coming back."

He'd just shake his head. "I'm going to do it," he'd insist. "You watch."

His wife, Tara, was there every day, all day, and we

spent hours talking while he was taking tests or napping. She was a pretty, down-to-earth woman with short dark hair, who was as outgoing as her husband. She constantly mock-complained about his demanding personality and busted his chops, but it was clear she was devoted to him.

They had met when Tara was just sixteen. Timmy had dreamed of being a firefighter the whole time he was growing up, she said. At the age of thirty-nine he had already been with the department for seventeen years. He was one of those guys that lived the job. He had played on the department football team when he was younger, brought his wife to firehouse events, and talked about work constantly at home.

They were devout Catholics, already close to Father Judge and Monsignor Thomas Brady, their wonderful pastor, who was a retired fire department chaplain. They had five kids at home. In the many long months of Timmy's recovery, I never heard Tara whine or complain about what had happened to her husband. Both of them just accepted it, rolled with the punches, and moved on.

Up at Jacobi, Scott LaPiedra shocked everyone by hanging on. Addie had been right about how strong he was.

Privately, I wondered—along with many others—whether it would truly be worth it for him to survive in such an impaired state. But Addie held strong to her faith that he would pull through, and swore she would care for him no matter what. For someone who had seemed so fragile and dependent on him the first time we met, she had an enormous reservoir of spirit.

Once, I watched as a roomful of doctors confronted her. They told her she had to face the fact that he was no longer the man she married and never would be. "What am I supposed to do, walk out on him?" she asked angrily. She walked out on them instead.

In the first couple of days after the fire, she and I hadn't talked a lot. Both of us were too upset, and the scene was too hectic, with firefighters and relatives coming and going constantly. I think she didn't fully trust me or my motives then, either. Was I there for publicity? Or out of a mere sense of duty? She had the attitude of a lioness protecting its cub.

But as I went back almost every day, as Scott stabilized and the crowds of the first night thinned out, Addie and I often ended up in the conference room where she had ensconced herself, deep in conversation at the corner of the big table, talking about faith and hope. To lift her spirits, at least a little, I kept trying to make her laugh, especially with jokes about Scott's side of the family.

Addie told me about Scott's love of the job and his hunger to move up to a leadership role. She reminded me that a few weeks before the accident, I had interviewed him for a position in a new squad we were forming. But he hadn't been a captain very long, and I had felt he needed a little more experience.

It was a nasty jolt. "Do you feel that I did this?" I asked. "Do you feel that the reason Scott is in here is because he didn't get that job?"

She put her hand on mine. "No, no. I don't blame you." In fact, she said, right after the interview, Scott had been asked to join the Special Operations Command, our elite crew of firefighters, by their leader, Chief Ray Downey. He was only days away from starting, and had been covering a shift for an absent officer in Ladder 176 when he was hurt.

STRONG OF HEART   179

One of the inspiring things during those days was the devotion of Engine 80, Scott's old firehouse; Squad 1, where he had worked a decade earlier; and Ladder 176. Together, the men in those houses devoted themselves to providing round-the-clock care for Addie while she kept her sad vigil. On the second day after the fire, a bunch of them had lifted a refrigerator onto a hospital gurney and wheeled it into the conference room. They kept it stocked with drinks and food and made sure she had three meals a day. They brought in furniture to make the room comfortable for her and less antiseptic. On their days off, they volunteered for 24-hour shifts guarding the floor to keep away reporters and ensure that Addie had some privacy. They constantly ran errands for her, sometimes bringing her home so she could visit the kids, or ferrying in relatives to sit with her. They ran several blood drives for Scott. John McLaughlin, a tough lieutenant who trained for marathons with Scott, became Addie's faithful friend and protector. He never left her side during those harrowing weeks.

It was the best of the department on display every day, the stuff that showed how small and insignificant the bad moments were. There was no reason all those guys had to be there. Addie had sisters, loyal friends, and all the hospital staff. But those guys felt it was their duty to serve her, to show their devotion and love for a fallen comrade. They were looking out for their own, and knew Scott would have been there the same way for them.

Addie lived at the hospital for a month. She spent her days with Scott, in the conference room, or sitting on the stone wall outside the emergency room. Every night she slept in the hospital administrator's office. The mayor's chief of staff, Tony Carbonetti, had asked the executive if he would give it over to her at night so she would have a comfortable room to stay in. Every night after he went home, the staff rolled in beds.

They were very rough days. Scott would make small improvements, then take huge steps backward. He was constantly at risk of infection. His hand was amputated. Some of his burns were down to the bone. He suffered a rupture in his esophagus and was only saved after Dr. Prezant spent several intense hours on the phone with a specialist in Boston and performed an emergency procedure to repair the tear. Every day, it seemed, there was a new crisis.

Some of his old friends were convinced that such a physical, active man would hate to survive with the kind of crippling infirmities Scott had.

But Addie wouldn't give up. She was convinced he could hear and feel her and was trying to speak. No one wanted to dash her hopes.

Nearly a month after the fire, on the evening of July 3, I drove out to meet my family in Montauk for the Fourth of July holiday. With Scott still in critical condition, I hadn't been sure whether I should go, but Addie assured me they would be fine. The day before, she had convinced a reluctant Father Judge to go ahead with a long-scheduled trip to Prague. She told Lynn Tierney not to cancel her planned visit to friends in Maine. Addie seemed as concerned about us as we were about her.

I arrived in Montauk around dusk, interrupting a family feast. I stuffed myself with seafood and drank too much wine, relieved to be with them for a respite. Then I went to bed.

Around midnight, I got a call from one of Scott's doctors. His blood pressure was up, his breathing shallow. He was bleeding profusely. I needed to get back.

I had eaten and drunk too much, and gotten too little sleep, to leave immediately. But after a nap, I rose, well before dawn, threw on shorts and a T-shirt, slipped away, and sped back to the hospital. All the way I felt heartsick for Addie, hopeful I would get there in time to help her somehow.

When I pulled up, I saw her sitting on the stone wall outside the emergency room. I tried to act casual when I walked up, making another dumb joke. But she knew why I had come back, and I could see she was upset.

Throughout the day, more firefighters and friends quietly slipped in, as word of Scott's condition spread. Bill Feehan came by. So did the mayor. Lynn drove all the way back from Maine, turning her car around just hours after she'd arrived. Every half-hour the guys in Engine 80 called Lynn on her cell phone to make sure she stayed awake on the road.

Addie was in agony, watching us gather and feeling helpless. She spent most of the day pacing, crying, and praying with her sisters. She refused to go see her husband. It was as if she felt going up to see Scott would be giving him permission to say good-bye.

At one point she left the conference room and ran into Bill Feehan in the hall. "Everyone's given up on Scott," she said, near tears.

"Don't you give up," he told her. "You hold on to that hope."

"Am I wrong to hold on?" she asked.

Bill took her hand. "Don't *ever* give up that hope," he said.

* * *

By late afternoon, relatives who had been sitting with Scott came in and told Addie it was time for her to go see him. She agreed. She asked her sisters, the mayor, and me to go with her.

We all went to the door of Scott's room and dressed in the protective gowns, masks, and gloves that protected him from infection. I felt a little funny about going in. As a city official, not a relative, I felt I was imposing. But Addie had led us there. As she went in, the mayor grabbed my arm gently and pulled me along.

As soon as Addie entered the room, Scott's heart rate dropped to 56 from 113. The only sound was the beeping of the machines that were keeping him alive. Despite his incredible fight, he looked even worse now than he had a month earlier.

Behind us in the hallway, relatives and firefighters were huddling and watching through the window. Several nurses were there too, crying.

The mayor and I each held one of Addie's hands.

"Please don't die, Scotty," she said. "Please stay with me. Tell God no." The machines kept beeping.

"Please," she whispered. "Please."

The mayor started yelling, "Tell him no, Scott! Tell him no!"

I couldn't say anything. Tears poured down my cheeks as I squeezed Addie's hand.

A few minutes later, at the age of forty, Captain Scott LaPiedra died of injuries sustained in the Atlantic Avenue fire. When he finally stopped breathing, Addie leaned over and gently kissed him.

That night, Engine 332, the house where Jimmy Blackmore had worked, was down at the East River on an assignment meant to be a relief for them. It had been my brother Roddy's idea. They were on what we called "brand patrol," helping to keep an eye on the Macy's fireworks display. It was almost certain to be light, fun duty.

When the fireworks ended, Roddy climbed up and started the rig. Just as the radio came on, it was broadcasting the four fives—four sets of five tones—that signified a death in the department.

He shut the rig down and went back to the riverbank to tell the guys what had happened. Then he walked off by himself for a minute to cry for Scott, for Addie, for the department, and for all they had been through since June 5.

In June of 2001, three years after the accident, Lieutenant Tim Stackpole returned to full-time active duty in Ladder 103. It was a great place with a group of super guys, dedicated and undisciplined mavericks who had missed him while he was away. He had passed the captain's test, and within a few months would be promoted.

Timmy had spent three long years in rehabilitation. During some of that time, he did light duty at headquarters—working with the troops in our Bureau of Health Services. I had seen him there often, and we had gotten even closer. It was a real lift to come into work and see him sitting there with that big goofy grin on his face.

Timmy would always have discomfort in his legs. Though he had passed a physical, they were badly scarred. He still couldn't bend them perfectly or run as fast as he had before. On his ankle he had a lump of scar tissue the size of a fist.

I rode with him for a couple of hours on his first morning back in the field. After all the times I had seen him in his hospital gown, then in gym clothes, it was funny to see him wearing a new hat and coat and boots. He had a wide smile that he was unable to suppress the whole time.

"I knew I'd be back," he told me.

"If this is what you want, then this is what I want," I said. "You're going to be uncomfortable, you know. Every time it's too hot, or too cold, your skin is going to hurt. Every time you stretch, too. But I'm happy for you." I loved Timmy. I was so proud of him, but I discouraged him: I didn't want him to come back, because I thought he had suffered enough.

He shrugged. "I feel fine," he said. "This is where I want to be."

Investigators spent much of the rest of 1998 investigating the fire on Atlantic Avenue. The investigation revealed that a supporting wall underneath the floor that collapsed had been removed more than thirty years earlier to make way for the restaurant. It was a major code violation in a city-owned building, but one that inspectors had missed for years.

At first it was reported that an oil burner had caused the fire. But later we thought that something else may have transpired. Based on the information our marshals were able to gather, it seemed likely that the fire was started deliberately, and originated in a pile of valuable comic books.

But we could never gather enough evidence, and as a result, no charges were ever brought in the Atlantic Avenue fire.

18

IT'S EITHER OUTSTANDING OR UNACCEPTABLE

One day a hilarious piece of propaganda that was going up on firehouse bulletin boards came across my desk.

It showed an elaborate fire truck that had a number of unusual accessories. There was a snowplow for clearing streets. There was a spray nozzle "for painting street lines." A holding pen was set aside "for humans, truants, animals, and homeless." There was a mail slot, a garbage hopper for trash and recycling, an aerial bucket that could be used both to fight fires and maintain light poles, and, best of all, a tow hook "for derelict vehicles and to carry fat union leaders home after huge meals."

It was described as our new multidepartmental vehicle. Its slogan was "We'll take the call for nothing at all." The phone number to call for help, it said, was 1-800-NO-RAISE.

Best of all was the vehicle's name: the Von Yessen mobile.

I knew it reflected, in the best tradition of firefighter humor, some doubts about my reforming impulses. As I pushed for change in the fire department, the ripples often alienated people.

VONYESSEN MOBILE

N.Y.C.'S new multidepartmental vehicle

TOW HOOK
for derelict vehicles and to carry fat union leaders home after huge meals

GARBAGE HOPPER
for trash and recycling

EMS COMPARTMENTS
for medical emergency supplies

HOLDING PENS
for humans, truants, animals, and homeless

HOSE BED

STREET SWEEPER
for use on runs and bldg. inspections

PUMP PANEL
for fire operations and crowd control

MAIL SLOT
for mobile post office use

SPRAY NOZZLE
for painting street lines

SNOW PLOW
for clearing winter streets

AERIAL BUCKET
for use at fires and for tree & light pole maintenance

00334 314

FDNY
EMS
CORPS

OUR NEW MOTTO

"We'll take the call for nothing at all!"
DIAL 1-(800)NO RAISE

The early days: Ladder 42 in October 1974. I'm in the back row, second from the left.

With my wife, Rita, Mayor Giuliani, and my four children, Tom, Pam, Erica, and Marc, on April 22, 1996, the day of my swearing in as the city's Thirtieth Fire Commissioner.

Celebrating my election as UFA president in 1993 with my brother Roddy (left) and my old friend Danny DeFranco, who was voted back in as sergeant-at-arms.

My official "proby" department photo from 1970

Engine 73–Ladder 42 on Prospect Avenue in the Bronx—my firehouse for nearly sixteen years. This photo was taken at the rededication ceremony on September 10, 2001.

La Casa del Elefante, Ladder 42, 1990. I'm second from the left.

Mayor Giuliani presents me with my commissioner's helmet at my swearing-in ceremony.

Pitkin Avenue, Brooklyn, December 1997.

The Atlantic Avenue fire and collapse on June 5, 1998, took the lives of Lieutenant James Blackmore and Captain Scott LaPiedra.

Timmy Stackpole's first day back to work after a three-year recovery from injuries sustained in the Atlantic Avenue fire. Timmy was later lost in the attack on the World Trade Center.

Searching for three brothers buried in the collapse at the Father's Day fire on June 17, 2001. (I'm visible in the white helmet just left of center.)

Firefighter John Vigiano and his brother, Emergency Services detective Joe Vigiano. Both were killed in the World Trade Center attack. Their father, retired fire captain John Vigiano of Ladder 176 (shown below at a City Council meeting with me in 1988), came to the site every day to search for their remains.

Attending one of the many briefings with the mayor in the days after 9/11 (from left): Police Commissioner Bernard Kerik, Mayor Giuliani, me, and Richie Sheirer, head of the Office of Emergency Management.

"Sphere for the Plaza Fountain" by Fritz Koenig, which had been the focal point of the World Trade Center plaza, symbolized peace through world trade. After 9/11 the sculpture was taken to Battery Park, where it served as a temporary memorial.

Touring the site with the mayor and President Bush on September 14, 2001.

Eating pizza and pastries with President Bush, Mayor Giuliani, and family members of Engine 55 in Chinatown on October 3, 2001.

Squad 1 from Park Slope, Brooklyn, lost twelve members on September 11. Many of their names are etched in the dust on the truck. Andrew Esposito's father, Mike, was the boss for Squad 1 that day.

Ray Downey, Deputy Chief
September 19, 1937–
September 11, 2001

With Father Mychal Judge
(bottom left) May 11, 1933–
September 11, 2001

Bill Feehan, First Deputy
Commissioner September 29,
1929–September 11, 2001. With
grandson Connor on a fireboat
in 1998.

Pete Ganci, Chief of Department
October 27, 1946–September 11, 2001

With Governor George Pataki at Ray Downey's
memorial service on December 15, 2001.

The scene at Pete Ganci's funeral, Farmingdale, Long Island, September 15, 2001.

Seeing my granddaughter Rita after a funeral helped brighten my spirits a little. Here we are in front of St. Patrick's Cathedral after Terry Hatton's funeral.

But I thought their parody was great. In a department of 16,000 people, it's inevitable that someone who tries to bring change will meet resistance. But that's the job of leaders. I thought of myself as a reformer. As a leader, I believed it was better to try something and fail than to play it safe. That approach, I knew, was guaranteed to draw criticism. But that was okay with me.

As I'd said at my swearing in, my biggest priority was improving safety. A major fire in late 1998 dramatized how badly we needed to do it.

Two days before Christmas, shortly before 10 A.M., fire broke out in a luxury nineteenth-floor apartment on the Upper West Side. An electric heater short-circuited, and the sparks reached the couch nearby, igniting it. The flames then spread to the Christmas tree.

Once fire hits a dry pine tree, it's all but over. The tree lit up like a torch in a matter of seconds.

The apartment belonged to Patricia Brentrup, the mother of the actor Macauley Culkin and four other children. A servant discovered the fire soon after it began, and the family and staff were able to make their way out safely.

Though terrified, Ms. Brentrup had managed to knock on her neighbor's door to alert them, and had the presence of mind to call 911 twice. She had gotten one of her sons to call the security desk downstairs to let them know what had happened.

On her way out, though, she left her front door propped open with a welcome mat, apparently to make it easier for the kids coming behind her—some of whom had been sleeping when the fire was discovered—to find the door. They left it open, too.

After the family left, air rushed in through the open door and fanned the flames. Like a thirsty man in search of a drink, the fire was drawn toward the hallway for more oxygen.

Soon the hallways and stairwells of the fifty-one-story building began filling with black, acrid smoke.

Firefighting in Manhattan presents special difficulties. There are many more high-rise apartments and commercial buildings than in any other borough. Most are modern fireproof structures, with concrete and steel fixtures that limit damage. But some of those very features make fires in Manhattan tougher to put out. High-rise fires can be difficult to find. The fireproof materials and shatterproof glass frequently prevent the fire from venting itself by popping windows or reaching outer walls. Though that generally confines the fire and smoke to a small area, restriction causes the heat and flames to build into a concentrated furor that is unusually potent and stubborn.

I reached the scene a few minutes after our men had gone upstairs. By then it was a four-alarm fire. It sounded as if it had been an inferno. The fire hadn't vented outside; the windows hadn't shattered. Flames had shot out from the apartment and scorched the long hallway, filling it with intense heat and smoke.

The firefighters needed to use two large hose lines, blasting full bore ahead of them as they crawled slowly down the hallway. The heat and smoke worsened with every step. But with the early warning, the rigs had at least reached the building quickly and contained the fire to the immediate area around the apartment.

As always at a scene, I wanted to see it for myself, so I trudged all the way up there—the elevators had been

shut down almost immediately—right behind Ray
Downey, the chief who ran our Special Operations Command, which responded to many major fire scenes in the
city. A stream of water cascaded down the stairs under
our boots.

By the time I reached the fire floor, the fire was out.
The hallway was completely destroyed, a blackened
shell, and the damage in the apartment was extensive. A
tough job, but a good one, I thought, with no loss of life.

After a couple of minutes I was called back downstairs
to brief the mayor, so I started the long walk down. In
the street, I ran into Jerry Hauer, then the head of the
city's Office of Emergency Management, who was on his
way up to get me.

"Tommy, they just found two people dead on the
thirty-second floor," he said.

"You're kidding."

"No," he said. "They were in a stairwell." Apparently
the smoke and heat had leaked from the apartment and
funneled up the stairwell as if in a chimney.

"We're going to have to search the whole building," I
said.

There weren't enough firefighters on the scene yet to
do the job. Some backup units had been stuck in traffic;
with Christmas coming, there was a gridlock alert. But
as Jerry pointed out to me, there were a large number of
emergency services cops standing around with nothing
to do. We could send them in.

Of course, given the long-standing rivalry between
cops and firefighters for control of scenes, I knew our
troops would be angry if we sent police in to search the
building at a scene we controlled instead of waiting for
our firefighters to arrive.

Even so, the building needed to be searched immediately. So for the first and only time as commissioner, I issued an order and sent the men in. Later, I would hear plenty of grumbling because of it.

But the police confirmed what Jerry had told us—and found two more bodies. All four victims had died not from the fire but from the smoke and heat that had funneled upstairs and overtaken them as they tried to escape.

The fire had been the latest in a series of difficult ones that made 1998 a bad year. Only the week before we had lost three firefighters at a fire in a Brooklyn high-rise.

The disasters galvanized us, and the city, into a major effort to overhaul building fire codes. Headed by Donald J. Burns, one of our most seasoned fire chiefs, the effort resulted in March 1999 in passage of an ordinance, Local Law 10, a landmark measure that upgraded many fire regulations. Among other things, it required that automatic sprinklers be installed in all new or heavily renovated existing residential buildings that house four or more families. Additionally, apartment residents must now read and sign a detailed fire-escape plan once a year.

Meanwhile, in January 1999 we had added twenty-five lieutenants to our Fire Safety Education Unit, hired another ten civilians, and begun a massive campaign to teach fire prevention to landlords and tenants throughout the city. We emphasized, for instance, that when fleeing a fire, residents should always close their doors, to contain the fire in an enclosed space. We reminded people that when a fire broke out elsewhere in their building, the proper procedure was to stay inside, with the door closed, and wait for firefighters to come rescue them.

We launched aggressive campaigns to promote Christmas tree safety, and warned residents when we saw a steep rise in candle fires. We plastered posters and billboards all over the city. We sent firefighters to schools. We reminded people that when it was time to change their clocks, they should also change the batteries in their smoke alarms.

The efforts paid dividends almost immediately. Fire deaths had already started heading downward in 1996, but in the year 1999, after we accelerated our efforts, they were lower than they had been in half a century—in good part, I'm convinced, because of the heightened awareness of the citizens.

In 1970, the year I joined the force, there were 3,508 serious fires and 310 civilians killed. In 1999, with 3,504 serious fires—just four fewer—only 110 civilian lives were lost.

Inside the department, meanwhile, I had turned much of my energy toward reforming the way we managed our chiefs. After my early moves to add training and other programs, I had become convinced that this was the root problem we needed to address.

As firefighters, called to make critical decisions quickly, our chiefs were among the best in the world. But our structure prevented us from making the most of their skills.

At headquarters, we had long had two dozen chiefs overseeing most major staff functions. But that made no sense. The chiefs had been trained to fight fires, not run departments and deal with budgets.

A year into the job, I overhauled the whole system. I sent half the staff chiefs back into the field and replaced them with civilians. Some of them, not wanting to return to active duty, chose to retire instead. For that, I was criticized in the ranks.

But I felt the move was necessary to increase accountability, and therefore our overall performance. The chiefs had been tenured under union rules, which inhibited a commissioner, for instance, from taking action against one who was doing a bad job. The civilian employees, in contrast, were directly answerable to him, just as he was to the mayor.

In rethinking how to deploy the chiefs, I benefited from the detailed knowledge and strong support of Bill Feehan. Bill told me not long after I started that he felt it was a big problem that the chiefs weren't accountable and that their performance wasn't measured, and he truly believed that the troops and the city deserved better. Coming from Chief Feehan, such views angered many of his peers. From my perspective, they were proof that I was on the right track.

Unfortunately, I could never be successful in some areas involving the chiefs. Winning support from the chiefs in the field on some policy changes, for instance, was often tricky. Like the staff chiefs, they were tenured and gained promotion by passing a test, so they were unaccountable to the department leadership. I had my own staff, but it was the job of the chiefs to enforce policy with the troops. If they didn't, nothing got done.

One time I sent a request for information to one chief, but didn't hear back for weeks. When I asked him what had taken so long, he told me, "Well, I was away and didn't see any mail till I got back."

"So nobody opens your mail?"

"No. Not when my name's on it."

"Why wouldn't somebody open your mail for three weeks while you're on vacation? Wouldn't it be helpful?"

"Well, we don't do that. We don't open each other's mail."

For me, one solution to the problem was to find creative ways to promote better people. In late 1998, I used a loophole to reach into the chiefs' ranks and appoint a new chief of department. It was one of the better moves I made.

Peter J. Ganci Jr. was in his early fifties, with a ready smile and a cocky swagger. He had been on the job since 1968, joining after a stint as a paratrooper in the air force. He always told people he had decided to become a firefighter at the age of sixteen, when he realized that the only one of his parents' friends who seemed to be happy was the one who belonged to Ladder 120.

Pete had worked in a couple of tough houses in Brooklyn and become a lieutenant in 1977, captain in 1983, and chief in 1987, a rapid rise through the officers' ranks. He had loved being in the firehouse. His favorite piece of advice, delivered often through the years, was: "When you leave home on the way to the firehouse in the morning, don't smile. Because you don't want your wife to know how much you're looking forward to going there."

As he made his way upward, Pete was known as a tough, hard-ass firefighter who was fearless. He was cited for bravery repeatedly. On just one occasion, as a lieutenant, he'd led a group of men up to a burning third-floor apartment. They had been told there were children inside. When Ganci saw an opening in the wall of flame, he ducked through it, then started throwing burning furniture left and right as he searched for the kids. Absorbing tremendous heat and smoke, as the engine men behind him were spraying the fire, sending the heat in Pete's direction, he found an unconscious five-and-a-half-year-old girl and gave her mouth-to-mouth before passing her through a hole in the wall to other firefighters. He had saved her life. Even then, he stayed to help remove two other victims with little regard for his own safety.

But Pete was also the sort of stoic who downplayed his achievements. Well after he'd become an officer, he'd answer people who asked what he did for a living by saying, simply, "I'm a firefighter."

Pete loved fires and firefighters so much that even as he moved up in the city, he remained a volunteer member of the Farmingdale Fire Department out where he lived. He continued going to scenes there whenever he could.

Long after he came to headquarters, working first as head of fire investigations, then as chief of operations, he spoke wistfully of missing the action of the firehouse. "It seems that I spend an excessive amount of time trying to resolve one conflict or another," he said. "Most of the issues I face daily are problems of some sort. It doesn't leave much time to acknowledge the good our guys do every day." He always said he wanted to be remembered as a good fireman and a good chief.

But Pete was smart and a capable manager, and said he saw working at headquarters as "giving back to the FDNY." I liked his enthusiasm. We didn't always see eye to eye, but he sincerely wanted to improve the department.

Personally, Pete and I had a lot in common. We had

come up during the same time, and we both thought of ourselves as firefighters first. He had the relaxed personality of someone who knew what it meant to be challenged in the heat of the moment and therefore didn't need to put on airs the rest of the time. Around the office, Pete was laid-back and charming. He was always talking about his kids, his boat, and golf, interests that seemed to dominate his off-duty time. At the end of a long day, he was often the first to lead the parade toward unwinding. Down in operations, where he worked, he'd turn to his guys, smile, and announce, "It's time to get ice."

Pete could be a great storyteller. In 1999 we attended a conference in Washington, and in the bar he held everyone spellbound with tales of his fire-fighting days. He had worked in Bedford-Stuyvesant during the War Years, where things had been so busy that the dispatcher would sometimes have to call out an alarm and then instruct, "*Don't* stop at any fire but your own."

Years later, he still had the concerns, problems, and comfort of the troops uppermost in his mind. At the same conference, I remember hearing him describe his frustration over the fact that so much initial antiterrorism money was going to federal and state agencies when he knew it was people on the local level, like his firefighters, who would be on the front lines.

In our department, the most elite group of frontline firefighters we had belonged to the Special Operations Command. SOC, as we called it, comprised all our units with special skills. They included the Hazardous Materials (haz-mat) Unit, structural-collapse experts, fire rescue units, and, at the time I became commissioner, two squads of elite firefighters who responded to all major incidents in their areas.

SOC had long been run as a small fiefdomlike corner of the department. It kept itself separate from many other operations, like a commando squad in the military. It had its own headquarters, over on Roosevelt Island, and even its own budget.

Its chief, Raymond M. Downey, was a tough, taciturn man in his late fifties, with piercing eyes, a shock of snow-white hair, and a poker face matched by a dry sense of humor—so dry that you might not know at first when he was joking. Ray was somewhat of an anomaly in our department, a man who had built an outside reputation because of his expertise in special operations such as building collapse. He had overseen the rescue operation after the World Trade Center bombing in 1993 and had headed the federal Urban Search and Rescue team that led the recovery following the Oklahoma City bombing in 1995. His extensive outside network and reputation gave him an unparalleled Rolodex when it came to tapping resources. It also won him the nickname "The Master of Disaster."

Ray had joined the department in 1962, following in the footsteps of his two older brothers, and had worked in several different houses in his early years, including the Times Square area in Manhattan and Rescue Company 2 in Brooklyn. In 1977, as a new captain who worked at the training school, he had been picked to create the first special operations squad, Squad 1, a fully equipped engine company of elite firefighters, which also carried a full complement of ladder tools.

He next became commanding officer at his old Rescue Company 2, where he continued to sharpen his exper-

tise. Rescue companies were our most elite units. They
had originally been formed at the turn of the century to
rescue firefighters, but had evolved into units that responded to all working fires, motor vehicle and industrial accidents, major emergencies, water incidents, and
other atypical events.

What was great about Ray was that he didn't limit his
knowledge to the confines of the FDNY or the material
he might need to master for his next officers' test. He
was a voracious reader of all kinds of texts, documents,
books—anything that would expand his realm of
knowledge in his chosen area. He never stopped trying
to widen the scope of what he knew.

Ray was always trying to teach others, too—though
he was known as an unusually tough and demanding
boss. When I was president of the UFA, I regularly got
reports from firefighters that he bent the union rules. His
men weren't allowed to go sick, it was said; worked
overtime in violation of the union contract; and were required to undergo all sorts of additional training. They
were known for being arrogant; it was said they often
just showed up at scenes and took control.

When I became commissioner, I was determined to
break up SOC. I firmly believed that no chief should be
allowed to run his own private operation. Ray had to
play by the rules like everyone else.

So early on, Bill Feehan and I went over to SOC for a
meeting with Ray and his people. I planned to dismantle
the command structure of special operations and spread
their units among the battalions.

But when we sat down, Ray started talking about all
he was doing and all he wanted to do. He was increasing
haz-mat training. He was worried about the threats of

bioterror, such as anthrax. He was constantly upgrading physical fitness requirements for his men, and regularly drilling them. He had laid down stringent demands and always transferred out anyone who didn't measure up.

The more I heard, the more I realized that Ray was basically building his own army of super-firefighters, men who would be ready to head into the most serious situations and save lives.

Ray himself was cool-headed. He was detailed and methodical, but didn't tell me more about any one operation than I needed to know. If I asked follow-up questions, though, he answered them.

We talked for more than three hours, and what I saw going on there made me incredibly excited about special operations and the prospects for our department. I left that meeting, as did Bill, convinced that Ray was doing what *all* our chiefs should be doing. During the ride back to headquarters, Bill and I talked enthusiastically about Ray's innovations and what they would mean for our department. We agreed that rather than dismantling SOC, we should expand it.

We created five new squads to add to the two that SOC already had. Besides increasing training and expertise in many more firefighters, the expansion would enable a squad to respond to almost every alarm box in the city, which would mean a SOC presence at all fires, large and small. That would certainly make all major fires safer scenes because it would give every battalion chief more highly trained soldiers to deploy.

In the years ahead, Ray would become a familiar presence at many firefighting scenes. I remember watching him in the summer of 1998, when scaffolding collapsed at the new Condé Nast building in Times Square, killing a woman in a nearby hotel.

As rigs flooded the scene, Ray arrived and quickly assessed the scene as very serious. He advised the mayor to close a six-block area, a huge decision since that included Times Square and the heart of the heaviest traffic in Manhattan. But the mayor respected Ray so much that he did it immediately.

Two years later, in July 2000, I saw Ray in action at two collapses in two days. The first was in Cobble Hill, Brooklyn, where a massive gas explosion destroyed several homes. Ray was there for nearly 24 hours straight, supervising the recovery. Then, just as that operation was winding down, an antiques-filled warehouse in the East Village collapsed, leaving a two-story hole. Ray raced over to that scene.

When he arrived, he saw firefighters conducting a search in an unstable building. Without delay, he ordered them all out. About two minutes later, a large portion of the building caved in.

That night, outside the scene, a tired-looking Ray told me that his wife, Rosalie, was giving him grief for working so much. I asked the mayor if he would mind helping Ray out.

Quickly, the mayor pulled out a notebook, jotted a note to Ray's wife, and gave it to him. "Dear Rosalie," it read. "Please excuse Ray's absence. He's been very, very busy."

One of Ray's best traits was the way that as he moved up he made a habit of finding, hiring, and training the best young firefighters out there. Many went on to become captains and great officers in their own right.

Groups of Ray Downey's men stayed in touch through the years, sometimes gathering on their own to talk about particular jobs they'd had and to share ideas on how to improve.

One of the finest of these firefighters, one of Ray's real golden boys, was Terry Hatton. None of the squads, or other safety measures we implemented, would have worked without Terry and exceptional firefighters like him.

Terry had grown up two doors away from me in Rockville Centre. Even as a young kid, he had been incredibly conscientious and demanding of himself. He worked as a volunteer firefighter in the neighborhood and began studying for lieutenant even before he actually joined the department in 1980.

He had risen quickly through the ranks, in the old-fashioned way: through hard work and intensive studying. He was always looking to do more, to reduce unnecessary risks in the job. As a young firefighter, strapping and broad-chested, with short, neatly parted hair, he had brought a host of concerns to our union safety committee.

Terry could be intense—too intense, in the eyes of some firefighters. He became the kind of officer who'd wake people up in the middle of the night to drill them on how to force open a car door in the snow. But that was because he pushed constantly for excellence in himself and his men. "It's either outstanding or unacceptable," he used to tell his men. He was the model of what all captains should be, and to me he was always a soldier. When, in 1998, I named him captain of Rescue 1, it was a dream come true for him.

Terry had an interesting personal life for such a

straight arrow. One day not long after I became commissioner, I spied him walking down Barclay Street with Beth Petrone, the mayor's longtime personal assistant.

I called Beth that afternoon and teased, "Did I see you with one of my young captains?" Apparently they had started dating a few weeks earlier.

On May 16, 1998, Terry and Beth were married at Gracie Mansion. Mayor Giuliani officiated. On the desk in her office, Beth kept a picture of Terry in his bunker gear, covered with soot.

When I asked Ray to create the five new special ops squads, he tapped Terry to head up the recruiting of 125 firefighters. Terry set up a challenging obstacle course of expectations that weeded out most candidates but ensured that the ones they got were the toughest and most qualified.

The men in our rescue units were truly among the best firefighters in the world. We wanted the squads to become a training ground for them.

With the efforts of Terry, Ray, and the firefighters assigned to the new units, we vastly increased safety for the firefighters and city. The new squads, we hoped, would be a permanent addition that would upgrade the whole department. Getting them in place was one of my proudest achievements.

19

THE FATHER'S DAY FIRE

In the spring of 2001, I became embroiled in the biggest battle of my tenure. And it never should have happened.

For years the city had been planning to upgrade its radio system, and for months we'd had our radio people working with a group of staff chiefs on a plan to replace the handie-talkie radios used by our firefighters and EMS workers. We had spent millions of dollars on the project.

The goal was to supplant the older analog system that had been in use for decades with a more modern digital system. It was expected to work better in high-rise buildings—perennially tough places for radio transmissions—and offer us more frequencies for transmissions. Once it was in place, more of our personnel would have access to a radio that reached across the entire department system, which had widened considerably when we'd taken on EMS.

By late winter the radios were finally ready to be field-tested. Unfortunately, the timing couldn't have been worse.

Not long before, I'd locked horns with the chiefs and unions again. At headquarters, we were reconsidering a long-proposed plan to rotate battalion chiefs throughout the city. We thought that by rotating them through the neighborhoods, they could learn about different types of fires in other areas. The program would also keep the chiefs from getting too complacent. We wanted our less active areas to feel the impact of our young hard-chargers from other parts of the city. We thought it would shake up the ranks, maybe even prompt a few chiefs who didn't want to work as hard or make tough calls like enforcing safety rules to consider retiring and clearing space for younger leaders.

As part of the process, I asked our forty deputy chiefs, the second-highest-ranking civil service chiefs in the department, to submit evaluations of the battalion chiefs under their command. Most sent them in, but a few balked initially.

When I pressed them, the evaluations finally arrived. It quickly became evident, though, that some deputy chiefs had simply filled out an evaluation, rated everything "satisfactory," and photocopied it for thirty people. It was an insult to the city and the department, and epitomized for me the accountability problems I'd fought to correct. These city employees, who made $120,000 a year apiece, were saying it didn't matter how they or their employees were evaluated.

I launched an investigation into what had happened. But as I started questioning chiefs, I got heavy flak, especially from the fire officers' union, the UFOA. In the newspapers I was ripped by union members as a "tyrant" and "Mayor Giuliani's puppet." All my previous conflicts with the chiefs were dredged up.

As I continued the probe, the anger deepened. I was in my office one evening early in March 2001 when my assistant, Ray Goldbach, came in to tell me that the UFOA board had passed a no-confidence resolution against me. Additionally, nine division commanders had formally resigned their titles, a symbolic move that didn't affect their jobs or pay but was meant to express their dissatisfaction with me.

The actions hurt—a lot more than I wanted to admit. Of course, it was all politics, albeit of a particularly disingenuous stripe. I knew I was right. I knew I was only getting blasted for daring to ask questions that the chiefs didn't want to answer.

But I also knew the action would be reported across the country. Many people would read that our chiefs had no confidence in their boss, but they wouldn't know the full history and context of what the chiefs had done. Others would think that a no-confidence vote from a union was a badge of honor, but I cared too much about all the terrific officers in our department to feel any pride in it.

Right in the middle of it all, the new radios started to arrive. We sent 3,800 of them into the field on March 14. But the implementation was badly botched. Our radio technicians and the staff chiefs did not communicate with each other during the development. For instance, the radio technicians hadn't alerted the training staff so they could properly prepare the firefighters to use the new radios.

And this was a far more significant change than simply swapping an old piece of equipment for a new one. The new radio had many more frequencies and features than the old one. The technology itself was completely different.

Almost immediately we started hearing complaints from the field about their complexity. A firefighter told us he had been trapped in a basement fire with his air tank running low, but his mayday calls hadn't been heard by colleagues nearby. Fresh off the no-confidence vote, the unions started rapping us for deliberately handing out bad equipment. City Council members started questioning the whole program. Reporters picked up the story.

I pulled the radios immediately upon hearing about the firefighter trapped in the basement, and accepted full responsibility. It was clear that the chiefs, and the department, had let the men down by not preparing them for such a major change.

But I made matters worse when I wrongly told reporters that the same system was already in place in Chicago and Boston. I accidentally passed on that incorrect information from the manufacturer, when I should have had it checked first. Almost immediately, the press learned the right information, and I was forced to eat my words.

My mistake fueled the shellacking, as my critics now accused me of deliberately lying to cover up our ineptitude—or, some hinted darkly, malfeasance. The UFOA had already been demanding a major investigation; now they called on me to step down. Alan G. Hevesi, the city comptroller who was running for mayor and had long battled the mayor over how city contracts were reviewed and awarded, accused us of flouting city purchasing rules because we hadn't bid out the radios. Advised by the mayor's office, we believed we were covered under our existing contract and didn't need to.

While the charges heightened the nastiness level, they

also marked more or less the crest of the battle. Nothing came of any of the investigations, in the end. Nothing could have; we were guilty of nothing more than a few mistakes.

Certainly the fact that our people treated the new radio as just another model was very serious, and we were lucky that nothing really bad happened. But the UFOA's attack, and the subsequent challenges by Alan Hevesi and other local politicians, were very hurtful to firefighters and officers. The radios we pulled were a better product than what we had—but the politics of the situation required us to hold back their implementation, and created bitterness among the troops. The fact that they weren't in the field by the summer of 2002 was unconscionable.

For me personally, the battle sowed bad blood with the UFOA that made my own union days seem like a distant memory. I never completely broke the ties with my old friends in the UFA. But it was clear that in the unions' eyes, I had gone from being considered a former ally to being considered the enemy. The distance saddened me—not least because it was so unnecessary.

Two months after the radio battle, we experienced a far darker event that cast all the political battling into proper perspective.

On Father's Day, June 17, 2001, early in the afternoon, two boys, one thirteen years old and one fifteen, were spray-painting graffiti in the backyard of Long Island General Supply, an enormous, block-long hardware store in Astoria, Queens. One of them knocked over a can of lawn-mower gasoline. Scared, the boys ran off.

But the gasoline trickled down a ramp into the basement and across the floor toward the boiler pilot light. The fumes ignited, and fire broke out.

Within five minutes of the initial call at 2:20 P.M. reporting a fire in the basement, Rescue 4 had responded to the scene. Firefighter Brian Fahey went toward the basement, while others searched the upstairs apartments, and another team tried to enter the building through a rear door. Minutes later, Ladder 163 arrived. A member of its crew, John Downing, worked with another man from Rescue 4, Harry Ford, to vent the windows.

At 2:47 P.M., a small explosion rocked the building. A minute later, a much larger one occurred. The second explosion shook the entire street, shattering windows and knocking over firefighters in the whole area. When the smoke cleared, firefighters saw that one whole wall of the building had tumbled down and part of the roof had collapsed. Injured men lay everywhere in the street. Instantly ambulances were summoned and more alarms were called, upgrading it to five-alarm status. In all, some 350 firefighters from seventy-five units were called to the scene.

A quick roll call revealed that three men were missing. Harry Ford and John Downing had been hit by the falling wall. Brian Fahey wound up in the basement.

Out in Rockville Centre, I had just finished working out and was getting ready to go to my daughter's house for a Father's Day dinner when my driver came in and told me what had happened. We responded immediately, me still wearing my sweaty gym clothes. I pulled in right behind Ray Downey, our expert in structural collapse, who had also come from home.

The whole block looked like a disaster movie. Brick, glass, and rubble lay everywhere. Paint, buckets, and other debris were scattered about. Dense smoke still hung overhead. Dozens of men were hurt—many lying on stretchers, a few still in the street, some just leaning against walls waiting their turns. EMS workers were running around frantically, performing triage on the wounded.

The focus of almost everyone there, though, was on those missing. Over a sickeningly large pile of bricks and rubble, the former wall of the store, dozens of firefighters were scrambling around looking for Harry Ford and John Downing.

Once again we were seeing the fine line that separates the routine from the disastrous, that suddenly exposes the horrible danger and potential sacrifice that underlie the firefighter's job. And it was happening on a beautiful early summer afternoon, on Father's Day, of all days.

I went with Ray to where the mayor stood watching the rescuers dig through the rubble. Unflappable and stone-faced as always, Ray took one look and shook his head. The scene was much too disorganized. He marched out and ordered everyone off the pile. Then he quizzed the chiefs, made quick calculations of velocity, distance, and timing, and determined where the missing men were most likely to be. "Start digging right there," he told the troops.

It was hard not to be inspired by the way Ray could stride coolly into the middle of a chaotic scene and instantly create order and discipline.

As I watched the work proceed, I was more frustrated

than usual by my commissioner's role as an observer. So I ran out to the pile and started lifting bricks and scraping dirt alongside the other rescue workers scrambling to get down into the rubble.

At that instant I didn't feel like a commissioner, or a city official, or anything except a firefighter with three of his brothers missing.

Within a few minutes, shortly after 3 P.M., we pulled Harry Ford from the pile.

Harry, at fifty, had been a larger-than-life hero in the department for a long time. Tough and irreverent, a strapping walking muscle, he had been cited nine times for bravery in his twenty-four-year career, and celebrated for a series of heroic rescues—such as the time he ran into a burning building on his day off, in bare feet, and saved the life of an elderly man. As both UFA president and commissioner, I'd found him to be a complete pain in the neck—in the best sense. He was one of those old buffaloes who are so tough, so fiercely independent, that they can't help but quarrel with people sometimes. In the department yearbook, for instance, Harry was the only guy in Rescue 4 who hadn't worn the proper uniform to get his picture taken. As his battalion chief would say at Harry's funeral, "Harry liked to say, 'Don't give out too many orders. The firefighters might follow them.'"

But when the heat was on and you needed him to be there, he was *always* there. He was the kind of guy you wanted most in those moments, the one who wouldn't give up and wouldn't lose his cool.

Praying he was alive, we carried Harry to a gurney nearby. Dr. Kelly, the head of our Bureau of Health Services, administered heart massage to him as we ran a block to a waiting ambulance. But Harry never moved. He was declared dead at Elmhurst Hospital Center just after he arrived.

A short time later, we found John Downing. Forty years old, an eleven-year veteran of the department, Downing was also declared dead at Elmhurst.

It took the rescuers four hours to reach Brian Fahey, who was deep under debris in the basement. In the very first minutes, he had transmitted a mayday. "I'm trapped in the basement by the stairs," he had said. "Come get me."

The men tried everything to get to him—breaching walls to get to the stairway, cutting through concrete. Ray Downey and Pete Ganci had both tried to reach him by crawling through a tunnel from the building next door. But they couldn't.

By the time the rescuers reached him, it was late in the afternoon. Sadly, Brian, forty-six, was already gone. The men removed their helmets and bowed their heads in respect as his body was carried to an ambulance.

Elmhurst Hospital was a mess. Fifty-seven people had been injured in the explosion, and most of them were rushed to Elmhurst. The halls and beds were so crowded that the hospital could give us only one room for the families of the victims. Normally we wanted separate rooms, so the families could have some privacy and avoid being exposed to one another's grief. But we had to make do.

John Downing's mother, sisters, and brothers arrived soon after we did, but his wife, Anne, was shopping and couldn't be located immediately. We sent a contingent to wait for her at their house and escort her to the hospital. The Police Aviation Unit had been alerted and was standing by to bring her by helicopter as soon as we located her.

The Downings were horrified and desperate to get in touch with Anne. John's mother looked at me with terrified eyes and asked, "Why?" I had no answer.

Denise Ford arrived next, along with a few relatives. She was a tough, vigorous, and attractive woman in white pants and a blue shirt. She looked strong; I later found out she had once worked installing phone lines. The expression on her face when she arrived and introduced herself to us made it clear that she was ready to hear that her husband was critically injured or seriously burned, but nothing more. Like everyone, she believed Harry to be indestructible.

At first Denise refused to accept his death, shaking her head and crying out, "No, no, no, it can't be true." The mayor lurched forward to embrace her, and I followed, but she kept shaking her head as she burst into tears.

Mary Fahey arrived some time later. We had sent a representative to sit with her during the search, but he hadn't told her what was happening. When she arrived at the hospital, expecting to find Brian hurt but learning he was dead, she was shocked, then inconsolable, and cried in her brother's arms. Within minutes she started asking about the other firefighters, and their wives, and how they were doing.

When Anne Downing was finally brought to the hospital, I felt especially terrible for her. She was a tiny woman with a thick Irish brogue, and I instinctively felt protective toward her. But before long, she was gently consoling *us,* telling the mayor she was sorry we had been through such a trying day. We looked at each other and shook our heads in disbelief. We knew we were in the presence of real courage.

The Father's Day fire was among the most devastating events of my career, and a hard one for our department. We once again lost great firefighters, colleagues, and friends. We once again endured a round of funerals, wakes, and investigations. It seemed the worst disaster any of us could imagine.

But going to wakes and funerals reminded me again of the decency and goodness of so many of our men. At John Downing's funeral, I was struck again by the strength of his wife, Anne—by the whole family's, in fact. The Downings had been planning to travel through Ireland that summer, meeting the rest of Anne's relatives and visiting the important places she had long spoken of. Their relatives had planned a huge welcome for them. Instead, they all traveled to New York to bid John farewell in a moving display of family support.

I hadn't known Brian Fahey. But for me one of the most revelatory images of the days that followed was his wake out in East Rockaway. Brian had devoted a great deal of his spare time to training volunteer firefighters at the Nassau County Fire Services Academy. When I reached the Perry Funeral Home, I saw hundreds of volunteers he had trained lined up outside, literally for blocks. He had touched hundreds of lives, and there were so many people who wanted to pay their respects.

As I took my place in a long line of people who were patiently and respectfully waiting their turn to get inside, I remembered that our department housed thousands of good people who were loving spouses and parents and devoted community volunteers as well as good firefighters. I'd never met many of these people, who never told their brothers what their lives were like or what they did for others. To them, it was just part of life.

The investigation revealed that the owner of the hardware store had been storing more highly combustible fluids in his basement than permitted. The explosions had been set off when the fire reached them. But it was more a case of negligence than of criminal intent, so no charges were ever brought against him. For their part, the boys had stepped forward, admitted what had happened, and apologized.

By the time the funerals and wakes had ended, it was late June. The end of the mayor's term was six months away, and we were starting to get nostalgic about the ride we'd had.

At Harry Ford's funeral, I was standing in line with the mayor when we saw Ray Downey from afar. The mayor and I started talking about the way Ray had so quickly brought order to the search for the men in the pile.

"Look at this guy, still working," I said to the mayor. "I'd love to do something for him."

"Why, is he retiring?" the mayor asked.

"No, he doesn't want to retire. But he's got to pretty soon. He's almost sixty-five. And when he does, nobody's going to know all he's done for the city the way that we do. We were the only ones who saw so much of it. It makes me think what a shame it is that the things you feel about someone don't get said until their funeral."

Ever so gently, I was hinting how nice it would be to do something for Ray while we were still in office.

"Why don't we give him a dinner?" the mayor asked.

"Really?"

"Sure. He deserves it."

"That's a great idea. I guess we could raise some money pretty easily and find a hotel."

"Why don't we do it at Gracie Mansion? It would be a really nice thing for his family and some close friends from the department."

"You sure?"

"Absolutely."

"You going to pay for it?"

He smiled. "Yeah, I'll pay for it. Why don't you call Beth and we'll set something up?"

The mayor had set aside some of his last weeks for farewell events, and expected that Ray's dinner would fit easily in there, some time in November or December. But when I spoke to his assistant, Beth, and she told me there was a midsummer date open, I grabbed it. I knew the mayor was apt to fill up his schedule quickly. When he found out what I'd done a few days later, he was a bit surprised and thought briefly of rescheduling. But he decided we should go ahead.

So on a beautiful night in late July, eighty people gathered to honor Ray, including Bill Feehan, Pete Ganci, and members of the SOC, among them Chief Charlie Kasper, Ray's close friend and likely successor. The rest were friends and family. All Ray's children and grandchildren were there. They beamed in gratitude and pride.

To me, Ray had always epitomized the tough, stoic, and experienced kind of leader that was among the very best our department had to offer. That night I got a glimpse of the father and husband, the one the grand-children called "Poppy," who ran around and laughed heartily and joyfully with them as they played in the twilight at Gracie Mansion. Later, in his speech, after he'd thanked the mayor and me for our support, and mentioned some other people in the department, he turned to his wife, Rosalie. She was the reason he had made it so far, he said.

I will always be glad that we had that dinner before September 11, that it didn't get postponed, that Ray Downey, for one night, saw how much he mattered to so many people. Thousands of New Yorkers who never met him owe him a debt of gratitude, too.

On August 28 we had another tragedy, when a twenty-seven-year-old proby named Michael Gorumba died of a heart attack as he fought a three-alarm fire on Staten Island. Michael had worked at Engine 163 for just a few weeks before his death.

On the first night of his wake, we heard that Michael's sister, Diane, was planning to be married in the middle of September. Michael had planned to walk her down the aisle, because their father had died only the year before.

Diane had gotten to know the mayor in the days after her brother's death, as we sat with the family and helped them plan a funeral. She wondered out loud whether he would be willing to stand in for Michael and give her away at her wedding.

I called him up to ask, and he agreed immediately.

* * *

And so August passed, and September began. The city was preparing to elect a new mayor. The Yankees were making another run at the World Series.

In the Giuliani administration, as we entered our final season in office, we were growing more nostalgic by the day. I was proud of our record at the fire department. We had promoted a strong team of officers and civilians. We had forged a strong relationship with a mayor who loved us and, fortunately, wanted to support us as much as possible.

We had instituted fundamental changes in the training of firefighters, started building them a new, state-of-the-art academy, and obtained the most modern, effective equipment we could get our hands on.

We had created five new squads, vastly increasing the amount of experience and skill we could bring to every major fire and laying the groundwork for more expansion in the future.

Through our fire safety and education efforts, we had helped bring the number of fires and injuries to a fifty-year low and passed landmark legislation on high-rise fires that will surely prevent deadly fires in the future.

To be sure, I felt sadness over the radio battle and heavy sorrow over the tragedies we had endured. There would always be fights I would wish we had avoided. There would always be more work we could have done to improve firefighter and citizen safety, and more reforms of our management structure that would increase accountability.

But overall, I believed I would be leaving behind a vastly improved fire department when I left office at the end of the year—a department, in fact, that was the strongest it had ever been.

PART THREE
BE NOT AFRAID

20

SEPTEMBER 12

Then, on a beautiful, sunny morning, the towers came down, the department was ripped apart, and everything we thought we knew was turned upside down. And I was suddenly facing a task that was harder and bigger than any I'd ever imagined, at a time when I was teetering on the edge of a sadness so deep that at times I thought it would swallow me whole. I didn't know how I, or the department, would ever get through it.

Early on the morning of September 12, 2001, as we returned to the Police Academy—grief-stricken, overextended, exhausted—I felt as if nothing in my career had prepared me for the situation in front of us.

I hadn't had time to ponder the historic import of it all. But when the mayor opened the 7 A.M. staff meeting by summarizing where we stood, he said the Port Authority estimated that at least a couple of thousand people had died in *each* tower. People around the conference table started comparing it to Pearl Harbor, where 2,400 had died.

I was stunned by the magnitude. *Twice the number of Pearl Harbor?*

I thought of the generals who had been in that war, and the job they faced putting that place back together while preparing for battle. Then I compared it to our situation. *Okay, here we are,* I thought, *and I've got to step up to this challenge.*

From the beginning, I kept careful notes on the many meetings we attended; there was so much going on I would have felt even more overwhelmed without them. The whole city was in a state of suspended animation. Southern Manhattan, the oldest part of New York, the center of city government and international finance, remained completely shut down. The offices were empty, the subways halted. Tens of thousands of people who lived below Canal Street weren't being allowed home. Throughout the city, schools and bridges were closed.

Across the nation, all airplanes were grounded. Only the military F-16s were in the sky, patrolling what was now a war zone.

Dazed relatives of the missing were already starting to wander the streets of the city, to visit the emergency rooms, bearing photos and flyers portraying their loved ones as they clung desperately to fading hopes that somehow those missing had survived.

All of us feared another attack might come at any minute.

As we met that morning, three hundred workers were toiling at the site. Four bodies had been found overnight, including those of two firefighters, which brought the total to ten recovered so far. There were 120 trucks waiting to carry debris to the Fresh Kills landfill on Staten Island.

Chiefs Cruthers and Fellini continued to organize the

rescue. But it was a logistical nightmare. The way the rubble had fallen, the site was divided into four different sectors that were almost cut off from each other. Heavy equipment couldn't go in because of the fallen pedestrian bridge on West Street. The only debris coming out was whatever human hands could lift.

There were almost too many people. Along with the hundreds of firefighters and police officers who had flooded the scene the day before, there were eight teams of federal rescue workers dispatched by the Federal Emergency Management Agency, as well as hundreds of volunteers. More would arrive that morning, and in the days ahead, including untold numbers from other cities. It was difficult to determine which volunteers had specialized skills.

Even so, at that moment the chiefs were taking whatever manpower they could get for the bucket brigades. And it was heartwarming to see how many people wanted to help. Whenever I went down to the site, I'd pull up and see a heavy rescue truck from Stamford, Connecticut, or Roslyn, Long Island, or see people bringing the firefighters food and clothes and whatever else they thought we might need. For days, people lined up along West Street to cheer any fire truck or ambulance or official-looking car that drove by.

There were still many dangers there. The entire site encompassed sixteen acres and two very different landscapes. The "pile"—that is, the mountain of debris—was a deadly obstacle course of treacherous, twisted steel beams and slippery rubble. The "pit"—the space beneath the towers—went down seven stories. At the bottom lay more compacted debris.

Firefighters and volunteers alike scrambled between

beams and into holes and voids in the debris, often moving quickly, even carelessly, in their eagerness to find survivors. On the perimeter and even underground, fires continued to smolder. Water mains were bursting, threatening the support wall underneath. Communications would be spotty for days.

In hindsight, it's a miracle we didn't lose anyone else.

We made progress, but haltingly. Every few minutes, work would be interrupted by alarms of another building collapse or shifting rubble. That would force the chiefs to clear an area, sometimes for several hours, until it could be determined that it was safe to go back in.

Whenever someone heard a ping or some other sound that suggested a buried survivor might be trying to communicate, word would go out across the entire area to hush while rescuers searched for signs of life. During those moments a throb of hope would pulse like an electric current through the ranks. If it proved to be something else, as it always did, everyone would feel a little more crushed.

Just keeping the rescue going was a monumental job. But besides the work itself, the chiefs had to worry about things like securing the perimeter and making sure all the workers wore their gear—like safety goggles, or the masks, and later the respirators, that were supposed to filter out asbestos and other toxins. That was very tough in the first days, since many men found them uncomfortable. With all the muck in the air, it wasn't long before workers began to develop the stubborn hacking cough that would become known as "the World Trade Center cough."

I came down with it, too, and fought it for the next few weeks. It would come up suddenly and make me feel short of breath. But I just shrugged it off, and I was lucky that it eventually went away. That is certainly not the case for everyone who worked at the site. Some, I'm sure, will have long-term lung problems.

Even harder was knowing how to deal with the heightened emotions. A spirit of unity and a desire to work hard were balanced by short tempers, grief, anxiety, depression, even anger. Firefighters were literally desperate to go into the pile and rescue their brothers. They considered it a sacred duty.

But we also had to make sure our firehouses were staffed, and that the best people were being deployed for the many jobs at the site. Often the decisions rankled. Every time I went down and made my rounds, I ran into disaffected workers who felt they could be doing more if the chiefs weren't holding them back. I always tried to explain how much the chiefs were dealing with, and how the safety of the rescuers was a top priority.

We still harbored hopes of making mass rescues. But even on that Wednesday there were portents of the disappointment to come. The hospitals, after preparing for thousands of wounded, were strangely calm. Very few people, in the end, had needed treatment.

At a staff meeting that day, the medical examiner, Dr. Charles Hirsch, told us he expected the destruction to be so bad that most victim identifications would have to come through DNA testing of "biological stains," not the recovery of bodies. The phrase made some people in the room gasp.

That meant a lot of families would have to wait weeks, maybe months, before knowing the fate of their loved ones. Some would never know. It also infinitely complicated the recovery operation, as every piece of debris would have to be searched for signs of what had once been life.

Still, for days I waited for a phone call telling me that the men had broken through and found a cave or subway station with a dozen firefighters inside. With the ingenuity of our men, that just had to be the case, didn't it?

Up at the academy we were scrambling to get resources, tools, and assistance for the site, while mapping out the city's future.

The mayor held court in the conference room. There were several staff meetings a day, attended by key aides and commissioners. In between, a running series of meetings went on about a range of subjects, from economic development to determining the proper place and format for a citywide memorial service. Aides from every department shuttled in and out constantly for terse, to-the-point conversations. Governor George Pataki came and set up a desk to help coordinate recovery efforts and contacts with Washington.

I was asked to attend nearly every meeting, along with Bernie Kerik and Richie Sheirer, the resourceful head of the Office of Emergency Management, whose agency was working to get all the supplies and aid we needed. It was strange for me, as fire commissioner, to be so involved in everything; but the mayor wanted his disaster-recovery team at hand for planning and strategy.

Every half hour, it seemed, something new came up. Con Edison reported that it had lost the substation that powered much of lower Manhattan and would need months to build a new one. Verizon, the phone company, said a piece of steel that had impaled its brick building next to the north tower had destroyed a network of wires. The basement of the building was flooded due to a water main break that took days to fix. It would take weeks to restore full phone service to lower Manhattan, including the New York Stock Exchange. From across the city, we got a steady stream of bomb threats and evacuation orders.

When problems weren't coming in, the mayor peppered us with questions, almost as if he was trying to *will* the city back to normal. How soon could the schools reopen? He wanted that to happen as soon as possible. What about the bridges and tunnels and stock exchanges? Where were the black boxes from the two jets? Who was dealing with the families of the dead and missing? We had to get to work on benefits and information gathering right away. What was the immediate economic impact on tourism and travel, what was happening to hotel occupancy and restaurant reservations, and what could we do about it?

Some of the most time-consuming dilemmas of those first days never became more than theoretical. Someone would wander in and ask, "What about the drinking water?" and we'd start asking whether it was being poisoned by leaking fuel. That led to a discussion of the sewer system and whether there was a danger that fuel might ignite a fire down there. We worried about the freon tanks beneath the towers after someone said they would leak deadly phosgene gas into the air and kill any rescue workers in the vicinity. Later we found out that the gas had already leaked out, harmlessly, in the collapse.

Through it all, the mayor barked, pleaded, commiserated, prodded, and questioned, just as he always had. At every meeting he wanted to see measurable progress on what you had been working on earlier; he demanded the latest facts and figures from the site; and he piled on the tasks. If you couldn't deliver, he made it clear, you had to get out of the way.

He pushed himself as hard as anyone. When he wasn't with us, he was talking to the White House or members of the congressional delegation, speaking on TV, visiting the United Nations, walking the site. On the Sunday after the attacks, he even kept the promise he had made to Diane Gorumba after her firefighter brother, Michael, died in August—to stand in for him and walk her down the aisle.

It was inspiring and a little intimidating. At times I'd look at him and think, *He's doing it, so how can I not? He's putting in the hours, so how can I, or anyone, complain about doing the same? At least we're alive.*

When my alarm went off early every morning, I'd lie there for a second thinking that maybe it had all been a dream, that the towers still stood and we hadn't lost all those people. But I'd shake it off quickly and get up and out the door because I knew the maniac was waiting in the conference room for an update.

Indeed, on the very day after the attacks, he started talking about this book he had begun reading on Winston Churchill and the bombing of London. In search of inspiration, he had wanted to see what Churchill told the British people as they suffered through raids night after night.

When I got home late at the end of a long day, I was lucky to get my clothes off and make it to my bed before passing out for four or five hours of sleep. This guy was going home after these killer days and *reading*.

All day, thoughts of the men we'd lost came to me. In past crises, from Atlantic Avenue to the radio debacle, I'd had Bill Feehan to share my burden and confide in; I'd had Father Judge to turn to for comfort in dark moments.

Without them, I felt incredibly alone.

I found strength, sometimes unexpectedly, in little moments: a glimpse of the mayor or an expression on the face of a worker at the site. For all the agony, there was a strong shared sense of duty, the feeling that as horrible as this was, we had to get through it together.

Almost every hour the list of the dead and missing grew longer and more specific. A number of companies, including Cantor Fitzgerald and Marsh & McLennan Securities, had taken huge hits. Dozens of workers had died at Windows on the World, the top-floor restaurant. The NYPD had lost twenty-three officers, the Port Authority Police another thirty-seven.

At every meeting, staff members tossed out more names they'd heard. At that first meeting on Wednesday, the mayor said that John O'Neill, the former head of the New York FBI office, was missing. It was one more jolt. I'd gone out for a drink several times with O'Neill—a colorful, swaggering, and incredibly smart man—and really liked him. In the lobby of the north tower on the day before, I'd even seen him striding by, and he'd muttered to me, "We've got a good one here." John had left the FBI just weeks before and taken charge of security at the towers. He had been warning for years that the towers remained vulnerable even after the bombing in 1993.

The losses to the FDNY, of course, were especially

devastating. I carried a fresh update to every staff meeting. At headquarters we had a platoon of people calling firehouses and starting to coordinate funerals. I couldn't be too involved with the families in those first days. I knew it was an important, overwhelming job, one that we had to handle sensitively. Normally I would have been intimately involved in the funerals and spent hours with the families to comfort them and do what little I could, as I had in the past. But the scope of this disaster prevented that. I knew from the start that we were never going to be able to give all the families what they needed and deserved. That was probably the bitterest disappointment in our recovery work for me.

When I could, I stopped by a couple of firehouses, too, to thank and comfort the guys. I wished I could do more. But as nice as it would have been to devote days to consoling them, I just didn't have the time. Not everyone understood that, unfortunately, then or now. But along with the police and emergency services, we were trying to organize every operational detail, while dealing with officials at all levels.

I also knew that at a time when there was so much to get done, there was only so much grieving I could take if I was going to be able to function. It was hard even with a little distance. Every half-hour a report would come up: "We found a helmet." I'd say, "Did you find any remains?" Usually the answer was "Not yet." And I'd sit and think about what that meant while I continued to work.

It took a few days to winnow the list of our losses down to its final figure of 343, including two paramedics. At its height on Wednesday the 12th, it was some fifty names higher. Many of them represented the cream of our department, guys with experience and guts and know-how that I didn't know if we could ever replace.

Among the missing was Captain Patrick "Patty" Brown of Ladder 3. One of our toughest firefighters, he had also been one of our most colorful characters: an active bachelor, Vietnam War veteran, yoga enthusiast, often-decorated firefighter, and absolute maniac who loved every new piece of equipment and backed every step we took toward improving safety. Within a few days of the attacks, we were hearing stories about how even after the order to evacuate the north tower was issued, Patty had been taking his troops up the stairs because he had a mayday from Rescue 1 and needed to respond. He was, simply, a warrior.

Ray Murphy was a good guy I had worked with in 42 Truck. He had recently made lieutenant, and I'd placed him in Ladder 16, where the firefighters had loved him. There were two other guys lost from 42 Truck too, Brian Ahearn and Peter Bielfield. Brian Ahern was another new lieutenant; I had worked for many years with his father, Ed.

Jonathan Ielpi, a member of Squad 288, was the son of a decorated Rescue 2 veteran I had known well named Lee Ielpi, who was now retired. Another old-timer, John Vigiano, who had retired as captain of Ladder 176 and was legendary for his toughness, was missing two sons: John, a firefighter, and Joseph, an emergency services police officer. Both men came to the site every single day for months, vowing not to leave until they found their boys.

Kevin Pfeifer was the brother of Joe Pfeifer, the battalion chief who had been first on the scene. Dennis Oberg was the son of a wonderful Brooklyn lieutenant who had briefly been my personal assistant. His dad, also named Dennis, had been so proud of his son on the day he graduated from the academy—just two months earlier.

Eddie Geraghty was on the list, too. Seeing his name, I remembered how hard Eddie had worked when he was my assistant and how he had pushed to return to the field. He had been on a fast track, soon to become a deputy chief and certainly a possible future chief of department.

Horribly, another name on the list was Timmy Stackpole. That one was especially senseless and cruel.

How could Stackpole have been killed? He had just come back, just spent three horrible years fighting like hell to return to the job he loved, just been promoted to captain, in fact, on September 6.

How could he be gone five days later? I didn't know how I would ever be able to face Tara Stackpole again.

Sitting at the table, reading that list, was like being dealt blow after blow after blow after blow after blow. I grieved for every one, and for the entire department, too. Every man left a specific hole in our ranks, one that would be hard to fill as we moved forward.

Rumors and misinformation plagued us in those first days. On Wednesday we heard of an injured firefighter who had been in the collapse and taken to Bellevue Hospital. The mayor and I clambered into cars with the rest of his entourage and formed a convoy for a visit to the bedside of the injured hero.

We swept into the hospital and sought the hero out. We all crowded around his bedside. As fire commissioner, I was the spokesman. "Where do you work?" I asked him.

"Verizon," he said sheepishly. "I'm a volunteer fireman, but I work at Verizon. One of your guys gave me some clothes to wear down there."

All day long I would get calls from people at the site asking about a rescue they'd heard of, or some other story they'd seen on the news. Invariably they'd say, "It's confirmed." Then my team of people would be unable to track it down and I'd end up screaming at them out of frustration. After we'd spent hours pursuing them, most of the reports would turn out to be false.

On Thursday, while we were in a staff meeting, TV reporters picked up on news that five firefighters had been pulled alive from an SUV after being trapped under the rubble for fifty-two hours. Some channels aired dramatic video that showed the men being hauled out of a hole while rescue workers chanted "USA! USA!" At the academy we started getting calls from reporters and firefighters at the scene, the mayor's press office, more reporters, and the families of the missing, asking, "What's going on?" The mayor started pressing me for information. Everyone was hoping it was true.

Yet we didn't know what was happening. We had gotten no reports from our chiefs about the rescue. I told my brother Roddy to get on the phone and find out what the hell was happening.

Anxious minutes passed. While the news continued making its rounds, providing a little hopefulness in the midst of the horror, Roddy kept coming back and telling me he couldn't get any information. "Not good enough!" I screamed. "Find out what's happening!" I was frantic for information. The mayor kept demanding, "What the hell's going on?" Roddy was punching numbers into his phones and getting nowhere. In the conference room, we could see reporters on CNN talking about the rescue. Officials of the fire officers' union were describing it as a "miracle."

Finally Roddy brought us the information we hadn't wanted to hear. According to the chiefs, the men shown being rescued hadn't been caught in the collapse at all. They were rescue workers who had fallen through the debris and been lifted back out only a couple of minutes later. The reporters hadn't verified the story with any chiefs before they went on the air, and the story had taken on a life of its own.

I could see how it had happened. Restricted from the site, reporters were constantly quizzing passing workers about what they knew. Most of those guys had no more clue about what was going on than the press did. Some character a block away must have seen the guys coming out of the hole in the distance, heard the "USA! USA!" chant, asked the guy next to him what happened, and been told, "Five guys!" The story had snowballed then, changing a little with each retelling, like the children's game of telephone. The reporters, who wanted to recount an upbeat story, had seized on it.

Understanding, though, didn't excuse it. I was furious at the way the story had generated hopes in the department and among family members, only to dash them. When Roddy told me what had happened, I started slamming desks and bellowing curses across the conference room. The mayor encouraged me to say something at the next press conference, and that night I did:

"Because someone has a coat on with a yellow stripe and it is black, you should not assume that person is speaking for the New York City Fire Department," I an-

STRONG OF HEART   235

grily reminded the reporters. As for the firefighters, I told them to quit talking to the press: "It is not helpful. You're not doing your brother firefighters, or anyone else at the scene, any good."

After the lights and cameras went off, a few reporters came up and told me they were sorry for what had happened. I could see that most of them were as confused and upset as any of us, and trying to do their own job in very difficult circumstances. For the most part the media were sensitive and insightful during the aftermath.

Not every false rumor came from the press. The day after the attacks, I received a seemingly solid report from an officer at the scene that rescuers had found the body of Terry Hatton, the husband of the mayor's assistant Beth Petrone. I immediately passed it on to the mayor, who told me he wanted to tell Beth himself. She was out in Rockville Centre that day, staying with Terry's parents.

Only a few minutes after he had spoken to her, I got another call correcting the first one. They *hadn't* found Terry.

It was horrible. I was enraged that we would pass on poor information and make the burdens and suffering of people like Beth worse. It felt as if we were piling our sloppiness on top of everything else.

The guy who made the mistake felt terrible and said he wanted to tell the mayor himself, but I said it was my job. So again I knelt down by the mayor and told him what had happened. I saw his face tighten as I spoke, and his eyes start to tear. When I started apologizing and cursing, though, he put a hand on my shoulder. "Don't do that," he said. "Things like this are going to happen. Don't worry about it."

I told him I wanted to phone the Hattons and tell them myself what we had done. Kenny, Terry's father, was inconsolable. "How could this happen?" he asked. All I could tell him was "I don't know what to say."

21

A LIFT FROM THE PRESIDENT

On Thursday morning at the Police Academy, the mayor and governor had a staged, somewhat awkward phone conversation with President George W. Bush. I could see the president on TV, pacing back and forth behind his desk in the Oval Office, as his voice came out of the speaker on a table between them. He promised money and moral support to the city, and thanked the mayor and governor for their extraordinary efforts. They thanked him in return.

The mayor had told us before the call that the president was thinking of taking a trip up to New York to see the site. We all knew it would be an enormous honor. We also knew that logistically it would be one more huge operation to mount in the middle of everything else. We hoped he might wait a little.

But then he told the mayor he planned to come see us *the next day.* Everyone smiled. I thought, *Oh God.*

The president planned to come up early on Friday afternoon, following a memorial service at the National Cathedral. We scrambled to arrange a suitable tour at the site, which would enable him to see the damage and meet the workers but keep him secure. Secret Service agents swarmed the area right away, mapping escape plans and tightening security even further.

First the mayor and governor would take the president on an aerial tour of the site. Then he would be briefed on specifics by me, Bernie, and Richie. At a staging area near the remains of the north tower, he would make a few remarks to the workers, then head uptown to meet some of the victims' families.

I spent Friday morning walking the site in my bunker gear. It was a gloomy day, with intermittent rain and clouds overhead. The smoke rising from the ruins added to the gloom. We hadn't found anyone alive in two days, and workers were getting tired. But the pedestrian bridge was almost removed, and the convoy of dump trucks continued to haul away debris.

Around 1 P.M. I walked north to the liaison point, met Bernie, and waited. In the sky several large military helicopters were whirling around. The Secret Service, we were told, had deployed several of them to confuse potential attackers. Up close I could see that they were powerful machines, as impressive in their way as the F-16s that had been passing overhead since Tuesday to keep the airspace clear.

I'd never been much of a war buff. I'd barely had time to think about the fact that we were now at war against enemies who wanted to kill us. But seeing the strong blades slicing the air, I found it hard not to think, *Okay, you guys had your best shot, you destroyed a big part of our city and took away a lot of our best men and women. But now YOU better be ready, because we're still standing, and we're coming back.*

One copter finally descended from the sky, settling down a few blocks from us at the Wall Street Heliport. I started to feel a little apprehensive, thinking that in a few minutes I would be meeting the president and talking to him about what had happened to my fire department. All of a sudden the fire department stood at the center of national events. It still seemed unreal.

Soon we saw a line of big black limos approaching. Several rows of police officers and firefighters stood at attention along the route. The vehicles stopped short of us, and the president bounded out the door and started shaking hands. I could see he had an instant rapport with the men, as he fell into easy conversation with them. He was dressed in ordinary clothes, a gray spring jacket, casual shirt, and slacks.

I'd met George Bush two years earlier, but back then he was just a governor beginning a presidential campaign. We'd invited him to speak at our department's annual Memorial Day ceremony, where we honor our dead. He made a short, respectful speech. Obviously he wanted to get some pictures of himself honoring firefighters. The mayor and I took a little flak for making the ceremony political, but we pointed out that he was a genuine presidential candidate who wanted to pay his respects. We wouldn't deny anyone that chance.

He and I had only shaken hands and exchanged pleasantries that day, but he had seemed like a decent, sincere man, not just another politician who wanted to make a speech and get out of there. He had lingered a while to speak with firefighters, and seemed able to talk to them in the same direct, teasing manner they use.

Eventually he and the mayor made their way to our platform, and the president, looking sad, stuck out a hand. "Oh, hey, Commissioner, how are you doing?" he asked, grabbing my hand with an air of familiarity. "You guys sure took a hit. How are you holding up?"

"Okay, sir," I said. "It's been tough, but we're okay." For ten minutes we described the site to him, told him of the pit and the pile, of the risks the rescuers were taking, and of the efforts of the bucket brigade. We couldn't see too much from where we stood, at the staging area. Even so, I noticed as I stood pointing out where the towers had been that the president's eyes were locked on the landscape. He seemed first to be simply awed, absolutely flabbergasted by the scale of the destruction. Then he seemed to grow angrier.

His concern and sincerity were palpable. His resolve seemed to strengthen with every minute he stared at the site. He looked like a man preparing himself to take action.

I thought about the burden he had to bear. All week I had been thinking, *How could someone do this to my city, to my department?* The weight of that thought had seemed enormous. He must have been thinking about the nation and all Americans, and the fact that we couldn't stand for this. He had to formulate a response to an unprecedented attack. At the same time, I could see in his face how moved he was. He was our leader, yet he was also a human being, filled with determination but wrenched with sorrow.

* * *

It was time to drive down to the staging area for his remarks. A huge Cadillac pulled up, and six of us climbed in. The president, the mayor, and the governor sat on one side; Bernie, Richie, and I faced them. I sat directly across from the president. The door sucked closed behind us, drowning out the noise outside and hermetically sealing us in.

We moved silently through the devastated streets. It felt a little uncomfortable. No one said anything. How do you make small talk with the president?

Then he broke the ice himself. "Man, Commish, you look really tired," he said. "Are you getting any rest?"

I don't know why I responded the way I did. Maybe I was too tired to think straight. Maybe I just didn't care. Maybe I'm not mentally healthy.

But looking at this guy with the friendly eyes and slightly curled lip, thinking about the way he had talked to the firefighters, I had a feeling he was someone I could joke with. Like a lot of firefighters, I often open my big mouth during tense moments. It's my way of trying to ease the tension and maintain my sanity. My gut told me the president had a similar sensibility.

"Well, it's been tough," I said matter-of-factly. "But I got lucky last night. My wife came home and took care of me. So I'm feeling much better today."

The silence was deafening. The president looked at me with an expression I'll never forget, a quizzical, surprised look, not at all angry, that seemed to say, "I can't believe this guy just said that to me." The governor looked like he was about to have a stroke. The mayor, more familiar with my irreverence, just shook his head.

After a beat, the president cracked a smile. "Well, I guess you're the only guy in *this* car who got lucky last night," he said.

And we all burst out laughing, deeply, and with relief.

I know this story is not the most politically correct moment in American history. But at that time, in those circumstances, he had said the perfect thing. I don't know if I can convey how badly all six of us needed a laugh just then, after that long, horrible week. During a private moment, we were briefly away from the glare of the spotlight and the burdens of our jobs. It was as if we were sitting in the firehouse kitchen after knocking down a really tough fire, and it helped a little to be able to joke, to look at the president and think, *You're just like one of us.*

Almost as soon as we got out of the car, we each started sharing the story with friends and family. Finally, amid all the darkness, we had something a little light-hearted to talk about. Humor always helps you get through horror. The story became a much-needed running joke around the command center.

Our command post stood beneath a large tent right in the middle of West Street, which had been a thriving artery for the whole city before the attacks. We pulled up in front, and I introduced the president to Chief Nigro and some of the other officers. Firefighters and rescue workers gathered around, standing on rubble and old cars. The president spent a few more minutes shaking hands. I noted how carefully the Secret Service moved to maintain a clear pathway between him and the car.

It was clear that the president's presence was providing a big boost for all the troops. I could almost see their spirits rise as they shook his hand. They were urging him on and exhorting him to go after the terrorists. He was thanking them for their work. It was a moment when the typical symbolism and rituals of politics took on real meaning for the people who were there.

After a couple of minutes, someone handed him a bullhorn and pointed him toward the roof of a car that had been reserved as an impromptu speaking platform. A few minutes earlier the Secret Service had asked a worker nearby, a white-haired retiree named Bob Beckwith, to climb up and test the roof because "someone" was going to need it in a few minutes. Bob was still there when the president climbed up, but when he moved to get down, the president threw his arm around Bob's neck, pulled him close, and kept him there the whole time he spoke.

The president stood soaking up the scene for a minute, while the rescue workers started chanting, "USA! USA!" Then he raised a hand to quiet them.

"I want you all to know that America today—that America today is on bended knee in prayer for the people whose lives were lost here, for the workers who work here, for the families who mourn. This nation stands with the good people of New York City, and New Jersey and Connecticut, as we mourn the loss of thousands of our citizens."

That was when somebody shouted out, "I can't hear you!" and the president delivered his famous response: "I can hear you! I can hear you. The rest of the world hears you. And the people who knocked these buildings down will hear all of us soon!"

A huge roar rose up and the chants of "USA! USA!" started up again.

I was paying less attention to what was said than I was to the wave of enthusiasm sweeping the crowd around me. It had been just what they needed. But as the president spoke, it did hit me with new force that this really was a war. The World Trade Center hadn't been just one day, but the beginning of something. *More people are going to be killed,* I thought. *More mothers will be mourning their children.*

After he finished, the president let go of Bob and clambered back down. One last time we shook hands and he wished us luck. The way he said it, I knew he would be watching and thinking about the fire department and all those who had lost so much long after he returned to Washington. He was with us and would stay with us.

From there, the president drove with the mayor and governor to meet with some families of the victims. He made time to meet with each one personally. Then they bid him good-bye as he headed back to Washington and the war.

There was an incredible photo taken of the moment before he got on his chopper. The president stands in the center of the picture, between the governor and the mayor, his back to the camera. On the right, the governor is patting the president on the shoulder. On the left, the president's hand is placed soothingly on the back of the mayor's head.

It is the face of Mayor Giuliani that moves me so deeply. Viewed only in profile, a little bent, a little tired, the mayor looks as if he is about to start crying. But he is holding back. It seems almost as if he is drawing strength from the president's touch. Knowing the mayor as I do, I can believe that he was inspired, if not by the touch, then by the look in the president's eyes and his own faith in the office, the *institution*. For all the criticism directed at the mayor over the years, not to mention the mistakes he might have made, for all the political rhetoric any public figure must expend, I knew the mayor's belief in democracy, in our system, to be deep and abiding. I saw it captured in that moment.

To see the mayor's own need for strength expressed so clearly, to see the way he drew strength from the president the way I and others got it from him, was incredibly moving to me. It told me the burden of recovery was shared, and therefore a little lighter for each one of us.

Nearly a month after that trip, the president returned to Manhattan. Among his stops, he planned to visit a firehouse in Little Italy: Engine 55, or "Cinquante Cinque," as they call themselves. He wanted to buy the guys some pizza, talk to the troops, and meet the widow of a man they had lost.

I was supposed to be waiting with the firefighters when he arrived, alongside the mayor and governor. But I got held up at a funeral and arrived when they were already in the kitchen eating. When I walked in, one of the men offered me his seat, next to the governor, but then I heard the president calling, "Commish! Over here!" and saw him pulling out an empty chair for me. "Sit here," he said.

I went over, shook his hand, and sat down. The guys passed me a plate. "How are you, sir?" I asked.

The president leaned toward me with a friendly leer

and raised his eyebrows suggestively. "So, Commish," he said. "How are things at home?"

As I laughed, I thought, *This guy could hold his own in any firehouse kitchen.*

22

THIS ISN'T YOUR FAULT

It was always one thing after another in those terrible days just after the 11th. After the president left that Friday afternoon, we went right on to the next thing. That night, it was the wake for Father Judge.

He had been one of the first victims whose bodies were recovered. After he died in the north tower lobby, before the building even came down, firefighters carried his body to Saint Peter's Church nearby, where he was laid out on the altar. From there he had been taken to the quarters of Engine 1 and Ladder 24, across the street from the Franciscan community where he lived, Holy Name Province of the Franciscan Friars, on 32nd Street. That was where his wake and funeral were to be held.

I had stayed at the site after the president left to visit the families, and I ended up lingering too long. By the time I realized I had to go, I hadn't left enough time to get home and change, even though I was covered in soot and grime. I figured I could at least grab a quick shower at the firehouse.

I dropped in just as the guys, who had been close to Father Judge, were getting into their formal uniforms for the wake. "I've got to take a shower," I said to the lieutenant there, whom I knew. "You mind?"

" 'Course not," he said. He eyed my dirty clothes and asked, "You need to borrow any extra clothes, Commissioner?"

"Nah, that's okay." I thought he was going to offer me some of his own clothing.

"No, really, we've got a load of clothes here from the Garment District." The house was right in the heart of that area and had been inundated with donations.

"Oh, in that case, sure. I'll take a shirt, pants, underwear, socks, the whole bit."

Up in the bunk room, I peeled off my grimy clothes and got in the shower. As soon as I turned on the faucet, a blast of water exploded from the showerhead. I looked at it and saw it was a really old-fashioned head, which felt great. But we had gotten rid of many of those showerheads years ago because of all the water they used. *We should put a reducer in there to save some water for the city,* I mused.

Then I caught myself. *No wonder they call me a micromanager!*

When I emerged, dripping, I saw that the lieutenant had left me a sport shirt, tan cargo pants, and a pair of black designer underwear. It was more cutting-edge than I'm used to. The pants had zippered legs and huge pockets on the front and back. I walked out the door thinking I must look like Boy George—that is, foolish. Halfway across the street, I slipped a hand into the back pocket and it just kept going. I realized there was a hole right in the seat. With my fingertips, I felt a big piece of cloth flapping around. *Great,* I thought, *now everyone at the wake will get a lovely view of my designer underwear.*

There was no time to run back and change, though. I could only hope everyone would think that's how the pants were supposed to be.

As soon as I entered the apse, all those frivolous thoughts went away. Immediately, palpably, I could feel the sadness. The chapel was packed with firefighters and monks. Media trucks had been everywhere outside. In the distance, by the altar, I saw the casket.

One of the priests said hello and steered me to meet two women sitting in the front row. They were Father Judge's sisters. I told them how sorry I was and how much he had meant to me. One of them, Dympna, asked me if I would say a few words.

Once I passed Father Judge and found my seat, I entered the same dazed state I'd been in on Tuesday. I don't remember most of the service, or even what I talked about. I just remember an ache of unbearable sadness at his loss, and a feeling of exhaustion threatening to overtake me. It was the first time since Tuesday morning that I'd sat down without a phone or a file or a report in front of me, the first time I had nothing to do but dwell on what had happened. I knew I could lose myself in grief, but knew if I let myself go, I might never get back.

Afterward I was standing in a mob of people when I spotted a familiar face out of the corner of my eye. It was Tara Stackpole.

All week long I'd been dreading the moment when I would have to see her and face the reality—and enormity—of what she had lost. Much as I'd thought about her and the other wives and what they were going through, I'd been so busy that I'd kept that deep grief at arm's length.

Looking at her now, just fifteen feet away from me, her arms open, her face indescribably sad, I couldn't hold back anymore. I started crying. By the time I reached her, I couldn't even speak.

We hugged tightly. I tried to whisper how sorry I was, but could only get out a few incoherent words.

Tara pulled back, wiped one eye with her sleeve, and fixed me with a glare.

"This isn't your fault," she said. "Don't even think that for a minute. Do you think there's any way you could have stopped Timmy Stackpole from going back to work, even if you'd wanted to?"

I didn't know what to say. I wanted to believe she was right, but I felt too terrible about Timmy. I just hugged her again and didn't want to let go, as the tears kept flowing.

I found out later why Tara had decided to come. She had been at the families' meeting with the president, and after seeing him, had taken a seat on a sofa in the corridor to rest. Exhausted, she'd shut her eyes for a minute. Then someone had started rubbing her shoulder, trying to comfort her.

She opened her eyes. It was the mayor. He had searched the room to talk to her.

"Do me a favor," he said. "I want you to tell Tommy that it's not his fault, what happened to Timmy. I think he's blaming himself."

Tara decided to do it right away.

After all she'd been through, the years of suffering as Timmy struggled to come back only to lose him in the cruelest way imaginable, here she was, worried about me? And here was the mayor, in the middle of the greatest crisis in the city's history, concerned about my grief and guilt? Such bottomless compassion gives me more comfort than I can ever say.

23

AT ALL RANKS,
WE ARE VULNERABLE

The next day, Saturday, September 15, was a lovely, sunny, breezy day, the nicest since the morning of the attacks. But as hundreds of firefighters gathered outside Saint Mel's, a quiet neighborhood church in Flushing, Queens, we had a grim duty to perform.

We had come to bury Bill Feehan.

Before that week, I never could have imagined attending a line-of-duty funeral for Bill. But this was just the start. We would be burying Father Judge, Pete Ganci, and firefighter Ray York later that same *day*. Hundreds of other funerals stretched out before us like a dark tunnel.

A breeze whipped through my hair as I stood across the street from the church entrance watching the procession. Row after row of marchers from the department's Emerald Society Bagpipe Band paraded solemnly by to the beat of their lonely drums. In every direction I could see officers and firefighters standing at attention.

Bill had been a parishioner at this little church. He could have had, and certainly deserved, a hero's ceremony at Saint Patrick's Cathedral. But it seemed fitting to me that his family had chosen this place to bid him good-bye. I remembered being here a few years earlier for the funeral of his wife, Elizabeth.

The large hearse crept up slowly. With great gravity the pallbearers removed the casket and marched toward the door as the bagpipers struck up a mournful "Amazing Grace." The rest of us followed behind.

Inside, a woman stood by the altar singing "Be Not Afraid" as the mourners streamed by the casket:

> Be not afraid,
> I go before you always,
> Come follow Me,
> and I shall give you rest.

As at all the funerals and wakes except for Father Judge's, Bill had to have a closed casket.

I took a seat in the front row of the middle section of pews, by the mayor. People poured in behind us, quickly filling all the seats. Other mourners lined the back wall and crowded in the doorways.

There was an uneasy sense of expectation in the air. We were here for Bill, but I could feel a larger, shared grief in the room for the city, the country, the time before everything changed.

The priest entered, and we rose and crossed ourselves while he prayed. We listened to the Bible readings. Daniel chronicled a "time unsurpassed in distress," while Saint John wrote that "we are God's children now." The reading from the Gospel of John told of when Jesus visited the tomb of Lazarus and raised him from the dead, saying to Martha, "I am the resurrection and the life." I had heard all the passages before, and right then, they didn't sound like much more than words to me.

As the priest delivered his homily, I looked around the room. Bill's two sons, two daughters, and their families were sitting together on the left. They were fine, good people. One of Bill's sons was a firefighter. The other, Bill Jr.—or "Guillermo!" as his father greeted him on the phone—was a handsome and graceful lawyer. I knew how proud Bill had been of them all.

There was a lot of warmth in that room. Officers and old-timers, some of whom I hadn't seen in years, packed the place. I could look from face to face and remember what favors Bill had done for each one. Some younger troops had come, too, and I felt sorry they hadn't known Bill the way I had.

When it was time, I got up to receive communion, as I was to do at every Catholic funeral in the weeks ahead. The old ritual of receiving the bread and wine was deeply familiar to me from childhood. Back then, I had believed in the almost magical promise of the Eucharist, of swallowing the body and blood of Christ.

Now, I was more skeptical. Taking the wafer felt comforting in the middle of all that sadness. But the most I could muster was a vague hope that there was something more behind it than this.

Once the formal mass ended, the eulogies began.

Bill Jr. spoke first. He thanked all the mourners and said he was proud of the workers who were trying to repair the city. He talked fondly of his father's integrity and humor and of how much laughter had been a part of his life. He evoked Bill's deep love for his family and his job. "There is no place on earth my father enjoyed more than a fire scene," he said. "That's where he wanted to be." He almost seemed at peace with the way his father had gone. At least Bill died the way he would have wished. And at least he had lived a rich life.

As I got up to speak next, I realized that the speech I had brought, written for me the night before by Mike Regan, was missing. I had lost it somewhere in the rush. So I was forced to improvise.

Looking right at Bill's family, I talked of his great talents and personal dignity. Bill had thought only of being a firefighter, but I had always believed he had the brains and drive to be almost anything. I spoke of the many different ranks he had held, emphasizing that chief was the one that had meant the most to him. Bill had always answered his phone, "Chief Feehan."

Nervously, I joked, "Nobody calls *me* chief unless it's a mistake."

Most of all, I talked of how hard it would be to fill Bill's shoes. All week long I had been feeling his absence.

"I can't tell you how much Chief Feehan meant to me," I said. "We won't be able to replace him. It's just not realistic to think we can. Someone will take the job, someone will take this department forward, but it won't be somebody like Chief Feehan. It won't be somebody who had every rank in the department.

"Wearing that white helmet is sometimes a heavy load, a heavy burden. Because of Chief Feehan, it was easier for all of us. It will be harder for all of us now. It will be very hard for us."

By the end, I was barely holding it together. I went back to my seat and put my head in my hands.

Then the priest introduced the mayor, and a long and

emotional round of applause broke out. It seemed out of place at a funeral. But I think it reflected the need everyone had to ease the grief just a little. Feeling raw, they looked to the mayor, as people had all week, for some reassurance.

The mayor seemed to know that, and to be speaking not just to us but to the rest of the city, even the nation.

"They may have taken three hundred men or more from us," he said. "That's a lot. That's a horrible, horrible thing. And the impact of it, I don't think we even realize yet.

"But the reality is, and I really believe this, we're actually going to be stronger as a result of what they're trying to do to us. The fire department is going to be stronger because there are eleven thousand firefighters left who were taught by Bill, by Pete Ganci, by Fire Commissioner Von Essen."

When I heard my name, I thought, *I must really be a wreck if the boss is saying that to cheer me up*. But he continued, generously, "You *are* a chief too, Tom. You're terrific. You've gone through a very difficult week, and your strength and leadership are incredible."

The crowd applauded, and I was shocked and embarrassed, thinking, *I wish I believed that*.

"We're going to get through this," the mayor continued. "The fire department's going to get through it, the city's going to get through it, and I hate to say this in a church, I probably shouldn't say it this way, but we're not going to let these miserable, horrible cowards that attacked our city, attacked our nation, and killed our people, they're not going to kill our spirit. They can't."

Firefighters, he said, live by the words of Jesus that

man can show no greater love than to lay down his life for another. "They all believe it, and they all carry it out, because they're the greatest people in our city, our fire-fighters, they're the ones who are respected the most. That's why the children love them so much. The symbol is a fire truck, but the reality is how brave they are.

"Bill was the best, and the reason he was the best is that he left it all behind. He left it in all those eleven thousand men and women that are there to protect us in life. They are stronger and better as a result of his life, as a result of his teaching, and ultimately as a result of his example."

As soon as Bill's service ended, the mayor and I climbed into his truck and rushed off to Pete Ganci's funeral.

We had been forced to make a horrible decision about which services to attend that day. Father Judge's funeral was scheduled between the other two. But we didn't have time to head back into Manhattan for that one and then out to Farmingdale for Pete's. We had gone to the wake the night before in part to make up for that. But it was awful to miss the funeral of one of my closest friends. I didn't have time to attend either the wake or the funeral for Ray York, a terrific guy who worked for us in fire safety education.

Pete's funeral was at Saint Kilian, the same church where we had held Jimmy Blackmore's service after the Atlantic Avenue fire. His helmet sat atop the casket. Again it was an overflow crowd.

The priest was Father John Delendick, our depart-ment chaplain in Brooklyn, who had narrowly escaped injury at the Trade Center and did the work of ten chaplains that first week. In his homily, he talked of Pete's lust for life and sense of humor. He remembered Pete's old line about never smiling when you left the house in the morning so your wife wouldn't be upset.

As I listened, I replayed those last minutes in my mind and wondered what it had been like for Pete and Bill. It was terrible to be there without them. But I knew they had died wanting to be with, and protect, their men. To send everyone else north while they went south seemed to me the height of heroism.

With those thoughts swirling through my brain, I found it hard to deliver my eulogy for Pete. My voice quavered throughout, and several times I had to stop to collect myself. Between Father Judge's wake the night before and the funerals that day, the emotions I had been able to keep back, at least somewhat, were catching up with me.

"Never could I have imagined a scenario that included holding funerals for Bill Feehan, Pete Ganci, and Mychal Judge on the same day," I said. "It really is a little bit more than I guess we're supposed to be able to take."

I looked out at Pete's wife, Kathy, his daughter, Danielle, and his two sons, Chris and Peter III. Peter was a firefighter in Ladder 111, one of the houses his dad had worked in, and my voice grew shakier. "Pete would never ask anyone to do anything he hadn't," I said. "That is what happened Tuesday, as he took charge of rescue and firefighting efforts at the World Trade Center. As the towers gave way, Pete and Bill were among the last to leave the command post. Only by seconds. It cost us all dearly."

I quoted Pete from one of his speeches: "We must

stand ready to face what comes. In this department, no one is invincible. At all ranks we contribute, and at all ranks we are vulnerable."

From then on, much of my time would be devoted to funerals and memorial services. I must have gone to more than a hundred. For weeks I went to at least one a day, and on many nights to one or more wakes.

The numbers were overwhelming. Often there would be four, five, six services scheduled on the same day—or more. One day there were eighteen. It seemed as if the parade of grief would never end for our department.

It was physically impossible to make every service. So every day, with the help of my staff, I made the wrenching decision about which ones I would go to. We coordinated with the mayor and his staff to ensure that at least one city official would be at every service to honor the sacrifice the deceased had made for the city.

Sometimes either the mayor or I would be specifically asked to come to a service, and we always tried to oblige. Occasionally a family would tell us they didn't want us there, either because of some problem in the past or because they wanted to keep it a family-only affair.

One of my hardest tasks every day was reading the obituaries my staff compiled on each man. Each contained the raw data of a human life, the awards and years of service, the spouses and children, the memories of firehouse colleagues. They seemed like unfulfilled promises, cruel reminders of what had been lost when these lives were cut short.

Normally, I would have spent hours with the wives of men we had lost, doing what I could to comfort and help them. Making that connection, sharing that pain, had always been very important to me. Now, often the best I could do was greet the family beforehand, tell them how sorry I was and how much we appreciated what their loved one had done for us, and spend a few minutes with them afterward. It was so little that I always felt I had fallen short of my responsibilities as commissioner. But there was no other way.

The whole department was stretched thin, in fact, by the need to care for the families. But so many workers helped. At headquarters, a number of civilians devoted themselves to making and keeping contacts with each family and trying to find out what they needed. Many firehouses, already strained by the losses they had taken and the ongoing rescue effort, stepped in to do more for the families anyway. We will never know how many small acts of kindness and generosity were performed in those dark days.

I'd start thinking about the funerals when I woke up in the morning, and sometimes even the night before. They never became routine for me.

Every service was some kind of revelation. One day we'd be burying a kid who had just come on the job maybe three months earlier. I wouldn't know him, his family, or even his company. But I'd go feeling horrible at the loss of someone so young. The next day the funeral might be for someone I'd known back when I was a fireman, or a union delegate. It might be someone I'd done some favors for, or had the privilege of promoting, or placed in a sought-after firehouse. Sometimes he would be from a company where I knew everyone. Those types of funerals would have a totally different level of pain. Sometimes they would be services for entire units—warm community affairs that could be deeply moving.

Every time, it was upsetting to me to see the widows and fathers and mothers of the men who had died. Sometimes I would walk in and see a young woman dressed in black, maybe about the same age as my daughters, and think how sad it was that she had lost her father—and it would turn out that she was mourning her *husband*. They were too young to experience so much pain.

Hardest of all for me were the children. So many young boys and girls lost their fathers at the World Trade Center that I lost count. I'd sit in the pew looking at these families, thinking of what they had been through, wondering how they would go on, and I would feel powerless.

It usually didn't take much to make me cry. In the office or at the command center, I strained to keep my emotions in check. It was traditional in the department to be strong and stoical, and that was the sort of man I had aspired to be all the way back to my childhood. But if it was too hard to keep it in during a service, I didn't. I just let the tears flow. I needed the release.

At just about every service I went to, I delivered a eulogy. In my remarks I usually tried to focus on the man and his life. Occasionally I tried to say something broader and more inspiring, but the motivational words were harder for me. I believed in the fighting spirit of the firefighters, and the goodness of our country. I wanted to think we would prevail in whatever struggle we were in. But I didn't know if I could say anything about them that would sound convincing. In my heart, I knew the department had taken a severe hit, and it would be a long time before we came back.

Most of the services I attended were Catholic. As with communion, there was something comforting to me in the routine, which I knew so well—the pews, the incense and the statues, the prayers. I knew by instinct when to cross myself.

Often, though, I wanted more. I listened intently to every homily, every eulogy, sifting the words for something that could help me understand why we were going through all this. So many times I wished Father Judge were still around. I didn't know how to make sense of God's plan in the middle of all this chaos; I didn't even know if I believed there was a greater plan anymore. I didn't know where or how the divine was at work. All I saw around me was anguish and misery and sorrow.

I could *almost* accept the idea of God taking away someone like Bill Feehan. It was hard, it was unfair, it was unnecessary, but as even Bill's kids had said, he had lived a good life, was seventy-one years old, had already lost his wife and raised his kids, had loved what he was doing, and was able to do it for forty-two years. There was some way to make sense of it.

But when I looked across the church and saw Tara Stackpole sitting there, or some other widow with young children, I'd think, *How could a loving God do this?* I couldn't accept it.

I'd never asked such questions before. Ever since childhood, I'd had a basic, simple belief in the existence of God. Now I found it impossible to believe in a God who would say, "Okay, let me take Stackpole. That makes sense." To take a young man who had just suffered for three years to get back to a job he could have walked away from, who had four inches of scar tissue on his ankle and five kids at home, was just not right. Nothing could make me believe that it was.

Sometimes, right in the middle of a service, I'd start arguing with God in my head. *If your purpose is to send a message, and you've consciously selected people to "come home" to you, you've made a mistake. It can't be these people—not all of them, not now.*

I wanted, and want, to believe that there is a God who looks after us and cares for us. Some of life would make a little more sense if there was a God. At least it would mean that people like Tara and Timmy really will be rewarded in another life.

But to accommodate that thought, I had to believe that God wasn't involved in every single thing that happens down here. *He must be very busy. He must allow people to become completely evil. It must be that some days we're going to wake up and have a terrible tragedy, and maybe hundreds of people are going to die in the United States or elsewhere in our world, and it must be that victims are going to be random, because there are evil people that want to hurt them, and God's not going to stop it.*

After communion, I would offer a conditional prayer: *If you're there, God, please help these families and please help me do as good a job as I can. Help my family to stay healthy. Just let me be the best I can be during this ordeal. Please, bring us peace.*

While hard, the funerals and memorial services also helped keep me going. They got me outside my head a little, and kept me connected to the larger community of firefighting.

While I didn't draw much religious solace from them, I was always moved by the pageantry of a fire department funeral—the drummers and marchers, the crowds of brothers who came by the hundreds, the solemn, flag-draped caskets. The traditions of more than 130 years lived on—and would go on after us, too.

At every service I came away with a memory of someone's life that I could keep, a quote or an image or a story. Our ranks included poets, singers, songwriters, artists. Some of the material they'd written and produced in their lifetimes was wonderful.

It was at the funeral of Captain Vincent Brunton, in the program prepared by his family, that a quote from Thucydides was evoked that says so much about the sacrifice of the firefighters: "The bravest are surely those who have the clearest vision of what is before them, glory and danger alike, and yet notwithstanding, go out to meet it." The words haven't left me since.

I drew strength, especially, from children. Whenever I was at a service on Long Island, near my daughter Erica's home, I'd ask her to bring my two-year-old granddaughter, Rita, over, just so I could see her, even for five minutes. Rita was too little to know what was happening. She was a bundle of innocence and joy. To be able to hold her, nibble on her cheeks, bite her ears, tickle her, make her laugh and laugh with her, was like a lifeline. Every time I saw her, it was a lift that could carry me through a few more hours.

I'd notice the awe in an altar boy's eye as he looked out and saw all the firefighters. I'd realize he was imagining how it would feel to be one of those heroes. I'd watch as a young son stood at the altar and spoke of what a wonderful man his father was, and while it made me sad, it was life-affirming too.

On October 3, I attended a memorial service in West Brighton on Staten Island for a thirty-four-year-old firefighter named Stephen Siller. I hadn't known him, but he had been a member of Squad 1, our Park Slope squad, the original squad begun by Ray Downey and an institution in itself. Incredibly, they had lost twelve of the twenty-seven firefighters assigned to the squad on September 11.

Steve had left behind five children, a wife, Sally, and fifty-seven immediate family members. He had actually gotten off duty just before the attacks and had been on his way to meet his brothers for a golf date when he'd turned the car around and gone back. He was last seen running through the Brooklyn-Battery Tunnel with his bunker gear under his arm.

It was all very sad. Yet the sight of the honor guard was moving and inspiring. It was made up mostly of men from Steve's house. But at the end of the line stood a boy who looked to be about fourteen, his hair slicked back, standing at attention with a serious expression on his face.

The governor's wife, Libby Pataki, told me later that she had spoken to the boy. His name was Andrew, he said. His father, Michael Esposito, had been a lieutenant in the squad and had also been killed in the attacks.

When she asked him why he was there, he answered simply, "My father would expect it of me."

24

RECOVERY EFFORTS

On Sunday afternoon, September 16, the fire department set up a makeshift stage and rows of metal chairs
in the brick courtyard outside our headquarters.

Within a day or two of September 11, I had suggested
to the mayor that we hold a promotions ceremony.
Though we still hoped to find survivors, we had suffered
a devastating blow to our command structure. Eighteen
battalion chiefs, twenty captains, and forty-five lieutenants were missing. We had to fill those jobs if we were
to go forward.

Making the promotions wasn't hard technically. In
our department, firefighters take tests to move up to
each rank, and once they've passed the test, their names
are placed on an eligibility list. When positions open up,
the next names on the list get the call.

But emotionally it was very tough to make the promotions. Everyone ached to think of the empty spaces we
were trying to fill.

Normally a promotions ceremony was a happy occasion. Officers brought their families, took pictures, and
applauded wildly at any chance they got.

This one, though, was joyless. As the mayor told the

crowd, these were battlefield commissions—and the atmosphere reflected that. Everyone seemed miserable. No one applauded the men as they accepted their new ranks. Very few family members came. No firehouses were there to urge on their brothers. All the speeches and remarks were short and very businesslike. No one took pictures of the newly promoted officers as we shook their hands.

At one point the mayor put his head down in his hand and, for just a few seconds, cried.

I hated every minute of it. But it was one more thing we had to do.

"We need you to help us," I told the men frankly. "We need you to help us recover the rest of our men that are missing. We need leadership. We need structure. We need to have you out in the field as soon as possible. . . . I need you all to go out there and help us do the very best we can to recover our guys."

Among the promotions we made that day, we included all the missing men whose names would have come up on the eligibility list. It wasn't standard operating procedure. But it would mean that the hard work they had put in, sometimes for years, to pass a promotional test wasn't in vain. It would also boost the pensions their families got. Additionally, we paid the missing men overtime. For thirty days, these were just some of the actions we took that violated normal procedure, but I was never one to do things to the letter when I could help firefighters instead. Eventually we would promote every firefighter who had been eligible when he died.

The ceremony was only the first step in rebuilding a badly battered department. Of the 343 men we had lost, all but two paramedics were firefighters. They had come from seventy-one units all over the city. Our elite squads and rescue units had been particularly hurt; ninety-one of those lost had come from them.

We had also lost more than ninety cars and trucks and untold numbers of masks, radios, respirators, oxygen tanks, infrared cameras, and any other piece of equipment you could name. My administrative team, led by deputy commissioner Tom Fitzpatrick, worked hard on replenishing all those supplies, and did a yeoman's job under difficult circumstances. Tom McDonald, our deputy commissioner of fleet services, who had done a great job of upgrading the service before the disaster, worked hard to replenish our supply of vehicles. Michael Regan, our former press secretary, who had left us some months earlier, returned to the department to take Bill Feehan's job, while his replacement as spokesman, Lieutenant Frank Gribbon, worked to make sure each departed firefighter was treated with dignity.

Our load was made a little easier by the enormous support we received—and not just from the government. It wasn't long before people were sending us money, or holding fund-raisers to buy us new rigs. FDNY hats and shirts sprouted everywhere, as a way people showed us their support. All over the city, residents brought flowers and cakes and other gifts to the firefighters, or just stopped by and asked if there was anything they could do.

Bags and bags of condolence cards poured in from world leaders, firefighters, and civilians around the globe. People sent paintings and poems and songs. Every grammar school teacher in the Western Hemisphere must have collected student tributes, bundled them up, and sent them in.

Sometimes, when I had a few hours on a Saturday or Sunday night, I'd go into the office, sit down in the conference room where the mailbags were brought, and read through a pile. The letters and drawings from children meant the most to me—especially when it was an older kid who had tried to write something thoughtful and from the heart.

From one pile, I plucked out and taped to my computer a pencil drawing we had received from a boy. It showed the towers burning, and smoke pouring out, while in the sky Jesus was rising toward heaven, holding his hands out to the victims.

Down at the site, meanwhile, we were building, and running, what was almost a second fire department.

By the end of the first week, the collapsed pedestrian bridge was gone, and cranes and heavy trucks moved in. The crushed rigs and ambulances were towed away. Many of the streets in the surrounding area were being cleaned.

Security had been tightened. A cyclone fence had gone up around most of the area, and the workers were issued security cards. Many of the volunteers from the first days were gone, the bucket brigades disbanded. Firefighters, police, and construction workers were handling most of the hard labor. Ironworkers sliced through hundreds of enormous, thick steel beams that had been the backbone of the towers, while the uniformed personnel searched for remains. It was time-consuming physical labor. At the same time, FBI agents were sifting the debris for criminal evidence.

The primary command center for the recovery was set up in a firehouse on Liberty Street, across from the site. It was the home of Ladder 10 and Engine 10. Engineers from FEMA and the city's Department of Design and Construction pored over blueprints and designs to discuss construction problems and recovery plans. Ken Holden, the head of the department, did an outstanding job coordinating everything. Fortunately, he stayed on past the departure of Mayor Giuliani and saw the operation through to the end of May.

The FDNY, which was overseeing the rescue efforts, was based under the tent standing at West and Vesey Streets. On every shift there was at least one chief, designated the incident commander, who was responsible for everything going on. In a trailer on the edge of the site, Chief Nigro, Deputy Commissioner Fitzpatrick, and other officials would coordinate larger issues of resources and planning.

The site had been formally divided into four quadrants. Each had its own chief on every shift who reported directly to the chief at the command post.

Debris was loaded onto dump trucks, taken to barges, and shipped out to Fresh Kills landfill on Staten Island, a facility residents had fought to close but that was reopened for the grim and elaborate work of sifting through the rubble. It was an eerie location in an isolated area at the end of a long road. Waist-high grasses waved in the breeze. It could have been Kansas.

At the crest of a hill stood a cluster of tents and trailers, which were assigned to agencies like the NYPD and the FBI. There was an office where workers, many from the Port Authority, NYPD, and FDNY, checked in and got assignments. The area, like the Trade Center site, was divided into four quadrants. Workers in protective goggles and clothing would screen material and pass anything they thought important on to the next quadrant, where it could be more finely screened. Sometimes they found human remains. There were wallets, jewelry, religious medals, and watches. Each one was bagged, tagged, and passed to police detectives, who would search for any identifying mark that could tell them whom it belonged to so they could bring it to a loved one. Any piece of debris that looked as if it could be an airplane part was separated from the load and brought to the FBI to be cataloged for further examination.

In the last stage, the rubble was placed in baskets and passed through a series of conveyor belts to be gently sifted by hand. The process was meant to ensure that anything that might help identify a victim was recovered. It was heartbreaking, tedious, and even lonely work, but it was critical.

Nearby was a lot that had become a vehicle graveyard. All the crushed, battered, and burned fire trucks had been transported there. They were parked alongside police cars, passenger cars, and taxis. I wandered through the wrecks seeing ghosts from the department. The rigs used by Squad 1, Rescue 2, and Ladder 18, the hazardous-materials truck—all were tangible, painful evidence of the men we had lost, and of what they had gone through down there.

For several weeks after the attacks, every firefighter worked 24 hours on duty and 24 off. We needed the manpower both to staff the rescue effort and run the firehouses.

Taking care of all these people was a huge logistical operation. In the first days the job of transporting and equipping the firefighters had been handled largely by a range of state, local, and federal agencies at the Emergency Operations Center, working with my staff back at headquarters in downtown Brooklyn. It was a constant challenge to get food, water, toilets, lights, masks, gloves, and a million other necessities down to the area. Everyone became resourceful and creative at locating and deploying everything. The Javits Center, on 34th Street, became a central depot where supplies were gathered before being sent downtown.

Volunteers remained around the site in support roles. Whenever workers went outside the fence, someone was offering to wash out their eyes, give them counseling, feed them cookies, take their blood pressure, or pray with them.

To reach the site, rescue workers were required to go to designated gathering points. In the initial days we ferried some people in, but eventually we had everyone meet at Shea Stadium in Queens before they headed down to the site. They'd report to temporary command posts, pick up tools, masks, clothing, and other equipment, and be assigned to a crew for the day. Then they'd be bused into downtown Manhattan, usually with police escorts, almost always past cheering crowds as they neared the site.

Once there, the crews were divided further, into teams of four or five. Each one had an officer in charge. The team would be assigned to search in one area.

It was grueling work. There wasn't much lifting to do, beyond picking up small rocks or pieces of debris, because most of the rubble was too heavy for one person.

Mostly they were searching for human remains. At any moment they could come upon a hand, or torso, or something similarly disturbing.

A clothing store inside the World Financial Center served as the temporary morgue. All bodies, and body parts, were brought there.

The dust and smoke remained heavy. Breathing without a respirator was tough; even so, some guys refused to put one on. Though necessary, the respirators were uncomfortable and impeded communication.

After their twelve-hour shift, the workers would be bused back to Shea, utterly exhausted. I can only imagine what horrors they relived from the day as they rode back on the bus together—or, even worse, as they drove home alone.

I was down at the site as often as possible. When there wasn't a funeral to attend, I'd head down in the morning. Other times I would go down there to accompany visiting dignitaries or just to talk to the guys. (I always called it "the site" or "the Trade Center." I never liked the expression "Ground Zero." It sounded too much like a catchy media phrase.)

One day while I was walking the site, I talked to Dennis Oberg, then, a few minutes later, to Lee Ielpi. Both were searching for their sons. Whenever I looked in the eyes of men going through that, and tried to understand their horrible pain, I could never find words to comfort them.

Near the command post, I saw, about a hundred workers were gathered. I realized that the tours were changing. I went over to shake some hands and say hello.

As I greeted the men, I spotted my twenty-nine-year-old son, Marc, among them. He had joined the department a couple of years earlier, and on his rotation I had assigned him to Ladder 176, a house with great traditions of spirit, concern for safety, and a high level of proficiency. Suddenly I thought of Lee and Dennis and all the other men I knew searching for a son or brother or father. *Why is their loved one gone, and mine here?* I didn't have a satisfactory answer. There was none. But I knew how lucky I was.

At the citywide level, we had settled into something of a routine after the first week. We moved the Emergency Operations Center from the Police Academy to the more spacious city-owned Pier 92 on the Upper West Side. Rows of desks were set up in a wide room that resembled a factory floor, and a range of city, federal, and military agencies, public utilities, and private corporations were given space. Every station was manned by staff members and executives. It was all just as we'd practiced in emergency drills for several years. Soon half-eaten sandwiches and half-filled cups of old coffee littered all the desks. The Red Cross, staffed by smiling volunteers, provided great meals all day, and everyone started gaining weight.

The city had slowly begun to return to normal. On the Monday after the disaster, the stock exchanges reopened after heroic efforts by phone and power workers to get the facilities hooked up. Schools started up again, and bridge and tunnel traffic resumed. City Hall eventually reopened, though the mayor continued to spend most of his time at the operations center.

But residents remained extremely jumpy, and with good reason. On October 12, just as fears of another

Trade Center–type attack were fading, we announced that anthrax spores had been discovered at NBC headquarters in Rockefeller Center, in an envelope sent to anchorman Tom Brokaw, which infected his assistant. Anthrax infections were reported at the *New York Post,* and more spores were found at other media offices. Then they were detected at one of the city's main postal processing centers.

In Washington, D.C., a particularly deadly strain was sent to Senate Majority Leader Tom Daschle. Within days the Senate Office Building had been shuttered, and it would remain that way for months. Worried postal workers were assured they had nothing to fear, but a few days later, several workers who had handled tainted letters died from inhaling spores. It was disgusting to see how the politicians had gotten special accommodations while the postal workers had initially been brushed off.

I was only peripherally involved in the anthrax investigation. Our haz-mat teams initially responded to every report, and for a couple weeks received a lot of calls from jittery citizens. We responded by creating "hammer teams" made up of firefighters and police officers who responded to calls in pairs. Their job was to determine whether full-blown resources were needed and whether the police had any reason to open a criminal investigation. It was a creative way to handle the increased volume of calls without overloading our haz-mat units.

At the command center, the anthrax added to our anxieties about another attack or situation that would threaten the citizens and tax our resources. Privately, most of us thought the letters were the work not of Arab terrorists but of some nut who had sent a few envelopes and crawled back into a hole. But it was a scary interlude, and an important wake-up call for all of us. Ray Downey had long warned of the need to better prepare for future threats like bioterrorism. It was painfully clear that the future had arrived.

After the president's visit, a parade of other leaders came to see the site. The mayor wanted as many people as possible to inhale the air and see the rubble up close. He would bring visitors to a small platform OEM had built at Liberty and West streets and describe what had happened while I stood behind him to answer questions.

So many dignitaries visited that I lost count. Muhammad Ali and Tony Blair, the mayor of Jerusalem and Ted Kennedy came down. Governors and senators and congressmen and foreign delegations did, too. Almost every one of them seemed horrified and overwhelmed by the scale of destruction, just as we all had been the first time we saw it up close. Most could say very little. President Jacques Chirac of France got tears in his eyes as we flew overhead in a helicopter. Gerhard Schroder of Germany did as well.

For a shaken Senator John McCain, to whom I spoke for about ten minutes, the scene evoked memories of his days as a prisoner of war. He opened up to me about his experiences, and I was reminded of the natural bond that exists among men who have worked in harm's way. I could see that Senator McCain, who had endured real pain and suffering, understood more about what our troops were going through than most people did.

On October 11, the one-month anniversary of the attacks, we escorted Saudi Prince Al-Walid bin Talal bin Abdul Aziz, a nephew of King Fahd of Saudi Arabia and the kingdom's most prominent businessman, around the site, along with his brother and a friend. They were there to present us with a $10 million check for the Twin Towers Fund, the charity that Mayor Giuliani had set up to collect money for the uniformed victims' families.

They struck me as cold men. While the mayor described the destruction, they surveyed the area indifferently, almost blandly. They seemed genuinely unmoved. It was as if this were a possible investment for them, not the cemetery I saw when I looked out there.

A couple of hours later the mayor called me. "Tommy, I think I may have screwed up," he said. "I told that prince we were with to take his money back."

Shortly after the tour, he explained, the prince had issued a statement criticizing U.S. policy in the Middle East. "We must address some of the issues that led to such a criminal attack," it said, and among those issues, the United States needed to adopt "a more balanced stance toward the Palestinian cause."

For the mayor, who had always been a strong supporter of Israel, the words gave the donation the taint of blood money. He was furious, but he'd still had the presence of mind to call the White House before he handed the check back.

"It's totally unacceptable, it's bullshit," he said. "The nerve of this guy, to say something like that. I don't need it. But I am a little worried," he admitted. "Maybe I've overstepped my bounds. Maybe it wasn't my money to give. What do you think?"

I just laughed. "What do I think? You've got nothing to worry about. You did the right thing. Those guys were a couple of phonies."

I think he hung up feeling better about what he'd done, and I was glad to provide a little reassurance.

From then on, I always referred to the prince privately as "Abdul Fangul."

The mayor and I were getting closer as we worked next to each other for many hours every day. Riding in his car or sitting in a helicopter on the way back from a funeral, he now felt comfortable enough to unwind and open up a little around me. We'd talk about men we'd lost, or about what a tough job the president had. We'd wonder how long the support for the war effort would last. We'd talk about the visitors to the site and the families we'd just met at services.

He told me once that he felt we had been in battle together, along with Bernie Kerik, Richie Sheirer, and many other members of our staffs. All of us shared a sense of horror mingled with great responsibility, as well as grief for our mutual friends. The emotion wasn't something we talked about much, but we all felt that connection.

With so much going on, we needed a private release for our emotions, and we often found it in humor—especially in stressful moments. Late one night, I was waiting at the morgue for some tests on remains, along with the mayor and his girlfriend, Judi Nathan. They had planned to go out for dinner about four hours earlier, but instead he had asked her to meet him here. Now we were stuck together in an antiseptic and somewhat depressing office—for a very grim reason.

I didn't really know Judi too well, but I'd seen enough of her to suspect she had a good sense of humor. So I tried cheering her up. "Pretty great date, huh?" I asked.

She laughed.

I went on: "Yeah, there's nothing like stopping by the

medical examiner's office on your way to dinner. Rudy Giuliani sure knows how to plan a fun evening." He started laughing, too.

Soon we were all riffing on fun nights with Rudy. I took a clean sheet of paper from my notebook and wrote across the top, "David Letterman's Top 10 Dates with Rudy Giuliani."

For weeks we kept adding items to the list, dredging up memories of the many crises he had responded to through the years—fires, West Nile virus outbreaks, hurricanes. All sounded like perfect Rudy Giuliani dates. Visiting critically injured people in the hospital? We put it on the list. There seemed no end to the myriad ways he could entertain you: a water main break, dangling scaffolding, a power outage—whatever it was, we agreed, Rudy Giuliani knew how to show a date a fun time.

Watching him work, I felt the city was lucky to have an experienced mayor at the helm. He had been in the job nearly eight years. From the first moment, he had known who to call with every question and concern, and had always been able to balance the details with the big picture—the need to make sure that New York would recover. Philosophically, he believed it was important to push the city forward by making decisions, even imperfect ones, rather than getting bogged down in the moment. He passed that energy and passion on to the rest of us.

Ten days after the attacks, we were at a staff meeting discussing a big memorial service the city wanted to hold at Yankee Stadium. But Deputy Mayor Rudy Washington reported that George Steinbrenner, the team's owner, was balking at some of our requests. He especially didn't approve of the big stage we wanted. The mayor wanted to fit all the state and local officials, religious leaders, musicians, and singers on one platform. But Steinbrenner was afraid it would hurt the grass.

"This is bull," the mayor said. He thought for a minute. Then he turned to Bernie and asked, "Are you guys there for security?"

"Yeah, I've got officers all over the place."

"All right. Go to the office and take the keys. Tell them it's a security issue. Take over the stadium, and Rudy, build as big a stage as you want."

Then it was on to the next item. The mayor got his stage. Steinbrenner was supportive in many ways, but probably never even realized the mayor had ordered a "takeover."

One of my favorite views of the mayor in action didn't come until early November, when the Yankees were playing the Arizona Diamondbacks in the World Series. The mayor flew out to Phoenix for a game, and arranged to bring along some children who had lost their fathers in the attacks. I was invited, too. The trip had been donated by Continental Airlines.

On the flight I was sitting near a group of mayoral aides. Soon after we took off, one of them, Manny Papir, started scrolling through his Blackberry checking e-mail messages.

"What's that?" the mayor asked.

Manny started to hand it over, but Tony Carbonetti and Sunny Mindel threw up their hands. "No! No! Don't give it to him!" Carbonetti pleaded.

"Give it to me!" the mayor barked. He pressed some buttons. "Show me how this thing works!" he said.

I knew the mayor had a good mind for technology and loved any tool that could help make him more efficient. For the rest of the flight, he sat fiddling with the gadget. By the time we landed, he was already e-mailing messages to everybody on the plane. Some were setting off the vibrations on people's beepers and waking them up. He was laughing.

"Why did you give that to him?" Carbonetti and the others asked Manny with mock angst. "Now he's really going to be a pain in the ass. He can get us twenty-four hours a day."

That was just what he did. Within a week of arriving back in New York, I noticed that the mayor had a Blackberry of his own. He was e-mailing people in the middle of staff meetings and reading their responses—even getting visibly agitated when he didn't like what they said. When he couldn't sleep in the middle of the night, he'd sometimes blitz people with e-mails at three in the morning. By seven he'd be calling to know why he hadn't gotten an answer back.

Even I had to get one. I called it a mulberry or a raspberry. But I don't think I ever turned it on.

One evening in early October, the mayor and I were riding the helicopter back from two wakes upstate when he got a call saying that the rescuers thought they had found Terry Hatton's body. We decided to go straight to the medical examiner's office. After the mistake we had made the first time, we both wanted to be sure before telling Beth.

The morgue had been transformed since the attacks. The whole area surrounding the building, from First Avenue to the East River, had been blocked off and tents put up where remains were collected. Inside, doctors and lab technicians sifted a never-ending repository of remains, performing autopsies and working to identify victims.

Probably no remains in any disaster have ever been treated with the deliberate care shown to the remains at the Trade Center. The entire recovery effort concentrated on getting all the human remains we possibly could and bringing them here for analysis. It was gruesome but vitally important work. Whenever we went there, we made sure to thank as many people as we could.

The doctors told us they were having a tough time confirming whether the remains they had found were in fact Terry's. But the mayor called Beth and asked her for the name of Terry's dentist. Then he called the dentist himself—at home, late at night. "This is Mayor Giuliani," he said. "I wonder if you can get us some dental records."

The dentist agreed—once he'd realized it really *was* the mayor calling—and went to his office right away to pass them on to a police officer we'd sent to meet him. The X rays helped the doctors prove that it was Terry. Finally we were able to call Beth and give her the news she had been waiting for, and dreading: her husband really was gone.

Only a few weeks earlier, Beth had discovered she was pregnant. Terry had died just before she found out.

25

EMOTIONS ARE VERY, VERY HIGH

On Saturday, October 20, I drove out to Staten Island for the memorial service of a young firefighter named Michael D'Auria.

Michael was one of six trainees who had died while on a training assignment before they even graduated from the Fire Academy. He had been working with Engine 40, near Lincoln Center, for only nine weeks before the towers fell. He was just twenty-five years old, a kid with his whole life in front of him.

His family and friends spoke of a bright, happy, outgoing man. He had been a chef before joining the department, but had long wanted to be a firefighter. At his wake the night before, surrounded by so many of his friends and family, most of whom were Italians, I'd felt as if I was back in Ozone Park in 1965.

Sitting in my pew, I figured this must be at least my fiftieth funeral or wake. My feelings were rubbed raw.

Since the attacks we had gotten a lot done, both at the site and within the fire department. But the work in front of us seemed endless. I worried that as hard as the days we'd just been through were, the trauma would ripple through the ranks, in the firehouses and families, for years.

Already the strains were beginning to show at the site. Picking through the steel and rubble, the men found body parts, photos, and many other terrible tangible reminders of what had been lost, but no signs of hope. Most wore catatonic expressions of grim determination. I'd talk to some who seemed clearly depressed.

I was picking up more complaints about the buses, the food, and the limits on the workers' movements. Firefighters were grousing about the use of volunteers, even firefighters from other states, for some of the work. They felt it was *their* job to find their own brothers.

I always tried to listen. But I also defended the decisions being made by our chiefs. They had an impossible job trying to deploy everyone as sensibly as possible, and there was just no way to please everyone.

Inadvertently, I fed the growing frustration. A week after the attacks, I had given a long interview to *60 Minutes II*. I had never done much press outside of fire scenes. In the Giuliani administration, the official spokesman was the mayor. But with the crush of media attention in the weeks after the attacks, the mayor had told me, Bernie, Richie, and other officials that he wanted us to cooperate with the press as much as we could. He saw it as a big part of our mission to make sure people throughout the country understood what we were going through.

At one point I had been asked about our morale. "The morale in this department is great," I said. "The guys love what they do, complain a lot, but they love what they do. . . . I told anybody who's got a problem to suck it up and move on. There's no problem that anybody that's out there today has that meets the problems of the three hundred and forty-three families whose husbands or sons or loved ones are missing, so suck it up and just do your job."

To some firefighters, those were fighting words. They only heard me blowing off their concerns and ordering them to suck it up. But that wasn't what I'd intended. During most of the interview, I'd emphasized my admiration for them and all they were doing. I simply meant that all of us needed to keep our pain in perspective, however great—just as I'd been reminding myself to do every day. Time and again I found myself having to explain the context of my remarks.

The trauma extended into every firehouse. We made counselors available to them early on. But the fact was that many men didn't use them. There seemed so much to do. Every firefighter had gotten used to the idea in his career that sometimes you needed to tough it out.

If we'd lost one or two men from a house, we would have been able to concentrate all our resources on that one group of men. I myself would have spent time there talking with the men and hearing their concerns. Now, though, I barely made it to any of the houses.

The truth was that there wasn't much time for *anyone* to grieve. We never pushed any worker who felt too upset or traumatized to work. But if he could, we wanted him in the firehouse or down at the site with a bucket and some tools. We were asking for an unbelievable sacrifice, and God only knows what the toll on the workers and their families is going to be in the years to come.

One day, after a staff meeting, the mayor cleared out the room and said to me, "Tommy, stay here a minute."

"What's up, boss?" I said when we were alone.

"Have you been talking to anyone?"

"What do you mean?"

"You know, a counselor?"

"No. Why, am I nuts?"

"Just the opposite, actually. You seem too together. I'm a little worried about you."

He grabbed a pad, scrawled out a number, and handed it to me. "Why don't you call this guy?" he said. "I know he's good."

I took it, but I never called. I had no doubt I was a wreck. I was getting up early and working late every day. I was crying so much my eyes were red all the time. I gained weight. My hair turned grayer.

But in the middle of it all, I was afraid that if I stopped and really thought about how I felt, I wouldn't be able to keep going. Maybe I'll talk to someone someday.

Almost from the start, there were doubts about how we were handling the rescue. One day, early on, I was walking around the site when I saw John Vigiano, the retired captain who'd lost two sons, looking through the pile. A former marine, he was one of the toughest men I'd ever known. He still looked strong. Beneath his gray hair, he had a determined expression on his face. Long ago, he'd had half his neck removed because of cancer and he'd still returned to work. He'd been a fanatic for discipline, training, and following orders—yet never hesitated to challenge directives from above if he had doubts. I had always thought of him as my kind of officer.

When John saw me, he dropped what he was doing and came over to me. "Boss, we aren't doing enough to get into this pile," he said angrily. "The chiefs aren't letting the troops really get in there and take the kind of risks we could take in the first days. They're treating everyone like babies. The guys are pros, and they know the risks they can take. The chiefs are holding them back."

I was a little taken aback. "John, I know where you're coming from," I said, "but the chiefs have to be in control. You know that. How could I not give my chiefs the power to do that?"

I knew my answer didn't satisfy him. But all of us, especially the mayor, were deeply worried about the chances of losing more men at that site. We felt obligated to do everything possible to prevent any additional losses.

It was always a tough trade-off, especially for men like John. He was thinking like a father who had lost two sons; a gutsy firefighter; and a boss who had been willing to make hard decisions. He knew how many risks he could handle, and they were higher than those the average firefighter could take. But all along, we were faced with a horrible balancing act between the desires of the men to push themselves and the need to contain them. There was never a right answer for it.

I felt terrible for him, and mad that I couldn't tell him what he wanted to hear. When I got back to my car, I slammed the dashboard furiously, in a futile effort to release some anger. For a half hour I was unable to talk, thinking about John Vigiano—all he had given, and all he had lost.

Before September 11, I had wondered whether I might be able to stay on as commissioner after the Giuliani administration. It seemed unlikely. But I so loved the job and the department that I thought I would work for just about any mayor that asked. I was still young enough to contribute, and felt I had so much more to accomplish.

But I could see now that the pain and heartache would stretch on for years. If I stayed, I would always be seeing close friends, widows, colleagues, at memorials and in meetings and at fires. The pain would be too much for me to take.

As I stood outside Michael D'Auria's funeral on October 20, thinking of what we'd been through and what we were still going through, it all crystallized, and the thought just flickered through my brain: *I am done.*

I couldn't stay. I didn't want to. The hurt was too deep.

Until that moment, I would never have imagined that deciding to leave the fire department would be easy. Being a firefighter had been a big part of my identity for more than half my life. I couldn't begin to guess what I would do without it.

But almost immediately, I felt relieved. I knew it was the right thing to do. I would work like hell until our last day in office, December 31. Then I would move on.

For the first time since my final weeks in the navy in 1970, I started counting how many days I had left in my job.

On the same night as Michael D'Auria's funeral, I had a chance to unwind. Knowing how tough things were, some of Rita and my childhood pals came to the city to spend some time with us. We met for a big meal at a steak restaurant in midtown that my daughter had recommended.

It was a great night: good food and good company. I

didn't have to talk about September 11 and the aftermath. We talked mostly about the old days, and remembered a lot of old stories. I hadn't been able to kick back like this and let my guard down in weeks.

After the meal, though, I had another event to attend. A few weeks earlier, Larry Levy, a City Hall attorney who had been put in charge of the Twin Towers Fund, had planned a fund-raiser and concert at Madison Square Garden. He had recruited a range of singers and actors to appear. A few thousand firefighters and cops, and many of the wives and children of those who had died, had been invited.

I had been asked to make an appearance, alongside the mayor and Bernie. But I'd had a funny feeling about it. I was always a little nervous that some celebrities and politicians wanted to use the strength and heroism of the firefighters to improve their own images.

We left our friends as they waited for dessert, promising we'd be really quick and meet them afterward at their hotel for a nightcap.

We rushed over to the Garden and through the backstage area. It was cluttered and noisy. A few people came up and expressed their condolences and gratitude to the department. I didn't recognize any of them, but they all seemed genuine and concerned.

It was also pretty chaotic backstage. I couldn't figure out what I was supposed to be doing or what the plan was. People were screaming directions from everywhere around us. Some crazy firefighter I knew came up and asked if he could go onstage with me. I couldn't find any one person in charge who could tell me precisely what I was supposed to be doing.

All of a sudden a woman with a clipboard and an ear-piece grabbed me and said, "Commissioner, they want you onstage."

"Are you sure?" I asked. I could see the mayor wasn't ready yet. I didn't know why, but I had a very bad feeling about this.

But the next thing I knew, I was being shoved forward onto the empty void at the back of the stage.

I peered forward, but it was pitch black in the arena. All I could see was a spotlight shining down on the microphone. The actor Michael J. Fox was introducing me.

Then he was finished, and I was walking forward, all alone, a little uncertain. And I was hearing *boos*.

As my eyes adjusted to the dark, I was able to identify some faces from the crowd. A lot of boos, I saw, were coming from the front row. Squinting, I saw a sizable contingent of firefighters sitting there, a few of them jumping up and down and screaming. One little twit was yelling, "Suck it up! Suck it up!" He had the same blank stare I remembered seeing years earlier on the stoops in the ghetto.

I heard some people seated farther away clapping and applauding, trying to drown out the hecklers. Looking around, I saw Joe Downey, Ray's son, whom I had seen at the site on the night of the attacks. He looked embarrassed.

I felt like I wanted to crawl into a hole. There was nowhere to go, and nothing to do but stand there, listening. I chewed on a bitter piece of gum, chomping over and over, nervously, smiling weakly but withering up inside.

I kept waiting for the mayor and Bernie to come out,

and waiting, and waiting. Bernie's name had actually been announced, but he hadn't appeared yet.

In my head, I knew that the booing didn't represent the feelings of everyone in the department. I figured some of the guys who were doing it were probably just going along with the crowd. They might have drunk a little too much. They might just have gotten swept up in the chance to let loose and show some emotion that wasn't sorrow.

I was also aware that booing the commissioner, or just about any public figure, had long been the thing for firefighters to do at some public events. Later on, I learned that several other people had gotten booed that night, including Senator Hillary Clinton, the actor Richard Gere—even Mark Green, the Democratic candidate for mayor whom the firefighters' union had just endorsed in the Democratic primary.

But in my heart I just couldn't understand why any firefighters would do something like that at a time and place like this. We weren't in a closed delegate meeting or contract talks. This wasn't the annual firefighters-versus-cops hockey game, where the only guy who doesn't get booed during the introductions is the Budweiser man.

This was a very public event, televised. The grieving widows and young children of men who had just made the ultimate sacrifice, people who were counting on the entire fire department to help them through the most difficult time in their lives, were sitting and watching. So were people all across the country at a time when the entire nation had been celebrating our men as selfless heroes and lavishing gifts and gratitude on them, when children everywhere had been talking about firemen and drawing pictures depicting our die-hard bravery and goodness.

And we were putting on the ugliest show imaginable of the petty bickering and internal disputes that at times almost crippled our department.

It seemed like an eternity before I saw the back curtain shake, and then finally Bernie walked through the curtains with his arm around the mayor. Once the boss came out, the booing subsided and the crowd started to roar. Clearly he was still at the height of his popularity.

I realized that only I had been stupid enough to come out alone.

As the mayor basked in the glow, the lights came up, and cheers cascaded around the arena. I was able to pick out a few more friendly faces in the crowd.

Joe Downey walked to the edge of the stage, and I bent down. He handed me two metal bracelets, and I saw they had his father's name on them. "I made these," he said, "One is for you and one is for the mayor. Could you give it to him?"

I took them and carried them over to the mayor, and told him what Joe had said. We slipped them over our hands.

When we were finished, I slumped offstage, feeling lower than I had in weeks. "I knew I shouldn't have done this," I told Rita as she gave me a hug. As we drove to meet our friends, I was quiet, and I felt sad the rest of the night.

For a week I felt rotten. Every other look I got from a firefighter seemed to be nasty. I hoped it would all go away, but before long reporters were calling me to ask about what had happened, and articles about the display appeared in the newspapers. Every battle I'd ever had with the ranks was again brought up, from the fight over digital radios the previous spring to the five-year contract with no raises for two years that had come early in the Giuliani administration.

There was a nice footnote to the concert, however. A couple of days later I was handed a phone message from Senator Clinton.

I didn't know her very well. In the past, I had never been a big fan of her or her husband. But since September 11, she had been to several staff meetings and made a real effort to help the city. I had been impressed by her sincerity and empathy. Besides lobbying the president for aid, she had gotten us more money for counseling and other services to help the firefighters and their families, support that was crucial in dealing with the psychological issues early on. Unlike some of the politicians who had been through the Emergency Operations Center, she had been low-key, self-effacing, nonpartisan, and businesslike. She seemed genuinely interested in getting things done, not just in trying to get herself into photos.

When I telephoned her back, she took the call right away. "I just wanted to let you know how bad I feel about what happened the other night," she said. She had gotten booed, too, but she was used to it, she said. She couldn't believe they had done it to me.

"No matter how often it happens, it's always very hurtful," she said. "It makes you feel bad. But you have to go on. And you have to realize that they're not really thinking about how the things that they do give pain to other people."

She said she knew I was the kind of a person that

wouldn't hold it against them. "It's hard, but you just have to try to put it aside and move on," she said.

I was really moved. "I didn't know you before this, but I can tell you I think you've been really classy since it started," I told her. The disaster, I was seeing, brought out the best in people, too.

26

DON'T SAY IT . . .
THEY AREN'T READY

From the beginning, we knew that dealing with the families and colleagues of missing firefighters over the sensitive issue of recovering remains would be painful.

All the way back on September 18, we had held our first meeting with family members of the missing firefighters to update them on where we stood and hear some of their concerns. We met in a huge ballroom at the New York Hilton in midtown. Hundreds of sad-faced people had gathered around tables, each one wanting to hear news we couldn't give.

That night we had asked them for DNA samples. Many of them carried bags with hairbrushes, dental X rays, and other items that might help us identify their loved ones. Police DNA specialists set up a private area in the back where they could gather the items for later testing.

I had dreaded nothing since the 11th, be it the promotions ceremony or Bill Feehan's funeral, as much as that meeting. I couldn't even begin to imagine what all these people were going through. As I mingled and asked how they were doing, along with the mayor and other officials, I could see that some were still almost too devastated to speak at that point. It was agony staring into the grief and helplessness in their eyes. Others grabbed my hand and expressed some hope for a miracle, while I forced a smile and said, "We can hope." They hadn't yet accepted the somber reality.

The encounters cut me deeply. In the lobby, when I ducked out to the rest room for a minute, I ran into an old friend, Richie Brower, who had once headed the officers' union. "You don't look too good," he said.

"I feel like I'm going to have a heart attack," I told him.

What had made it worse was the knowledge that I was about to deliver some terrible news.

Behind the scenes, we had been debating for several days about when to switch from a rescue operation to a recovery. In the first days, when we hoped to find people alive in the pile, rescue had been our major priority. No one had come out in a week, though. A collapse expert from FEMA had warned at an early staff meeting that it was a virtual certainty that no one had survived the titanic force of thirteen hundred feet compressing into a mere eighty.

We had known that, in reality, the rescue was over. Admitting it publicly would allow us to move in more heavy equipment, which in turn would help us find remains more quickly and begin a process we expected to take a year. But the words would be terrible for the families to hear. It would mean we were extinguishing hope.

That afternoon, we had decided that with this meeting, a week after the attacks, the time had come. I was to tell the families that all hope was gone.

* * *

As I was on my way to the podium, though, the mayor had grabbed my arm. "Don't say it," he whispered. "They aren't ready."

"What do you mean?" I asked.

"They're just not ready yet. Don't tell them that we're switching to recovery."

"You sure?"

"It would be devastating to them right now. They need more time to adjust."

"Well, when are we going to do it?"

"I don't know. But not tonight."

In the end, we never formally said it. Over the next week and a half, we slowly and deliberately escalated our public statements every day to move the city toward acceptance. Even without an official declaration, it was widely understood by the end of the month that no more rescues were coming.

Maybe we should have gone ahead and told the families. Though hard, I think it would have been more compassionate to be more honest with them.

Had we done so, we might have avoided some of the friction that developed a few weeks later.

By late October, a full-blown recovery operation was under way, and the site had become an enormous construction zone. Trucks and plows rolled around everywhere. Giant cranes lofted massive steel beams over the heads of the men below.

The hundreds of rescue workers down there continued to take big risks. Nearly every day the morning briefing from the chiefs included some tale of a near accident. A group of workers would be standing underneath a grappler hook suspending a beam, something would slip, and a heavy piece of metal would crash to earth and just miss someone. Despite warnings from the chiefs, large groups of men gathered regularly on the lip of the plaza that had been the center of the trade center complex. It was now considered a good area from which to view the destruction, even though it was in danger of caving in. One night, part of it collapsed just minutes after some rescue workers had walked off it.

With so many people working, it was a constant battle to make sure they were following proper procedures. Though many workers had come down with the World Trade Center cough, many still refused to wear their masks and respirators. People walked around without hard hats and safety glasses. Just as at a regular construction site, men were sitting down on whatever part of the pile they were working in and eating sandwiches without even washing their hands.

It was clear we needed to revamp our procedures. Quietly, the chiefs and outside safety consultants began working on a new organizational plan.

When I brought their concerns to the mayor, though, he told us to wait. He knew, as we all did, that scaling back the number of searchers and reorganizing the site would hit the firefighters hard. Even if it moved the recovery along and kept more men out of harm's way, fewer firefighters would have the chance to find a brother. They were already messed up, and continued to complain about the conditions down there. Increasingly we were becoming a lightning rod for discontent. This would only fuel those feelings.

But over the next couple of weeks, the mayor himself saw a few near accidents at the site and began to understand what the chiefs had meant. Once, he saw some workers escorting a crew from *Dateline NBC* right underneath a grappler hook holding a beam. Had it slipped, it would have taken out the whole crew.

On Halloween we unveiled a new system. At the time we had sixty-four firefighters on each eight-hour shift; a few weeks earlier it had been a couple of hundred. Under the new plan, we would limit the number to twenty-five. They would work with twenty-five police officers and twenty-five Port Authority officers.

The mayor hadn't participated in the planning. But before we announced the change, he asked me, "Will this be a big deal?"

"For some of the workers, maybe," I said. "But not the average guys. They'll understand."

We probably should have given the men a few days to prepare, but we implemented the plan immediately. The chiefs, after asking us for the change, didn't explain to the men down there why we were doing it.

Instantly, as the mayor had feared, the rescue workers were up in arms. Stories went around that we had simply given up on finding bodies; that the mayor wanted to speed the cleanup so it would be finished before he left office; that we had recovered gold from the trade center vaults and didn't care about anything else. (As it happened, on the day of the manning reduction, rescuers had recovered more than $200 million in gold and silver from a vault deep in the basement, belonging to the Bank of Novia Scotia; but neither the mayor nor I knew that.) Many asserted that although safety was the stated reason for the move, we were really just interested in speeding up the return of commerce to southern Manhattan. Union officials started telling the workers we were haphazardly trucking everything to Fresh Kills—a "scoop and dump" operation, as they called it.

I got some anguished calls from widows asking me if it was true that we were giving up on finding remains. I had become close to several of them, including Mary Geraghty, Eddie's widow, who was really struggling with his loss. Each time, I explained the full story.

But I felt terrible for them. It was outrageous that the rumors and myths going around the site had reached the ears of these wives and parents and added to their burden.

To protest the change, the two firefighter unions announced they would hold a march on Friday, November 2. The union leaders, Kevin Gallagher of the UFA and Pete Gorman of the UFOA, sat down with Deputy Mayor Tony Coles and told him they planned a peaceful march. They promised the police they would not go onto the site, and would only take the demonstration to City Hall.

That morning, more than a thousand firefighters massed outside the site. They chanted "Bring the brothers home! Bring the brothers home!" and "Do the right thing!" and "Rudy must go!" and "Tom must go!" Many carried signs that said things like "Mayor Giuliani, let us bring our brothers home." Several speakers fueled the crowd's anger by recounting their own experiences finding the bodies of relatives and by again accusing us of mounting a "scoop and dump" operation. Bill Butler, a respected retired captain, told the crowd, "My son Tommy of Squad 1 is not home yet! Don't abandon him!"

"Bring Tommy home!" the men shouted.

Police officers were manning the metal barriers by the site, beyond which firefighters were not supposed to go. As their anger built, however, some firefighters moved to get past the barrier, and a confrontation broke out between firefighters and cops. Punches were thrown, and the police tried to make some arrests. A group of firefighters then lifted one of the barriers and used it to push back some officers. In the end, twelve firefighters were hauled off to jail, while five cops were reported injured.

Eventually the police let the men through the barriers, and they gathered on West Street and recited the Lord's Prayer.

For the most part it had been peaceful, but scenes of the heroes of 9/11 clashing, less than two months after the attacks, quickly showed up on TV and made their way around the globe. The unity forged in sorrow and toil, which had so impressed millions of people, seemed to be coming apart.

At City Hall, the mayor was as angry as I'd ever seen him. At a press conference that afternoon, he said the actions of the firefighters were inexcusable.

"Emotions are very, very high for all of us," he said. "We have all lost people that we love. But you can't hit police officers. You can't disobey the law, and you have to have enough professionalism and dignity about yourself not to conduct yourself in that way. No matter how bad you feel, no matter how much you feel like crying, and no matter how much you feel like venting your emotions. . . . Whether you're the mayor, a policeman, a fireman, or a regular citizen, you don't get to violate the law, and you don't get to punch New York City police officers. For that you go to jail."

A reporter asked him if he thought his relationship

with the firefighters was ruined. "I love the firefighters," he said. "I respect them very, very much. I don't know if you've ever had a mayor that was as close to them as I've been. But I am not here to allow them to do things I would not allow anybody else to do."

Bernie was just as angry. I think he felt betrayed after the promises made by the union leaders. But I also suspected he had been jacked up by some of the men who worked for him. I had always known him to be controlled and fair-minded, and wondered whether he was getting the full story.

I was embarrassed and upset, too, of course. Asked what I thought of the scuffling, I called it a disgrace. Publicly, I offered Bernie an apology on behalf of the department.

But more than anger, I felt sadness. Beyond the fisticuffs, the people who had been there were feeling a lot of pain, and it was being fed by rumors and scurrilous talk. Most of the participants were so anguished they didn't know what to think.

Early the next morning I went down to the site. I wanted to take a good look at the situation and see how the new plan was working.

I found a lieutenant there who was friendly and knowledgeable. He was willing to show me around and explain the firefighters' problems with what we were doing. The biggest problem was that the fire chiefs hadn't taken control of all the workers. While seventy-five workers were assigned to each shift, the fire chiefs running the site were only keeping control of the twenty-five who were firefighters. The police and Port Authority had their own officers and were doing their own operations.

Everybody was obeying the old protocols and hierarchies that had always impeded the ability of the departments to mount joint operations. If one area needed a lot of workers, for instance, the fire chiefs in charge would still use only their own men. They wouldn't get the police involved.

Clearly, as I could see for myself, the confusion was slowing the pace of the work to a crawl and leaving a lot undone. Much of the work at that point required concentrated efforts. The grapplers would lift piles of debris up, and men would have to fan out and go through it in search of remains, as if they were on an archaeological dig. While I was there, workers found the remains of two people on one scoopful. Without coordination, I could see that the whole horrible process took much longer.

Later that day, I pulled out a video of the demonstration and watched it closely. The fighting, unquestionably, had been ugly. But only a small handful of men were doing most of the punching. A lot of good men were doing nothing wrong, just standing in the background embarrassed.

For several days tensions remained high. The police pressed for felony charges, arresting more men, and poring over videotape in search of additional offenders. The union leaders savaged us in the papers; Gorman called the mayor a "fascist" and referred to Bernie and me as his "goons," remarks the mayor termed sinful. Newspaper columnists ripped us.

I just wanted us to get past the whole thing. Hurt though I was by some of the criticism, I felt everyone had gotten too worked up emotionally. I told the mayor and Bernie I thought the arrests were overblown, and eventually all the charges were dismissed.

I reported what I had seen at the site to the mayor, and I asked him to increase the number of firefighters. He agreed, but was worried that they were too emotionally spent to handle the work. We added some workers, but continued going back and forth on how best to handle the situation.

Meanwhile, we agreed to hold another meeting with widows and firefighters to listen to their concerns. We scheduled it for Monday, November 11, which was Veterans Day and the two-month anniversary of the attacks.

That morning started terribly. Around nine o'clock, I was at my desk at headquarters, taking advantage of the holiday to catch up on some paperwork, when I started hearing a lot of traffic on the radio. American Airlines Flight 587, bound for the Dominican Republic, had just crashed in Rockaway Beach, a middle-class residential neighborhood on the eastern edge of Queens, minutes after taking off from JFK Airport. All 260 people aboard, and 5 people on the ground, were killed.

Fire trucks roared to the scene, as did the mayor and I and a host of other officials. All of us worried that this was another terrorist act.

The scene itself, 131st Street, was macabre, with engine parts and slippery blood and oil everywhere. The plane had come straight down on a residential street, and most of the victims were still strapped into their seats, horribly burned. But the damage was mostly contained on one corner, which was fortunate. The men did

306 THOMAS VON ESSEN

an outstanding job putting out the fires and removing the bodies.

After a terrible afternoon with the grieving families of the crash victims, we discussed canceling the meeting with the firefighters' families that night. But the mayor said he wanted to go ahead with it, given the emotions everyone was feeling. So we went straight from being with those newly bereaved families to meet with the families of 9/11 at the Sheraton.

This time, the atmosphere was far more heated than at the muted gathering of the first week. Eight to ten officials sat up front, including me, the mayor, the medical examiner, and others who had been involved in the recovery. Facing us, in rows of metal chairs, were about two hundred people, far fewer than had been at the first meeting. They included firefighters as well as family members. A lot of them looked furious.

For much of the next three hours, the mayor and I were called just about every name in the book. Again we heard the stories about gold in the vaults. Again we heard about the "scoop and dump" operation. One woman cried, "Last week my husband was memorialized as a hero, and this week he's thought of as landfill?" Another said we should have been ready for the deaths of 343 firefighters. "How many men are at a large fire?" she demanded. "Why wouldn't you be prepared for all of them dying?"

We didn't say that much. We started to share our thinking a few times, but it seemed to fall on deaf ears. Mostly we just let everyone vent.

What could we say anyway? As I tried to explain some of the considerations we were dealing with to the woman who asked why we hadn't been better prepared, she shouted, "Stop saying you are overwhelmed! I am overwhelmed! I have three children and my husband is dead!" There was no way to reply. She was right.

When Dr. Hirsch told the audience we weren't finding intact bodies or anything resembling them, though, several firemen angrily contradicted him. They said they were still finding recognizably human remains, even in the bulldozer buckets, and were worried that some were getting through to the landfill.

At first I thought they were exaggerating the size of the remains, but the next day I looked at some photos from our chief fire marshal, Louis Garcia, which proved they were right. Some of the remains being found were substantive enough to be considered intact bodies.

Toward the end of the meeting, I saw a short older man with dark hair and a dignified expression raise his hand and wait his turn to speak. When he rose, the room quieted down. It was Lee Ielpi, the retired firefighter I had seen at the site searching for his son, Jonathan, who was twenty-nine.

Lee had retired from the fire department a few years earlier after a highly decorated twenty-six-year career. He had worked in Rescue 2 and had been friends with Ray Downey, John Vigiano, and other lions. Lee had been known as one of our elite firefighters. His low-key, authoritative presence epitomized, for me and many others, the model of the stoic firefighter who spoke through deeds, not words.

I'd met Lee in the union, when a close friend of his, named Marty McTeague, was severely burned in a gas explosion. Lee had become Marty's chauffeur, friend, and constant companion, helping him out as much as he could.

Since September 11, Lee had been down at the site every day searching for Jonathan, who had belonged to Squad 288. I had often seen Lee crawling through tunnels and burrowing into voids as he searched sadly but steadily for some trace of his son.

Speaking in calm tones, Lee now told us that Jonathan was still down there, buried, he thought, in the area of the Marriott Hotel. He had left a widow, Yesenia, who attended the meeting with Lee, and two little boys. Lee said he believed we were trying to look out for the safety of the men. But, he added, getting those remains was the only thing that mattered to the families. He thought we could do a better job and run a better operation with more people.

"Mayor, would you and the commissioner come down to the site tomorrow and let me show you what I mean?" he asked.

With measured tones and tact, Lee had accomplished in a few minutes what many louder voices couldn't. The mayor was clearly moved and impressed that Lee was so articulate and in control. I told Lee I would absolutely meet him there the next day.

The exchange finally defused some of the tension.

Late in the evening, as the meeting dragged on, one of the mayor's aides came over and reminded us that the mayor had to attend an 11 P.M. press briefing on the plane crash and that he was cutting it close. Lynn Tierney said she thought it was time to wrap it up. "This can only get worse," she said.

I agreed. "Boss, I think we've heard everything here. Let's just take one or two more questions and get out of here."

The mayor shook his head. "We're here to answer their questions, and that's what we're going to do," he said. "We'll stay until they're finished. If they can take it, we can take it." He never made his news conference.

I went down to the site with Lee the next morning, and learned even more about the problems we had become aware of. In the following days, we agreed to just about everything Lee had asked for. We raised the number of firefighters at the scene for the second time since the demonstration, to seventy-five. We assigned each worker to a specific sector, which brought more order to the operation, and cut down the number of intrusive earthmovers.

Some bitterness lingered among family members and firefighters. But a few days later, when the mayor and I announced the manning increase, Lee was classy enough to come to our news conference, straight from an emotional funeral, and endorse everything we were doing. He said he knew we had honorable motives, and he made it clear that he harbored no resentment.

As I watched Lee talk about his son, it all closed in on me again. Tears came to my eyes, and I had to leave the room filled with reporters. I found a corner of the hallway and lost it.

The strength and decency of men like Lee Ielpi will never cease to amaze me.

A few days later, I saw John Vigiano searching through the pile. I walked up and stuck out my hand. "John," I said, uncertain of how I'd be received, "I hope we're still friends."

He looked me right in my eye. "Of course!" he said. He took my hand and started shaking it firmly. "You're still my commissioner."

27

YOU CAN ALWAYS BE CALLED

Till my last day in office, the pace of work never let up. There were still funerals and memorials and meetings and media interviews.

But as we got near the end of the year, and further away from September 11, the air of crisis waned. With every week I was spending less time at the Emergency Operations Center and more behind my desk back at FDNY headquarters.

Except for the immediate area around the site, all of southern Manhattan was open by December. On Wall Street, a few blocks from the site, there were enough people working and packing the sidewalks in the middle of the day that you could almost kid yourself into believing it had never happened.

The site itself remained fenced off, and most of the adjoining buildings were still unoccupied. But it looked a lot better. Truckloads of debris were being removed every day. The final skeletal spires of the towers were taken down in mid-December, and with them went the last noticeable outline of the buildings.

Remains continued to be found—and sometimes even intact bodies. The initial opinion of experts that we wouldn't find any had turned out to be wrong. The bunker gear we had fought so hard for in the union, which the mayor had finally gotten into the firehouses early in his tenure, had helped preserve some firefighters' bodies.

Even so, when the operation finally ended in May 2002, the medical examiner had identified remains for only about 1,019 people, a little over a third of the 2,823 who had died. We had found the remains of only 200 firefighters.

But the DNA tests would continue for many months. In all, nearly 20,000 different body parts had been found by the rescue workers.

A steady stream of people came down to the perimeter most days. For many, travel there seemed to be a solemn pilgrimage, an effort to understand better what had happened. For others, it was a way to honor those who were gone and those who were still working.

People took pictures and videotape. Some just stood and stared for a long time. Many wept. They left flowers and hastily scrawled notes. They hung pictures and poems and artwork. In the park by the river, relatives created a shrine of teddy bears. Thousands had been left by families.

It was still eerie for me to drive south, emerge on West Street, look up, and see—nothing. For most of my adult life, the towers had defined the New York skyline, and I couldn't get used to their absence. I remembered when my kids were small and my wife and I had taken them way up high to see the city. Many years later, on the weekend my daughter Pam got married, I had brought dozens of her husband's relatives from Kansas up to see the city laid out before them. New York, my home, looked like the most awesome city on earth from that vantage point.

I still feel that way about New York. But the city has been forever changed. I used to look up at those huge towers at night and think of their might. Now, when I look at tall buildings, I can't help thinking, *That could be a target.*

Even as the recovery progressed, we began, in those last weeks, to review the events of September 11 to see what lessons the fire department could possibly learn. Was there anything we could or should have done? Did we make mistakes? What went wrong?

It was difficult work, which some people resisted. Some officers bristled when we assigned members of our safety battalions to start gathering testimony of their memories. People were worried that after the firefighters had suffered so much, we were going to turn around and start criticizing them.

To some degree, I shared those concerns. The more funerals I attended, and the more stories I heard of the individual bravery of our men, the prouder I was of them. It is hard to comprehend how so many men rose above themselves that day and willingly put themselves in harm's way to help others. Many, I am sure, performed acts of bravery that none of us will ever know.

For people around the world, the indelible image of New York City firefighters on September 11 will forever be masses of people streaming down the stairwells of the burning towers as our men passed them going in the other direction. No one knows precisely how many people they helped to escape. We estimated it was more than 25,000.

So, in many ways, the darkest day in the history of the New York Fire Department was also its proudest. I hope that will never be forgotten. It is the obligation of those of us who are left to always honor what the rescue workers did there, and hope to live up to their example.

Ironically, although the attack on the World Trade Center was one of the most documented events of our lifetimes, even now we know very little about what happened there. We can never know exactly what went through the minds of the people inside in their last minutes, all the individual choices they faced and the decisions they had to make. The limits of human beings, even the bravest ones, are starkly underscored in a situation in which one person goes left and lives, and one goes right and doesn't.

What we do know is that none of us was prepared for the scope of what we faced that day. Only 102 minutes elapsed between the time the first plane hit tower one, at 8:46 A.M., and the moment the tower came down, at 10:28 A.M. And tower two, struck at 9:03 A.M., fell only 56 minutes later, at 9:59 A.M. Even while they stood, confusion reigned. The repeater systems for the towers, which bounce radio transmissions from outside the high-rise buildings to upper floors inside them, facilitating communications in skyscrapers, had been knocked out when the planes hit the buildings. Because of that, radio contact was sporadic at best. Bodies and debris were falling all around. The elevators were knocked out, leaving those of us on the ground far away from the fires. Although we imagined that the buildings could fall, no one was thinking that it could happen in 102 minutes. No one knew how much jet fuel was in those planes; no one knew how little time it would take for the combination of fire and jet fuel to melt the infrastructures of two of the world's tallest buildings.

Like many who were there, I've replayed those 102 minutes in my mind over and over again. I can't stop asking questions: What if we had ordered an evacuation earlier? Could more men, even one man, have been saved?

I don't think we can answer any of those questions conclusively. We don't now and never will know enough. All we could do at the time was count on the decisions being made by our chiefs, who are some of the most experienced and knowledgeable fire chiefs in the world. And we can be confident that they fulfilled their duty, making dozens of snap decisions under enormous pressure with limited knowledge at their fingertips.

But we must do more to prepare for the next attack. For if you listen to the experts, the only question is not whether such an attack will happen but where, when, and what kind it will be.

The Trade Center was a crushing, horrific lesson in how much the world has changed, and how much we need to change as well. When I was a young firefighter, during the period we called the War Years, the dangers I worried about were tenement fires and kids hurling rocks at our rigs. Those were real enough. Now, though, as first responders to disasters, our firefighters face a widening range of deadly threats, from anthrax to suicide bombers—or maybe even something we haven't yet imagined.

As time passes, the temptation will always exist to postpone hard thinking and planning for such threats, or to treat them as an academic exercise. We learned the folly of that on September 11. We had long talked about and discussed terrorism; and I believe, as a city, we were as well prepared as any city. Living through it, we discovered, was a different experience. The firefighters arriving at the towers faced a situation that spun wildly and rapidly out of their control, in a way we had never anticipated. Firefighters are accustomed to bringing order and control. In this case, that was impossible.

The next time, we need to be ready beforehand for a situation in which all our communications could go down; for thousands of people to respond to scenes rapidly from all over the city and suburbs; for our command structure to be devastated; for truly horrific disaster scenes spread out over wide areas. We need to be ready for bioterror and bombings.

We also need to expand our conception of what a firefighter's duty is, beyond the image of the lone, heroic man facing the flame with only a hose and his own courage. All firefighters will need better training to handle potential dangers, including detecting warning signs, mitigating threats, and responding to exposure to hazardous substances for themselves and others. A fast-changing world will require us all to keep pace with new developments and new enemies. Gone forever, I think, are the days when we could afford to rely simply on the innate bravery, skill, and dedication of the firefighter to be able to handle whatever comes up.

This is not just the responsibility of local fire departments. As Ray Downey testified before Congress in 1998: "The preparation, training, and equipment requirements should be approached from a bottom-up planning process. Permit the first responders to get involved with the many various agencies at the federal level that are preparing terrorism training programs that will ultimately affect them. . . . The federal government needs to provide assistance and funding, for training, detection equipment, personal protective equipment, and mass decontamination capabilities."

One of the hardest jobs of all will fall on leadership, inside the firehouse and out of it. Courage is the great gift of firefighters to citizens. But as we enter a frightening new world of multiple threats, we must acknowledge that courage alone, however inspiring, is not always enough. Too often in my career, I saw how much our leaders depended on the bravery of the firefighters. Too often, we sent men into fires without giving them all the training and discipline we could. No sacrifice should be spared when it might help save human life. That is the firefighter's sacred obligation. But it is at least conceivable that the time may come when we have to hold back or limit our response, to choose between two terrible options in a split second.

It's a horrible reality that this new world will demand both great courage and the discipline to temper that zeal if necessary. Finding the right balance will be the never-ending duty of chiefs, captains, and every leader in the firehouse, even at the risk, sometimes, of upsetting their own people.

Firefighters will always be hurt, even killed. Their job, which they perform willingly, is inherently dangerous. No matter how much we prepare, we can't eliminate danger and uncertainty.

But there will always be more we can do to protect them, to improve the odds. Just as the duty of firefighters is to protect the public, the duty of their leaders—of all of us really—is to make sure we have done all we can to protect the men who will respond to the next call. If we do not, we are letting them down.

For inspiration, we can always turn back to September 11 and its aftermath for examples of leadership. There was the leadership of Mayor Giuliani, who pushed the city forward aggressively, combining the willingness to face reality with a stubborn and hopeful spirit of optimism. There was the leadership of Bill Feehan and Pete Ganci, who felt they couldn't leave the site when their men were still there, and who paid the ultimate price. There was the quieter, less noticed, but deeply felt leadership of men like John Vigiano, who lost his sons John and Joseph, and Lee Ielpi, who lost his son Jonathan, but who went down looking for them every day with a sense of resolve and duty to family.

The greatest examples, of course, were all the firefighters themselves.

My last month or so in office was bittersweet, my pride and satisfaction in the job mingling with regrets and grief.

But I had a number of warm encounters with people that will always stay with me. In early December, I went to the UFA Christmas party, held for families of the firefighters who had died. Lynn Tierney had arranged for it to be held at the new Toys "R" Us flagship store in Times Square. Dozens of widows were there with their children. So many women came up and thanked me.

It was awful, though, to realize how many of them I hadn't met or didn't recognize. I hated knowing that after all this time there were hundreds of wives and kids of guys who had given their lives that I hadn't been able to do that much for personally.

One boy, maybe fourteen or so, came up to me and said, "My father was Pat Waters."

Pat had been a captain in Brooklyn and a good, tough union delegate as a firefighter. I had known him for many years. He had helped me get elected to the UFA presidency, driving me around his borough and telling men there that they should vote for me; and as a captain he had been devoted to training and safety. Looking at his son tore me up inside.

"Your father was a good man," I told him.

"You're a good man, too," he said. He spoke with the gravity of a thirty-year-old man. I thought, *God, Pat, what a great job you did, and what a loss for this boy.*

One day a few weeks later, I was in the office when Eddie Geraghty's widow, Mary, came by with her three sons. Mary and I had become quite close. She was a special lady who was really suffering without Eddie. She had come by to bring me a briefcase as a farewell gift.

To her youngest son, Colin, I said as I pointed at the row of helmets and caps that lined a shelf high up in my office, "Pick any hat you want up there. It's yours."

Right away he pointed at my white commissioner's helmet, the one the mayor had handed me the day I was sworn in. I pulled it down and gave it to him.

Mary was mortified. She started telling him that he had to give it back to me, that it was too valuable to keep.

But I didn't want him to give it up. I thought it was fate. It made me happy to think Eddie's son would have that helmet; Eddie Geraghty, a man who could have been chief of department one day.

"Mary, it's what he picked, and I told him he could have whatever he picked," I said. "I want him to have it."

The following week, on Saturday, December 15, I went to a memorial service for Ray Downey. His body hadn't been found, and we weren't sure it would be. His remains were finally identified in May, near the end of the recovery effort.

The December service was held in Ray's home parish of Saints Cyril and Methodius Church in Deer Park. I had decided I wanted it to be one of the biggest services we had. We had the full band, thousands of firefighters lined up, and a full honor guard. Irish tenor Ronan Tynan, who had become a friend of the department and performed at several funerals and memorials for us, sang. We brought as many rescue vehicles as we could gather to parade out front. Until then, we hadn't allowed any rescue vehicles or our caisson to leave the city limits; we couldn't spare them. But replacements were starting to be delivered to us, and it seemed an appropriate time to get back to normal.

Again it was a packed church, again there was a rendition of "Amazing Grace" followed by "Be Not Afraid." But the mood, somehow, was just a little lighter than it had been in the first days. There was a lot of sorrow in the room, but the shock of the attacks had somewhat worn off after three months, and there was a little more space for warm and celebratory feelings for Ray and the life he had lived. Besides the governor and mayor, Joe Allbaugh, the head of FEMA, was there representing the White House. He read a letter from the president honoring Ray.

In his homily, Monsignor Brendan Riordan described Ray as a man who never sought accolades, who insisted he was only doing his job. That was true. He mentioned that Ray, celebrated for his accomplishments, had been proudest of being a good father and husband.

I remembered how happy Ray had seemed playing with his grandchildren on the lawn outside Gracie Mansion a few months earlier. They had been cheated of a chance to know him as they grew up. I thought of my own granddaughter Rita, and how blessed I was to be with her. I thought of Pat Waters's son and Colin Geraghty and Andrew Esposito, of the hundreds of children and grandchildren who were now forced to grow up with only pictures and words and their own memories. I wondered what kind of world we would be leaving them.

A few days before Ray's service, searchers found the body of Lee Ielpi's son, Jonathan. Lee called me at home at 10 P.M. to tell me the news and say that he just wanted to talk. I was glad he'd found his son and could move on to the next phase of grief. I was honored, too, that Lee would call me the same night.

But it plagued me to know that, because the disaster was so overpowering, we were reduced to thinking that recovering your son's body was a good thing. It didn't add up to me.

The Ielpis had already held a memorial service for their son. Now they scheduled his funeral for the morning of December 28.

As it happened, that was the day the mayor had selected to deliver his final State of the City speech. It was expected to be a big event, the final summation by Rudy

Giuliani of his tenure, and his vision for the city's future. Finding a date for it had been a nightmare for the mayor's scheduler, Kate Anson. She had to factor in a million variables, from the best location and time of day to the media's news cycle and how to get maximum exposure to the availability of the dignitaries and invited guests. The ordeal had taken weeks, and consumed most of her time every day. Once the time and place had been set, press releases had gone out across the city. Everything had fallen into place.

Two days before the speech, I told the mayor about Jonathan's funeral. He had gained deep respect for Lee during the manning battle, and I thought he'd want to know.

After we spoke, he went over to Kate. "We're going to have to reschedule," he told her. "I want to go to Lee's son's funeral."

Three days before he left office, he paid his respects to Jonathan Ielpi.

On New Year's Eve, the mayor and I presided over a graduation ceremony at Brooklyn College for the first group of probies to join the department since September 11.

Within hours, we would be gathering in Times Square, where the mayor would pass the torch to the Bloomberg administration. Despite all the fears and terrors, the streets would be packed, the crowds defiant and hopeful, as we bid good-bye to the tragic year of 2001 and looked toward the future.

Inside the Brooklyn College auditorium, some somber feelings from the attacks lingered. But for the first time in a while, there was some real joy at a department ceremony. None of the new firefighters had any formal connection to the department before 9/11, though one had lost a brother that day. They were the first bunch of hungry young kids who would lead the department forward, just as Father Judge had said at the rededication ceremony at my old house on September 10. Even after 9/11 had shown the world what firefighters risked, they had walked forward to grab the baton from the men who had fallen, and carry it deep into the young century.

Even before we began, they were excitedly chanting, "Rudy! Rudy!" which prompted a happy Mayor Giuliani to smile and show off that row of Chiclets he has. Everyone knew these were his last hours in office, and that he had chosen to spend it with them.

Their drill instructor, a lieutenant named Joe Higgins, led them in cheers. He was one of my favorite young guys, an absolute maniac for firefighting and discipline. He'd lost his brother at the Trade Center. I had recently sent him on a mission with Father Delendick to visit troops in Afghanistan, where the U.S. Air Force had named a base after Pete Ganci.

I looked out in the crowd and saw all those young, eager faces, and remembered my own graduation, more than thirty-one years before. I could never see any proby class without remembering myself when I was in their place, a lean young man, hard-working and with high ideals, but fairly clueless about the world. As different as that world was, it felt as familiar to me as if I had graduated yesterday.

Though a little sad, I had never regretted my decision to leave as commissioner. I knew it was the right thing. Nearly four months after the attacks, the pain hadn't subsided any. Inside, I feared, I was a wreck. I knew I wouldn't be able to stay around with that heartache anymore.

I would miss my many great friends and colleagues, like Lynn Tierney, Tommy Fitzpatrick, and Ray Goldbach. We had been through the ordeal together, and it had bound us much tighter. I still had friends at all levels, and wondered whether I would lose touch with some of them.

But everywhere there were ghostly reminders of what had changed. Every time I drove into work, I'd see Bill Feehan's empty parking space—and feel his absence. Every day there would be a moment when I wanted to turn to Ray Downey and ask his advice on some logistical matter—and I'd remember. Sometimes in the evenings, I'd want to call Father Judge to talk to him about it all—but I couldn't.

I felt a little sad as I got up to speak at the graduation and realized that this was almost the last thing I would do as commissioner. Back at headquarters, half-packed boxes were scattered all over the commissioner's office.

I reminded the new firefighters that they were there not to replace, but to rebuild. "My message to you probationary firefighters, if I had to say it in two words, is 'Go slow.' Be careful out there. Listen to the good firefighters you run into in your firehouse. Listen to that officer. Listen to that battalion chief. Make sure that you're involved in continually getting better, because you have an awful lot in front of you, an awful lot to learn.

"And no matter where you go, no matter how active it is or inactive it is, you can always be called on to lay it all out on the line. Always remember that."

As we read the names of the newest members of the New York City Fire Department, as they marched across the stage to get their diplomas and shook our hands, a steady roar of cheers filled the auditorium. Family and friends smiled and applauded. Many of the new firefighters jumped up and down with excitement.

I understood why.

WTC Command Posts-9/20/01 1310 hrs

The fire department used this map of the World Trade Center site in the rescue and recovery efforts after September 11. The twin towers previously stood in the area bordered by West, Vesey, Church, and Liberty Streets.

Early on September 12, city, state, and other leaders gathered at the Police Academy to discuss how to put New York back together after the horrible events of the day before. In a spiral-bound notebook, I tried to record as much as I could of what we talked about, from the concrete details of the recovery operation to the larger issues and concerns being discussed, such as economic development. There was so much going on that I needed to keep track of it all.

In the days and weeks ahead, I continued adding to that notebook, and when I ran out of space picked up more. There was a lot to write. The pace remained frenetic for weeks. The intensity of the first days did ease a bit as the dimensions of the crisis became clearer and some of the issues we worried about most in the first days petered out. A lot of the initial information we received was imprecise; some was inaccurate and even, we later learned, false. But the crisis kept evolving, with new facts and new complications, such as the anthrax outbreak and growing concerns over safety at the site.

Once the funerals started, I found myself with a little more time to write, when I was in the car or helicopter traveling to or from a funeral. So the notebooks changed. Besides keeping records of what was discussed in staff meetings, I jotted down conversations, thoughts—almost anything that came up. The notebooks came to function as a combination of "to do" list, historical document, and outlet for private feelings, thoughts, frustrations, and joys. Taken together, they constitute a detailed record of what we talked about, and what I thought about, behind the scenes in the months after 9/11.

My notes ran for pages and pages and filled several different notebooks; below are selected excerpts. Though hardly a complete—or completely reliable—accounting, they convey a sense of what was happening day to day. A glossary of acronyms and abbreviations and a list of names appear at the end of this section.

SEPTEMBER 12, 2001

7 am

- 300 workers in rubble
- 150 in primary staging area
- Busing in hundreds to assist
- 4 bodies during night
- Asbestos found at epicenter—as you spread out less
- John O'Neill retired two weeks ago from FBI—took job as head of security for WTC missing—presumed dead—I saw him in the lobby and presumed he left and went to Command Center
- 2 "black boxes"—actually red—2 on each plane ... need to find
- Illegals in NJ ... bogus lead ... people in Massachusetts nothing either
- Barry Mawn, asst. director of FBI: "colossal loss of intelligence"
- 18 minutes between hits
- all four airlines were loaded for West Coast
- <u>fuel loaded</u>

8:30 am—Briefing

- More than 300 missing
- Dept. of Env. Protection able to shut down the water main at 140 West
- Big concern yesterday to keep Verizon working
- Cell phones from Verizon with Jersey Satellite for better comm. at site are on the way—will make a big difference
- 120 dump trucks to Fresh Kills last night alone
- Barges at three locations will be operating shortly

8:40 am

- Fire at WFC in a malfunctioning generator
- Should keep all schools on West Street closed
- RG wants to open as many schools as possible
- RG worried about psychological impact that this has on citizens
- We should talk to mental health experts to see if people are upset about being in high-rise bldgs.
- Need to get 3 markets open tomorrow. RG is under impression that NYSE is OK to function
- Governor arrives and RG briefs him
- Con Ed lost the substation. Gov has generator available to help get area going again
- GOV is staging vol FFs
- We need to make good contact and organize the help most efficiently
- Need to work with Port Auth to figure out list of passengers on the planes
- 1800 emergency room visits in metro area.
- Hospitals OK, probably will be overwhelming for morgue
- DCAS OK for immediate purchase
- GW outbound only, need to open some bridges to get food and supplies into City
- NYCHA been very helpful moving debris—trucks are being operated at Fresh Kills by FBI
- Keep Holland Tunnel closed . . . for emergencies only . . . Hopefully open up all the bridges and tunnels tomorrow
- FBI will go through the rubble as it is dumped
- The 120 dump trucks will be isolated and probably looked at later
- Governor will help set up relief and help at water resources upstate
- Joe Hoffman (Transit) did great job yesterday.

They shut down 14 St., Rector St. station
collapsed—he can get lines going pretty
quickly but needs heads up
— Calvin Drayton—Sheriffs were very helpful
yesterday
— Gov: Are the ATMS working? Yes . . . we're OK
— Bill Diamond—economic impact, tourism
— RG—meet with economic development people
today, tomorrow—look at big picture
— Flags should be at half staff
— "Asbestos will be a problem" . . . we are not
talking about exposure at epicenter
— Gov: PA estimates that we'll find couple
thousand people in each tower dead
— Building #1 began evacuation immediately
— Major League baseball canceled all games . . .
We are open and want them to play.
— RG on phone with White House re: airspace
security—if they are opening airports he is
requesting tighter security
— Carrier group in NY harbor
— 3-4 scumbags in each flight—slit throats of
stewardesses with box cutters
— How do we begin? 10 dead and hundreds to
follow
— Corrections—very helpful equipment and
people
— Asbestos sampling . . . 11 samples at the
fringe . . . 1% is a problem
— Much of site is higher. OK at this point. . . .
Will need respirators at core
— Gov.—people at PA lost /unaccounted for 200
— UN asking for advice
— Barry Mawn FBI . . . they think the UN might
have been another target, probably not
re-open

— Dennis Swanson NBC/GE calls me, wants to give mayor $10m for families. Will he take the call?

2 pm—Meeting on the Opening of the Stock Exchange
— Dr. Marcos needs to get list from hospitals of people injured
— Unconfirmed FDNY losses . . . 392
— Only when the ME says it's a body will it be counted
— Verizon at 1 pm said it was still getting water from a broken main—DEP says it's taken care of
— Phosgene gas a possibility under plaza—77 1000-gallon tanks of Freon under plaza will become a problem . . . if water hits the Freon it causes phosgene
— Goggles and masks are being issued—up to supervisors to make sure workers are wearing them
— Jane Hoffman—price gouging going on with gasoline and water
— Teams will help get communication back at City Hall

3:30 pm—Economic Impact Meeting
— City players, business, real estate, hotels, tourism et al.
— Want help, need coordination
— Still a week before we get power to lower Manhattan
— TVE offers to set up a small task force at FDNY to expedite building permits/faster approvals in midtown to help those displaced
— Morgan Stanley had horrible losses
— TVE gives out number for service of structural engineers, etc.

- Restaurants want to help
- Spinola REBNY shortage of labor and contractors—wants to coordinate the effort
- Jerry Speyer—willing to put up temporary structures in 2 months—would help in the short term—25 million sq. feet of office space—probably need 10 million immediately to absorb the space that was lost
- Probably have 20,000 sq. feet available in hotels that will be used temporarily
- Schumer and Clinton want to help
- Feds promise generators . . . anything we need to stay open
- Most identification will be DNA
- Verizon working to keep system open at Wall Street
- Congressman Joe Crowley breaks down when I tell him that his cousin John Moran is missing—a great chief
- FEMA—8 USAR teams are here for the duration long term recovery
- All FEMA requests come from City and State first
- "President Bush never affected by anything as much as this"
- Independence Plaza people want to be relocated
- We do a press conference
- We decide on 9/25 for new primary date 10/11 runoff
- Later tonight we'll have a staff meeting

SEPTEMBER 13
7 am—Meeting
- Need location for military type operation
- About 4700 people reported or known missing
- PD has 3737 missing person reports

- Morgan Stanley 1700 is down to 400 they have not been able to identify
- Talk to the President at 10 am

8 am—Meeting
- Richie Sheirer trying to get one OEM, multiple OEM not the way to go
- Mayor wants another road on east side for access to lower Manhattan
- Transit information that went out last night was false
- Funerals . . . we need a coordinator
- Interstate—1200 of 3700 are Jersey residents
- Governor will help with color guards, band, whatever, and wants legislation to pass today
- TO DO: EMS should brief me on Phosgene Gas precautions
- Pier 92 55th Street new OEM
- Javits . . . USAR and State Police
- 633 3rd Ave 32nd floor . . . Econ Coord at governor's office
- Anyone from SOC that worked in Oklahoma City
- How can we use volunteer EMTs and paramedics
- Gov will have them, we should use them
- RG asks Gov to help with funding for 400 Pol/FF/EMT death benefit/ pension costs
- If the guys get close, they have to wear protection
- At 9 am I get a call from Mark Kasper . . . horrible . . . his father wanted a full FD funeral. Told him I didn't know where we would wind up (note, 1/22/02 . . . received a beautiful note from Kasper family later on thanking us for everything)
- Need a public information officer here at the Command Center

- Gov. needs coordination for volunteers
- We want to consolidate /coordinate fund-raising
- Holden DDC should coordinate the inspections of structures
- Dr. Hirsch concerned about the level of expectation on identification of recovery victims—incredible compression—is going to make ID . . . going to need DNA coordination group
- Gov. suggests asking to bring in pathological remains team to help identify
- Rev. Calvin Butts and Ralph Dickerson arrive to tell us they have $11 million from the United Way
- Want direction on how to organize and direct $
- "the September 11th fund"
- Yesterday the Lilly foundation gave $30 million
- Levy and others are setting up the mechanism
- United Way—I explained many different interests . . . no real need will be determined
- Benefits make people in great shape financially
- People will want to help the uniformed forces
- Secretary Thompson is coming at 11:30 am
- We just evacuated 5 Penn Plaza . . . bomb scare
- We need to reassure people . . . should not be evacuating based on a threat . . . wait for a confirmation
- Bush arriving 3 pm Friday
- Sec. Thompson arrives and discussed similarities Oklahoma City—3, 4, 5th week is when we will need help. We need to start planning
- TVE asks for help with honor guards and help down the road with funerals

- We'll need to get FF dental records
- Need to bury body parts
- Massive burial of tiny body parts should be thought about for the future.
- Jerry Hauer arrives with Thompson also Stu ... Federal government
- Conference calls every day with City, State and now Feds will get involved to answer medical questions
- John O'Neill dead ... WOW
- Thompson will assign someone from CDC to work with Cohen
- Operations meeting with Nigro and Fitz
- 24 on 24 off 9 am to 9 am
- 4 USAR Teams ready to work
- FEMA Mike Byrne, 8 are here now, he has 28
- Ch 2 inaccurate information—rescue of 5 firefighters—collapse
- 4 pm ... Freddy Ferrer calls ... guys from Sq 41 would really like to be part of the dig ... their guys are under debris and FD is not using them

4:30 pm—Religious Leaders
- Unbelievable turnout ... RG asks their advice on memorial service ... nondenominational
- RG recommending a large service near the end of the recovery operations
- St. John the Divine—first to offer their location
- Committee of Religious Leaders (CORL) is an organization they have recently put together
- We would do a prayer tomorrow with the President for visual effect of everyone showing unity

- 9/23 is selected as day for a major service at MSG or a more appropriate place

6 pm—Cabinet Meeting
- TVE expresses anger at horrible reporting—finding 5 FFs story is not true—reported before verified with our incident commander
- Will open up Canal Street tomorrow
- RG says he wants to get help to run Armory. Already have thousands of families that are angry and upset.
- Rosemary O'Keefe is overwhelmed, needs help
- President might be interested in visiting some of the families tomorrow
- Manny trying to find a location where they are ... we are told some are meeting at UFA
- DOB inspected 200 buildings in area ... some need structural repair
- Secretary of State and NYPD helping to set up system for burials
- RG tells everyone about issues at Family Center
- Sec. Minetta ordering NY airports closed and nationally also (shortly)
- ME says we all need to realize we are not going to be recovering bodies but probably biological stains will eventually be used for DNA identification.
- Joe Miele—"The results of the air quality are OK, no issue of asbestos even at the epicenter"
- City Council passed home rule message today
- ME reps want to sit down with reps of police and fire
- Corporations that have damaged property need to meet and know how long it will be, if ever, before they return

- Suggestions that Governors Island would be available immediately for short/long term office space needs
- AMEX signed lease in New Jersey?
- Citibank looking at 1 million feet in New Jersey
- Pier 92 is not large enough for FEMA, they want to get Pier 90 also
- Con Ed—no power in lower Manhattan for some time (how long????)
- Gov. will sign legislation passed by both houses today
- Speyer called looking for nurses at Columbia Pres . . . they are burned out
- Red Cross here and the Mayor gives big support

SEPTEMBER 14
6 am
- Looks like 250 were taken or went to hospital on their own
- 100 Gold Street has more than 100 places to sleep, we should use it
- Need to encourage our people to slow down . . . wet, slippery
- Total missing more than 5000—duplicates in that number
- We need to formalize our own efforts
- No more volunteers
- We have firehouse back under control
- Bogus FFs
- Web site is updated, no info on conditions of people
- Debris on buildings will become issue, heavier as rain continues—worse case scenario are some roof failures

- Trains are running under the area we tested without people and no problems with vibrations
- 1 Liberty Plaza has a bulging façade but the building is not in danger of any collapse—design of this building is causing concern—people are looking at it thinking there is a problem . . . doesn't mean windows or brick isn't going to fall but at least building is OK
- Con Ed needs to relocate substation—will try to do it in 3 months (faster than the normal 9 months)—they will have part of necessary power back in 10 days, more in 3 weeks, the rest in 3 months
- RG probably moving the grief location from armory on 23rd to Pier 94 at 55th Street
- Transit offers buses to shuttle from armory to Pier 94
- Once the registration is complete we hope we'll have smaller numbers
- Rain will reduce the efficiency of construction by 1/3: weight, water, etc.
- Report of possible hurricane in 5 days . . . remote
- $ big issue—getting funding approvals
- Respirators being delivered . . . training sites being set up
- We need to consider no or restricted use of vehicles in Manhattan
- Need better media control—all groups complaining of some problem (FBI, FDNY, PD, Mayor, everyone)
- Speaking to publishers—RG doesn't want to do that yet
- RG orders media meeting—misinformation—very harmful and dangerous

- City Hall will be open but without as good a phone system
- Subways are ready to go—we should open so we shake out for Monday
- We need to make contact available for businesspeople
- 10,425 tons of debris   1,154 truckloads
- Normal weekday we take 20,000 tons of residential and commercial normally
- Gov—State and City putting joint proposal to request Governors Island
- City and State on 32nd floor working on economic issues
- DNA testing

SEPTEMBER 20
8 am—Staff Meeting
- Rain coming—will add to problem
- Event Sunday (Yankee Stadium)—3 small stadiums (Coney Island, Staten Island and Jersey)
- 4 religious leaders—10 min. each . . . Gov, RG
- 2-3 music and performance
- Program starts at 3
- RG—Met Opera and Phil is in town
- Yankees don't want huge stage
- Columbus Day Parade . . . we should have it
- FD Mem Service—canceled
- FD Lt. & Capt tests canceled
- Long/short term effect on economy
- Very heavy buying calendar
- Tax receipts last 10 days disastrous—hotels down to 45% occupancy . . . beginning to come back
- RG—NYC will bounce back . . . we need to work on plans to help economy

- US Senators to site (about 50) wants me to help with tour
- Richie Sardiello calls with free Club Med (260 rooms) Columbus Island—2 wks for rescuers, families . . . looking for partner for transportation
- Should we do Town Hall next week? RG wants to consider
- Greg Miley will coordinate the Sunday event . . . wants to invite all the affected agencies, large companies, etc.
- Back to 9 Metro
- Back to site—met 40 US Senators and Staff
- Sen. from Ohio—former Mayor Cleveland—very sensitive to needs of large Fire Dept.
- Senators Daschle, Lott, Biden, Kennedy, Schumer, Clinton, Harkin—all moved, all very concerned and supportive

5:10 pm
- Just came from Tim O'Brien vigil mass—Bob did great job eulogizing his brother (lost not just Timmy but brother-in-law too) . . . left before Boomer Esiason (very close friend of Tim) finished remarks. He put on a Phil Simms jersey because Timmy was a great Giants fan. Sean really broken up . . . church overflowing with folks from RVC . . . unbelievable tribute to a wonderful person and family
- Last night's show . . . 60 minutes . . . was very emotional . . . watching it in Bill Feehan's office with Regan, Henry, Fitz, Ray et al, I had to leave and felt shaky for first time
- I'm now in Donald Trump's plane . . . trip to Capitol and White House—he couldn't have his name any bigger on plane . . . I'm early and

waiting for Mayor, Gov, Kerik and a few reps of
the actual heroes ... Jay Jonas is our rep ...
solid guy, captain of Lad 6 ... was rescued ...
don't know details yet
— Ran into Kenny Hatton at my house ... he saw
car and came over to say hello ... told him we
would keep looking ... he asked that we bring
Terry home
— So hard to talk to friends, family et al
— Stopped at Mary Geraghty's house just to say
hello ... two kids in the porch out front ...
hugged and kissed them both ... they don't get
it yet thank goodness ... Don't think I could
deal with it if they did.
— Great having Freddy in today ... Rod picked
him up at airport and brought him in
— Sitting here on plane—Gov is talking to
someone in his office saying the estimates on
$$'s shouldn't be 50 billion because the #
sounds fake ... should be 48 or 52 (amazing how
much money this tragedy is going to cost) the
long range monetary impact is beyond all
comprehension
— Funerals ... the first 3-4 days ... already
will be causing problems ... logistics, etc.
— So many people really stepping up to the
plate
— Sitting talking to the Gov about how
devastating this is to economy is
fascinating ... if it wasn't for the
overwhelming grief and tragic results it would
be a great exercise ... the people part is too
too upsetting ... looking into the eyes of
those affected is just the worst ... widows and
dealing with their issues has always been the
worst part for me

— Denise Ford sent me this outstanding note last
  week that said when you lose a loved one,
  God sends you an angel to help. I called her
  yesterday to thank her for sending some fruit
  and candy to office. She thanked me for
  everything and said she prayed for my good
  health . . . it was important for me to stay
  healthy to get FD through this . . . she was
  sorry for the widows . . . she knows we can't
  help them out like we did for her . . . she knows
  that we can't hold hands with 340 widows, attend
  all the funerals . . . all the things we did for
  her . . . we just can't do for everyone else

SEPTEMBER 21
7:30 am
— Today show with Matt Lauer, 8:00 am
— RG not happy with Yankees . . . not letting us
  put up a big enough stage . . . so he tells Kerik
  to take over stadium for security reasons . . .
  tells Washington to build enormous stage . . .
  Kerik to get all the help and do whatever we
  want
— RG pissed off that first 10 bil $$ that is
  coming in is already being controlled by
  State . . . they should not take percentage and
  should not control the funds—city is where we
  need $$
— Cristyne Lategano—firefighter/police
  officers—? price to Broadway shows

SEPTEMBER 21
3:30—Staff Meeting (Big)
— Service at Stadium—Ask people to please use
  tickets that we give . . . otherwise seats
  will be empty

- Concern over disease, etc. . . . dead bodies on scene . . . Dr. Cohen says not a problem . . . perception should be worked on . . . doing that with Dept. of Health.
- Airports not being used . . . no one flying . . . running 80% of flights . . . load factor 35% . . . 250M a day in lost revenue for airlines
- Death Certificate issue
- Growing # of people that need a death cert now to get benefits
- Exec Order to accelerate for New Yorkers . . . not for foreigners or other state residents.
- Found John O'Neill . . . wallet in pocket . . . I saw him in the lobby . . . thought he was still working . . . only found out later that he had retired from FBI to become head of security at WTC
- Heard today that Chief Hoehl was disappointed he did not get that job . . . he is approaching 63 and must retire . . . I remember seeing him outside WTC totally covered in dust
- Black car industry —less money reflected in less people flying
- Lhota—expects all agencies to be fully operational . . . if not able to all be in Manhattan, then utilize people in other offices (boros)
- Only emergency employees will be hired
- Ken Holden is interested in buying wrap-up insurance . . . thinks it is a good idea . . . Harold Wilson says they use it all the time at SCA
- Dead 252 (34FD) 6373 Missing 76,000 tons removed, 5,476 truck loads
- Prayer service not memorial service—many people not ready to use word "memorial"
- Will do a service at site also

SEPTEMBER 25
Early

- Visited Squad 1 this am—tried to quell the absurd but typical B.S. Yesterday, a story about closing the unit . . . really a shame . . . dedicated, emotionally wrecked guys and they have to get upset thinking the Dept. would be so insensitive to close them (permanently) in a situation like this.
- In the middle of all this shit, we need politicians calling us and telling us we shouldn't be closing Squad 1.

Noon

- Visited Lad 4—Eng 54—Mrs. Bush and Mrs. Pataki . . . really nice ladies . . . very sincere. Mrs. Pataki offered to attend funerals for us
- Guys are very appreciative—supportive
- FF Foty detailed there—brother lost in Lad 7—wants clothing cleaned—blood, asbestos, whatever—nice kid
- Joe Nardone says we should go back to the Rockefeller Center exception for alarm responses . . . ridiculous responding to everything when the building complex is taking care of problem—Told him I'd take care of it.

Mayoral Advisory Task Force—Terrorism

CHEMICAL ATTACK—YOU WOULD KNOW ABOUT IMMEDIATELY
- 2KG of Sarin in enclosed football stadium would get everyone
- Low fatality rate if mixed in air supply at Grand Central Station

- Crop duster over Central Park would kill
  hundreds . . . indoors you'd be in good shape
- Clothes off and hosed down quickly helps . . .
  90% can be saved by removing clothes and
  hosing down
- Dario—We have equipment and injectors
  available on ambulances and support units.
- He doesn't think hospitals are as well stocked
  as they should be
- This scenario we are moderately well prepared

SECOND SCENARIO—TANKER TRUCKS
- tanker full of chlorine with valve left open
  on top of subway tunnel
- heavier than air—small scale event—
  tremendous # of walking wounded
- good clinician at site—critical to get on scene
  to evaluate problem and direct action

BIOLOGICAL—handout given by Dr. Ackelsberg (?)
- HVAC at MSG if they used biological . . . no easy
  detection, no symptoms
- no clue till they got to hospital (city and
  outside)
- # of days before flu like symptom . . . then
  worse
- without treatment—100% lethal
- if we get medicine into them fast enough we'll
  save some not all
- Smallpox is basically impossible to stop but
  very hard to control and antidote
  available . . . only through military . . .
  15 million doses available.
- Smallpox not the most likely—very difficult
- People who had shots many years ago would
  still have a possibility of resistance to it . . .
  what level is unknown.

- Salmonella used to contaminate salad bars years ago.
- lethality in these areas is very low
- would be such panic in fear factor that it would create same effect but would have fewer fatalities
- Smallpox—extremely difficult to weaponize
- Anthrax—more likely . . . easier access to terrorists
- Joel Miele—has told bldg owners in city to get better control of their mechanical systems in basements
- he is not worried about reservoirs . . . tested regularly and protected
- is worried about terrorist getting into basement of major bldg and poisoning water system

3:30 pm—OEM Meeting (large)
- people want to see site
- want to leave something
- want to take something
- first group tomorrow . . . gov and mayor will participate
- Mayor wants to do memorial prayer service at 30 day point
- Amb. Gargano—State is doing a lot . . . need to know how long before some businesses will get back in

DEP
- Area by Greenwich St. is not decontaminated enough
- If we want to open Greenwich we should use West—air samples are good but he needs more samples (a second day) ·
- DEP uses Dem method and is more conservative

- He cannot put civilians back on Greenwich until we remove debris to West
- 40 Rector ready to occupy in 4 hrs . . . cleaning in process
- 150,000 tons removed

OCTOBER 4
Staff Meeting
- Ken Langone (friend of mayor), sounds like character—Paul McCartney concert 10/20 . . . where? . . . 5000 cops/FF
- Kevin McCabe wants to do concert at Shea (Rock concert)
- RG agrees to help J&R—they stuck with City when Downtown was bad news
- RG—schedule some downtown event to help them get back on track
- Indications that we are getting back to normal because we are now concerned that some of the lawyers that are volunteering services are taking advantage of some families and offering their services to them post/tragedy at $$.
- Michael Carey—need to work with downtown restaurants and help get their business back . . . RG offers anything . . . just tell him what to do
- Kuriansky—Eliot Spitzer reports on billing fraud. Medicaid—big investigation complete
- RG—talking about Jewish holidays . . . says he hasn't had holiday. Dyson says he's Italian . . . someone said that Sukkoth is coming . . . I said that we've had 3 weeks that sucketh. I guess I've gotten a little more brazen with my humor since I know he's not firing me . . . "who would take this job right now"

- Should we go forward with construction at PD Headquarters—PSAC 2
- New OEM on lower floor?
- RG needs private meeting—won't say anything today
- Article in <u>News</u> on PSAC 2 construction at PD
- Norman Siegel (possibly a heartbeat from Mayor) was the driving force against security being ramped up at City Hall—first amendment rights et al. . . . public has right to know that
- RG wants to organize tours so we get control . . . he complains that he has said this repeatedly and no one is setting it up . . . gives job to Rudy Washington.
- Yesterday NYSE, Richard Grasso said he is the unknown "RG" . . . afraid that RG could have his job if he wanted it . . . walking around like conquering hero through the floor . . . amazing
- RG—our fiscal plan shows how it was more responsible than ever
- cutting taxes shows up to make more sense now . . . more than ever . . . if people are going to be afraid to live here, higher taxes will make it even harder to keep/draw people here.
- Jim Riches' son's badge found by volunteer from Canada—returned to me from Canada—I need to call Jim and get it to him

9 am
- Israeli airliner went down on trip to Siberia (just confirmed) . . . no info yet
- Oct. 28 Memorial (MSG too small) but best indoor location . . . work on a location
- Terry Hatton funeral—"Either outstanding or unacceptable". . . what a great statement about an individual (very true about Terry)—strove

for excellence—his whole routine was driven
by an absolute love of job, FDNY and desire for
excellence
- Can't believe this is happening . . . they were
married 3 years
- Mayor's remarks were outstanding (Lynn wrote
mine . . . really good)
- Ken Hatton, what an ability to hold it
together . . . great remarks
- Tim Brown, Lt. Pena—terrific remarks—Gov,
everyone
- Press at site
- 180,00 tons—30,000 tons of steel going to
Jersey for recycling
- Rita and Julia at funeral

OCTOBER 5
Staff Meeting
- Big discussion Re: lost revenue . . . RG says no
one will replace lost revenue for us
- RG runs City the way I ran my house—you don't
take $$ even if someone wants to give it to you
unless it is absolutely necessary. He would
rather cut wages to balance budget—or do
layoffs
- Shouldn't strap city with debt for future—he
believes we should deal with budget issues
without long term borrowing—"not a tin cup
brigade"—the city has always been out of
control in spending—need to get and keep
control.
- Warren Buffett says we are in recession
now . . . people will be glad to keep jobs if we go
into depression.
- RG believes we should do 10% across the board
wage cut . . . more prudent than borrowing . . .

lost revenue should not be solved by
borrowing.
- Lhota suggests real budget meeting on Sunday
  to deal and take lead—need to let everyone
  realize that we are responsible
- RG believes we need to solve 1.5 billion gap in
  current year . . . need to solve without
  borrowing . . . cut spending in all agencies,
  cut salaries 1 year (5-10%) need cuts and
  everyone must be part of it
- "Pathetic" that everyone is reverting to the
  tin cup routine—we need to straighten
  ourselves out . . . problems will not be
  resolved by going to Washington . . . every time
  you go to Washington for help, another big
  firm says let's get out of NY, they don't know
  what they're doing.
- The city needs to solve the lost revenue
  problem itself . . . the cleanup needs Feds help
  but not lost revenue
- Ring out the 39 billion $ budget—and solve our
  $ problem—Feds must help with lost revenue
  but we must solve our own problems with
  revenue
- Wow!—this will go over big—he has
  unbelievable ability to show love, compassion,
  "tough love" all at the same time
- Helicopter—Marathon—problem getting them
  up in air—NBC needs help—need them to cover
  worldwide event.
- Restaurant week —10/15
- Microsoft—10/25—RG will participate
- Street fairs are really the only event he wants
  to ban

7:30 pm
- Ray Murphy funeral—what a nice guy!

- McLaughlin, Blair, everyone showed up (from Ladder 42)
- Two boys—they will be big tough good men just like their father—very happy to be whatever they are
- Ray was a class act
- Glover spoke on behalf of L-42
- Jim Carney on behalf of family—terrific
- Ken Ruane L-16—outstanding-emotional-sincere-nice guy … knew after 1/2 hour working with Ray he was a "keeper"—so true—people are people whether poor in the South Bronx or rich in midtown—FFs try to help
- 2 Captains—L-16 / L-42 made me realize how tough it must be for them—want to write captains a letter —thanking and offering help
- Went to office—Meeting on expansion of counseling
- need to allocate $$ for counselors—site, etc.
- Kelly/Malachy doing good job
- Prezant seems to be getting more critical as days go by—probably sees the Admin coming to end and sees the future—less money, less money… such a pro … guys are really lucky to have him
- Told Fitz we need to get military people in to run operations—Chiefs can't handle it … not much time left—we need to talk to FEMA to get their help

OCTOBER 7
6 pm—After Staff Meeting
- Helicopter to Fred Ill wake in Pearl River (Ladder 2)
- Really glad I talked RG into attending—he remembered Fred when he saw his picture.

- His son (L-58) hugged me and thanked me. What a family . . . 2 nice daughters . . . wife really a sweetheart . . . whole family, supportive of mayor
- Guys lined up outside by rear door to give RG and me honor guard while entering . . . what a great group
- Mike Finer there—hugged me—told me he loved me—worried about me—his wife hugged me also
- Mayor comes back from Ill wake and does live TV (National) (didn't mention this to me). Rita saw him and said that he was asked how he is getting through this—he told Brokaw that he just left TVE and they went to wake together— he gets strength from Tom Von Essen. Amazing experience working with him.
- Best news ever last night—Pam said she is pregnant (2 weeks) very very early, please don't tell anyone. She'll know more this week . . . WOW! Hope all goes well with her. (Note: Pam had baby Jenna on June 13, 2002)

OCTOBER 12
8 am—Staff Meeting
- Positive anthrax at Rockefeller Center (NBC Studio) . . . more to come . . . FBI had info . . . Lhota pissed . . . Fitz on way to City Hall . . . I'll be back after funeral.
- Saudi Prince—$10M—RG tells to keep it . . . check with White House . . . they are OK
- Stopped at 9 Metro last night . . . conference room loaded with mail from all over the world . . . amazing the level of support . . . absolute #1 project for every teacher/student in USA to tell NYC Fire Commissioner how wonderful his troops are.

- Helicopter ride back from D'Attri service with Molinari and RG . . . first time Molinari saw site from air . . . very upset.
- Frank Gribbon overwhelmed . . . doing a great job under trying circumstances to say the least.
- Funeral for D'Attri . . . great remarks from guy in Squad 1 (tough little guy) . . . "we'll never lose our courage"
- Going to bathroom before mass . . . window open . . . heard pipers practicing (eerie sound) . . . Staten Island took major hit . . . people all over island affected by it.
- Mentioned it to FF in urinal next to me . . . he said he hears crickets at night and thinks it's the chirping sound of pass-alarms at WTC.
- Squad 1—some operation . . . lot of tough Italian kids and good senior men . . . great group

Anthrax Meeting—OEM/Health Experts/ Mayor, et al.

- 30 Rockefeller Center (3rd Fl.)—NBC (Channel 4)
- Will medicate people that operate on 3rd fl. and mail room
- Both have separate HVAC systems.
- 9/25 handled by 3 people . . . powder all over herself . . . she was touching herself . . . notified FBI
- Not long after developed welts . . . original M.D. thought spider bite
- Dr. Kornblu tested negative (DOH)
- She recontacted MD's and got a biopsy . . . DOH sent material to CDC . . . letter was

negative . . . culture not confirmed yet . . .
2 interns and mailroom employee . . .
being tested now
— She says she is very skin sensitive . . . she is
definitely tested positive for anthrax
through blood tests
— It may not have been from the exposure of this
letter
— <u>NY Times</u> received letter with powder this
am . . . moved it around, if suspicious, leave it
in room and leave . . . PD has it . . . on way to
DOH
— Rapid diagnostic test available
— RG wants a system that gives immediate
collection and test.
— Clear instructions on how to deal with mail

WHAT TO DO:
— Need to remain calm
— Most often a hoax
— Don't move it—very important
— Call 911
— Very manageable
— Person should be treated?

— NBC closed down evening news because of fear
of anthrax
— Organism if not virulent enough would have
needed a larger dose of powder
— Middle of meeting—report of UN getting a
package. I told OEM to just send NYPD . . .
treat as crime
— Isolate and evaluate
— Fox News—3 people with flu . . . month ago
Roger Ailes's assistant got letter . . . spilled
powder on pants . . . 3 people now have flu and

his office is in panic. These 3 people need to be in hospital . . . IV, chest X ray, etc.

— Quick decision to give all calls like this from FD dispatch or 911 to SOD at 911 . . . we'll then figure out the resources necessary to handle

— If you opened up an envelope with powder in it, seek help . . . if not, don't panic

— Doctors need to stop prescribing CIPRO

— Individual crimes need to be put in perspective

— But this is one day after FBI said we would be having another terrorist issue shortly

— Isolate and Evaluate

— 1 hour to test with microscope and know if it is positive

— If negative, need more time to test

— Lots of threats

— Very low credibility

— A top 10 date for Judi (Letterman) visit lady with anthrax exposure

— St. Vincent's helping with counseling

— 25 FF's starting Hazmat training on Monday

— Prezant—The community groups are not necessarily the way for our folks to be getting counseling/help

— "Confirmed" by DOD—This was given to me by OEM (confirmed)
    —Men in fatigues have stolen vehicle full of automatic weapons. Turned out to be false report. Actual: a nut at Forth Dix shot his gun in barracks, then stole car and was shot at Army Base . . .

— Mayor wants to scale back the Hazmat moon suit response . . . told him we already did . . . now working to maximize resources

— Letter to <u>NY Times</u> and <u>Post</u> is from same source . . . Postmark: St. Petersburg, Fl.

OCTOBER 13

— Memorial for Adam Rand (Squad 288) . . . nice kid . . . wonderful family . . . priest big sweetheart . . . makes political remarks . . . out of place . . . fiance said . . . "seems to me like summer camp without counselor"

— Dennis Murphy—just an unbelievable leader . . . really gets it done and keeps 'em happy at same time . . . would love to clone him

— Mass at Blue Point for Sr. Marguerite

— Late for auction at LeCirque (Rusty Staub fund-raiser)—told audience I have nervous habit of running hand through my hair . . . afraid tonight . . . could cost me a lot of money. Nice people . . . big money paid for wine . . . felt like some people are helping their conscience by donating money . . . they don't know how else to help

OCTOBER 14

— Anthrax hot issue of day

— Cop and two lab techs have minor exposure

— Just left Mike Horton (DDC)—Tony Coles— letter from Bechtel saying our guys and P.D. are taking great risks and are in danger of serious injuries . . . they recommend getting them off pile

— Mayor now seems ready for what Fitz and I recommended two weeks ago . . . now we need to figure how to do it . . . two locations where we had 6-7 guys under material on Friday . . . it collapsed on Saturday

— Another glaring example of lack of discipline and leadership by some officers in command at

site . . . proper protective clothing, training, position, you name it
— The exceptional chief carries out the mission

OCTOBER 15
— Helicopter to funeral of John Tipping
— Breakfast with HRM Prince Andrew . . . tells the Mayor the Queen wants to Knight him and make Bernie and I a CBE . . . Mayor said he was nice guy . . . I said very different from Prince Abdul Fangul (we laughed)
— NYPD Press leaked the urn ceremonial process with pictures at One Police Plaza . . . RG very upset . . . wants someone fired . . . no reason to be such Press "whores"
— RG been more than reasonable with manpower at site . . . we could have de-escalated three weeks ago . . . but his first priority was the feelings of FFs/POs and families . . . not the expediting of moving materials.

OCTOBER 16
— Yesterday Mike Regan had conversation with Tom Manley (UFA "Safety" rep). Manley said the guys needed to be taken off pile . . . not good for them. He admitted that he would not say publicly . . . hinted he will criticize us once we do pull them off . . . What a man!
— Bechtel report stating the unsafe procedures needs to be addressed—we won't get finality from meeting Fitz attended on Monday
— Hopefully by next week, we will have moved into next phase—Mayor is on board cutting back risks to those that are alive.
— Hanley calls to tell me article in News with unions complaining that B.I.T.S. is doing

questioning re: tragedy—God forbid we
actually find out what we did—what
happened . . . lessons to be learned. How
pathetic!
— Fire Safety Education Meeting
— Marino funeral—more emotional for some
reason—family—beautiful wife and 2 kids—
Parents of Ken were outstanding
— I felt like my remarks were canned after
hearing mother and wife—I didn't use my notes
and winged it.
— Wife thanked me, hugged me . . . what a nice
lady
— Did interview with Monsignor Lisante (PBS—
Catholic TV)—long interview—spirituality/
my trying to help families
— Wrote letter to all the Captains
(Note: never sent—was supposed to go in letter
about counseling and health services . . . wish
I had sent it)

OCTOBER 22

— Watching guys at E 54/L 4—they have had a
really tough time—Chief Joe Nardone . . . he is
truly a class act . . . did a great job eulogizing
Joe Angelini Jr. . . . . thanked the Mayor, me on
behalf of family
— Classic case of FF not taking anything
serious—guy from L-61 put powder in envelope
and sticks in mail to Burn Center
— Burn Center volunteer takes mail home, sees
powder, afraid for family, calls 911—HAZMAT
and police respond—Westchester—then he
hears it was a joke—too late—to their credit
our chiefs followed up on it, and we suspended
this guy—probably decent guy

OCTOBER 26

- Postal workers very anxious—CDC says keep calm—only a few pieces at this time
- Hard to argue with workers
- Six cases at 5 locations
- NBC—CBS—Post—No post office anthrax yet
- The union rep is saying if Congress bailed out, why shouldn't his people—they are no less important—he's right
- Helicopter to Joe Marchbanks funeral—outstanding man and chief
- Windy . . . worst flight so far—beautiful up the Hudson
- RG cancels Press conference to announce 11/18 IAFF Memorial
- Horrible story in News today about air quality (lack of it) at site
- RG hire Bechtel—if not them, we need to get big firm in to make safer for workers
- Last night, Rita said she did not know how I go through this . . . said I was unbelievably brave. I told her I'm not brave . . . a guy who goes up while passing a guy going down that tells him they have been ordered to evacuate but says he heard a Mayday above and he keeps going up . . . that's brave! Those of us that are left need to stand tall for those that aren't. Then she said, well, you're courageous—still no—I believe in what I am and what I do! I would not run away from my responsibility! That's not courageous . . . that's being a man who cares about his responsibility and will carry that out as long as he is able. "Proud with conviction, that's what I'm about"
- If there isn't enough to worry about the pilot

just turned around and said we can't land
where we're supposed to . . . winds and light
towers . . . he'll try but may not be able to . . .
I said, no problem! You land wherever you feel
good about landing!

OCTOBER 30

- RG—concerned about giving urns without
  death certificate—Roe says it will be very
  emotional . . . decides it is OK to start—let's
  try to expedite the death certif. process
- Mike Burton—Ken Holden DDC have been
  outstanding
- RG planning an address to City Council—wants
  them to lower taxes—if they are not serious,
  he doesn't want to waste his time—if they
  won't commit he won't bother to make speech
- 10 samples negative—anthrax
- 30 more samples taken but results not back yet
- NYPD rep with Bernie—sharp—anthrax
  spokesman or liaison whatever—so unreal that
  whenever new issue comes up a new sharp NYPD
  officer appears—so different at FDNY—can't
  get the really sharp guys off the line
- Quote in paper—We don't need independent
  investigation—told Frank Gribbon to respond
  "are you kidding"—Absolutely needed—will
  never get unbiased/thorough study done by
  insiders at FDNY
- Helicopter to Joe Vigiano memorial
- RG—"Why are we being nice to the unions that
  fucked you?" . . . I said, "It's about the
  widows." RG . . . "you're right"
- Spectacular ride to Deer Park
- Father Romano (NYPD chaplain)—outstanding—
  he talked about difference from hero and

warrior—those men that knew if they kept
going up it would probably mean disaster—how
many men can consciously make that decision—
"Joe Vigiano was one of them"

- "Mr. Vigiano"—all the cops kept referring to
  him that way—that his son wished he could
  bring him to work every day—he knew he
  couldn't so he surrounded himself with cops
  (ESU) like his father—heart, guts,
  determination
- John Vig—"My Brooklyn Flagship"—how proud
  I am to know how much he thought of me—all
  the notes he used to send me telling me to stay
  the course—how important the training was—
  how he was revered by some and disliked by
  others
- Joe Dunne—first thing he did when he took
  command of a precinct was to find out if the
  place was being run by the unofficial leaders
  . . . were they the heroes or the zeros
- If you say that in NYPD, it is accepted—in the
  FDNY it would be great insult that many of the
  brothers are zeros but we don't want anyone
  else to know—how absurd—it's impossible to
  improve and move forward without encouraging
  the hero and doing something about the zero
- People like the Vig, Downey, Hatton, Brown
  . . . you name it . . . they were willing to
  stand tall and make the distinction—many
  others not

NOVEMBER 1

- Told Scott Weinberger on NBC —no more for me
  after Jan 1, 2002—grief all of next year too
  painful—too much for me—will work hard till
  end and move on

- Gallagher of UFA met today with Tony Coles. Coles said "he's an idiot"—he threatened demonstration tomorrow
- Coles told him that is not the way to reach this Mayor. No support for all we've done, no desire to give us a chance to work out the problem ... if there is one
- No desire to prevent any more pain for families ... just wants Mayor to roll over
- In my time, the worst UFA president they have had
- Proby graduation today—really mixed feelings—6 FFs didn't live to graduate— normally a ceremony that is 100% positive ... not today

NOVEMBER 4

- UFA/UFOA have peaceful demonstration on Friday that goes bad—UFA lied to cops and decided to not walk to City Hall as promised but wind up charging barricades, lifting them, punching cops—horrible debacle
- 12 arrested—turns into media frenzy—Unions definitely win the media spin—they have everyone convinced we have almost left the site and all the bodies will be recovered at the dump
- I told Cassano 3 days ago to send something out explaining what we were doing but he never got it out
- I visited the site Saturday at 6 am and could see what the guys are complaining about ... Chiefs are not using the PAPD or NYPD—just our 25 guys
- Just came from Press conference at One Police Plaza

- PD overdoing it—today they arrested Gallagher and Gorman—it certainly won't help diffuse
- What a shame to add to pain of families
- Marathon today—the mystery tour in open car with mayor . . . best ever—every neighborhood (almost) loved him this year—I told him coming across Queensboro Bridge that he had some run—did a great job—he said he really had the City fixed—in good shape—he is really angry that is now a mess—with him leaving. I told him he can't prevent tragedy.
- I felt the same about FDNY —we made great strides forward—now it is a wreck—discipline, emotion—you name it—the tragedy would foul up any operation but with the lack of leadership/loyalty of top staff, even more difficult to fix—fortunately, we were in such good shape before tragedy
- NYPD wants FD brass available at next event—said that Nigro, Cassano were there but disappeared when things got ugly
- All roads lead to a lack of accountability of top brass—need to get control of the 40 deputies or you'll never solve problem

NOVEMBER 16

- Gov Ridge to site—big job—hope he is up to it. Mike Byrne with him (great kid) —he'll be great help to Ridge—asked him to help me find new Fire Commissioner—military man—leader tough—discipline—compassionate—Mike is a great example of how you can't really keep the super sharp guys at FDNY—PD has the ability to move stars like him up in the Dept—the

tenured Chief system in FD turns them off—
holds them back

8 am—Staff Meeting

— RG—really upset about News Editorial—
terrible to put President Bush in situation he
can't win—very harmful—our support in White
House is much greater than what we have in
Congress—Bloomberg should not be pandering
to Democrats—we don't need the $$'s
immediately—no reason to give us all the $$'s
upfront—we can wait—big mistake to pressure
President
— RG wants OP-Ed response—obligation to
intellectual honesty—we should not be
looking for $$'s for subway, rail lines, upstate
and $$'s not connected to WTC—Feds have been
terrific
— Great cop story—PO get call—pen with
powder on it and envelope—citizen puts both
in plastic bag—calls PD ... PO collects—
comes back later that afternoon says no
results. Citizen calls next day concerned—
turns out PO throws bag in garbage on
street—PD suspends him and is searching for
bag. I ask Joe Dunne if he is on my list to
move over to FD
— We can't understand—it would have been just
as easy for PO to call our Hammer team and turn
over
— RG believes we should get out word—Re: Twin
Towers Fund—to our families—put widows on
board
— United Way a disaster

NOVEMBER 19

- Ceremony at Medical Examiner—what a class act Dr. Hirsch is—all the doctors and people working at morgue seem to love him
- What a great job he did for us
- He told me "The vilification of you by some people is the worst thing I've seen happen since I came to NY in 1989"

NOVEMBER 20

- RG—forced IRS to change process by sending out our checks—not based on need but because this is what the donors wanted—IRS then changed their restriction—he believes they would not have done this without pressure
- RG—that's what politics is all about . . . picking and choosing. Having the guts to make leadership decisions based on the priority of need, benefits, etc. AND most important, having the courage to back it up
- Met Bloomberg today—he agrees with me completely—need strong military person to take over FDNY—big job in front of him—strong business background OK—no insider—need to continue all the change we've instituted—he believes diversity major problem at FD—told him not to expect loyalty from brass—when things get tough they will not support him—have not ever supported commissioner or mayor when going gets tough

NOVEMBER 22
Thanksgiving

- Great experience riding float with RG, Sheirer, Kerik, Roe O'Keefe, Joe Torre
- Support for whole team—for everything

firefighters and all the team did was
outstanding
— You could see the appreciation in the eyes of
thousands of people—very emotional
— I often describe Mayor as maniac and sometimes
think I shouldn't—I really mean it as a
compliment
— The other day he was describing what he thought
was a good mayor—we were talking about how
hard it will be for Bloomberg—especially if his
plan is to be a hands-off mayor—RG said he
studied city history and said the most popular
and successful mayors were Koch and
LaGuardia—both were "maniacs"—his word—
they served 24 hrs a day and worked tirelessly
to serve the city—knowing that in the end you
can't really please everyone but for your
conscience, you have to go 1000%

NOVEMBER 26
Staff Meeting—Gracie Mansion
— WTC—if you keep the focus narrow you can
defend it better later on—they "can pound
you" but cannot force you to waver or change
your plan if you have it written
— Squads: 24/48
— 1 rescue at site
— hammer team—1 FF 4 PO   11 originally
— we did not man on a regular basis—we in effect
showed that team worked without us
— 84 additional trained HAZMAT techs will be
complete
— need another 50
— trouble recruiting

NOVEMBER 30
Staff Meeting
— No good for Queen in January
— Do not talk to Barstow on NY Times story re:
  $$'s to FFs and PO—will be negative—he thinks
  too much money—we disagree—we compare to
  the millions awarded for a fall, jump in lake,
  accidents, etc.—no justice—these men deserve
  it

DECEMBER 2
— UFA Annual Christmas Party for Widows and
  Children at Toys R Us
— Someone brought Terry Farrell's son over to me
  to say hello—asked me if I knew his father—
  "knew him?" . . . his was the only firefighter's
  picture I had in my ceremonial office—"Mr.
  Nice Man"—front page of <u>Newsday</u>—Terry was
  our first bone marrow donor to little girl from
  Las Vegas—great guy—his kid was really nice
— Mrs. Larsen came up to thank me—3 kids and a
  baby born 2 days after 9/11—couldn't have
  been nicer—beautiful baby
— Mrs. Haskell—beautiful lady—thanks for
  everything
— Mrs. Geis—told her I would promote her
  husband (posthumously) at ceremony at E-288
  or in Freeport . . . wherever she wanted—
  3 great boys—really upsetting
— Christmas party an unbelievable feeling of
  pain for all these wonderful ladies and all
  they have gone through and will continue to
  suffer

DECEMBER 31
Last Staff Meeting

— RG tells Neil Cohen—best Health Commissioner NYC ever had

— Harding just shaking his head—tried to do both stadium deals and RG still trying to get some action on west side stadium

— Rosemary O'Keefe—"never thought I could do it" ... Mayor said when things get really rough some people get it done ... step up and accomplish great things ... you did and should be very proud.

— Denny Young—"Good Run!"

ACRONYMS AND ABBREVIATIONS

B.I.T.S.—Bureau of Investigation and Trials (FDNY)

CBE—Commander of the British Empire

CDC—Centers for Disease Control

Con Ed—Con Edison Co., a power utility

DCAS—Department of Construction and Administrative Services (NYC)

DDC—Department of Design and Construction (NYC)

DEP—Department of Environmental Protection (NYC)

DOB—Department of Buildings (NYC)

DOD—Department of Defense (U.S.)

DOH—Department of Health (NYC)

EMS—Emergency Medical Services (FDNY)

EMT—Emergency Medical Technician

ESU—Emergency Services Unit (NYPD)

FEMA—Federal Emergency Management Agency (U.S.)

FF—Firefighter

Fresh Kills—Fresh Kills Landfill on Staten Island

GOV—New York Governor George Pataki

GW—George Washington Bridge

HAZMAT—FDNY Hazardous Materials Unit

HRM—His Royal Majesty

IAFF—International Association of Firefighters

IRS—Internal Revenue Service (U.S.)

JAVITS—Jacob Javits Convention Center

J&R—J&R Music World, a record store

ME—Medical Examiner (NYC)

MSG—Madison Square Garden

NYCHA—New York City Housing Authority

NYSE—New York Stock Exchange

OEM—Office of Emergency Management (NYC)

PA—Port Authority

PAPD—Port Authority Police Department

PD—New York Police Department

PO—Police Officer

PSAC—Public Safety Answering Center

REBNY—Real Estate Board of New York

RG—New York Mayor Rudy Giuliani

RVC—Rockville Centre, in Nassau County, where we raised our children

SCA—School Construction Authority

SOC—Special Operations Command (FDNY)

TVE—Thomas Von Essen

UFA—Uniformed Firefighters Association

UN—United Nations

USAR—Urban search and rescue team

WFC—World Financial Center

WTC—World Trade Center

NAMES

Bloomberg, Michael—Republican mayoral candidate, then mayor-elect of New York

Brown, Tim—friend of Terry Hatton, worked at OEM

Butts, Rev. Calvin—pastor of Abyssinian Baptist Church in Harlem

Byrne, Michael—former FDNY captain and assistant to commissioner; now aide to former governor Tom Ridge at U.S. Department of Homeland Security

Ridge, Tom—former Pennsylvania governor; head of U.S. Office of Homeland Security after 9/11

Sardiello, Richie—director of transportation, Club Med, and an old friend

Sheirer, Richie—director of OEM

Siegel, Norman—executive director of the New York Civil Liberties Union

Speyer, Jerry—president and CEO, Tishman Speyer Properties

Spinola, Steve—president of Real Estate Board of New York

Spitzer, Eliot—New York State attorney general

Staub, Rusty—former New York Met, head of Police & Fire Widows' and Children's Fund

Swanson, Dennis—general manager of WNBC/Channel 4

Thompson, Tommy—U.S. secretary of health and human services

Torre, Sister Marguerite—principal of Nativity of the Blessed Virgin Mary School in Ozone Park, sister of Yankees manager Joe Torre

Von Essen, Fred—Von Essen's brother in Texas

Wilson, Howard—chairman of NYC School Construction Authority

Young, Denny—mayoral counselor

A SILENT AND SOLEMN GOOD-BYE

The Site,
May 30, 2002

It's warm and breezy today, almost as beautiful a morning as that one eight and a half months ago.

It's been sixty days since I was last here. Most of the trucks have left. The ground is swept. The pile is gone. All that's left is the pit—vast, clean, empty, looking almost like any other construction site.

Driving down here with Mayor Giuliani, I flashed back to all the trips we took to this area in the days and weeks after the attacks. Cheering crowds lined the roadway this morning, just as they did then.

Today, though, we have come for the closing ceremony. The recovery effort has officially ended. The grieving never will.

At 10:28 A.M., the moment the second tower fell, the fire bell tolls four sets of five, the traditional signal transmitted across the radio when a firefighter dies. The tones bounce off the walls and resonate in the air. Joe Pfeifer, the first fire chief to arrive at tower one that day, leads a slow, solemn group up the ramp. They carry an empty stretcher with an American flag draped over it.

Where we're standing, at the top of the long ramp that extends into the pit, I see familiar faces everywhere: firefighters, political aides, officers, widows. Jimmy Ginty, my dear friend from Ladder 42, marches by with the bagpipe band. A group of workers follow. I see John Vigiano among them, looking proud, strong, sad: the long, horrible task of searching for his two sons is over.

The ceremony is marked by silence. No speeches. No announcements. No words are spoken. Thousands have gathered to say a silent and solemn good-bye.

I look up at the space in the sky where the towers once stood and I am filled with a deep melancholy. The emptiness in my heart will never be filled.

And I know I will never find any comfort or good in any tragedy.

Today, and every day, I can't stop thinking about the children who will miss their fathers and mothers growing up, and the incredible grief of the parents who lost their children. No parent should ever have to endure such a loss.

"How will we ever get through this?" is the question I asked on the night of September 11. "How?"

Maybe the answer is here, all around me. Not just in the cleanup, not just in the purpose demonstrated by all who came and labored all these months.

The answer is in the enduring spirits of all assembled here. That, for me, is the miracle in all of this: having looked horror in the face, we bear the pain without losing heart.

After the ceremony, I race back home. My granddaughter Rita is there when I open the door.

"Gramps!" she squeals before I can say a word.

"Hey, squirt!" I say as she jumps into my arms.

As I hug her, I think that for her, for all the children, and for each other, we must be strong of heart.

We must.

EPILOGUE

In the last year and a half, the lessons about strength of heart have continued. And some of them have been more painful, and more surprising, than I ever could have imagined.

For weeks after September 11, 2001, I lived only in the moment, caught between contradictory feelings of almost paralyzing sorrow and the urgency of the task at hand. Firefighting had taught me how to work through difficult moments, no matter how tired I was. I'd learned that more than stepping back to ponder larger questions or deep mysteries, the most important thing was to keep going. And as we recovered from the attacks, our team and department always had so much to deal with that there was not enough time to accomplish everything, let alone reflect on it. We were just putting one boot in front of the other.

Yet the pain couldn't be brushed aside. It had to be lived, experienced, every minute, every second. During the weeks after September 11, time slowed into a long, endless blur, with a strange mix of emotions that left me frayed and drained, yet feeling greater pain than I'd ever known. I couldn't really grasp it all and make sense of it, yet I couldn't escape it. I could only live it.

I certainly couldn't envision the day when the crisis would be over and there would be less to do, when the pain had diminished and my life, along with all of those touched on that day, would somehow travel beyond the moment when so many other lives had been cruelly cut off.

I thought things might improve once I left the commissioner's job. The whole purpose of leaving a job I loved, after all, was to get away from constant exposure to the painful reminders that I knew would pick at the wound. Like it or not, by leaving the fire department after thirty-two years, I would be propelled into a new future. There would be time enough to come to grips with what we had been through that day.

In fact, though, that transition didn't happen, at least at first. For one thing, the feeling of urgency didn't just disappear as I'd expected. I threw myself into my new job, this book, meetings, speeches, firefighting events—anything, I think now, to keep busy. When I wasn't working, I was racing out to the suburbs to see my kids and grandchildren. The pain was always there, of course; it was inescapable. But it wasn't overwhelming as long as I kept moving and managed to avoid slowing down.

By the summer, my schedule was beginning to ease, I was getting some distance from the department, and I figured enough time might have passed that my emotions would begin to soften. But while my overall mood had improved a little, the daily crying didn't go away. The sudden, stabbing memories were as frequent and severe as ever. I'd be at the beach, a contented average guy with few visible cares, enjoying a beautiful day, watching my grandchildren prance around—and then, in an instant, I'd look at the ocean and remember Father Judge standing by the water after the crash of TWA Flight 800, and I'd be seized by an overwhelming sadness that was as strong as anything I'd felt before.

Emotions besides sadness stubbornly hung on too. Leaving the commissioner's office, I'd possessed some sense of completion and finality. But now I found that my head was filled with second thoughts. I would recall some of the bitter fights, like the battles over the radios at the World Trade Center and over the performance evaluations of the chiefs. During my time as commissioner, my administration and I had worked hard to implement a performance review system. Now, it seems unlikely to happen any time soon, and this lack of oversight could have implications on the safety of the troops for years to come. I still had strong ideas about training the firefighters and believed that both the troops and the officers could benefit from learning about the structure of the Marines and the principles of accountability and discipline that go hand in hand with the privilege of becoming a leader. Even after I left the commissioner's office, I was still anxious to know the internal probe's findings on the communications problems at the World Trade Center. When I read in the fire department's magazine that—just as I'd expected—the cause of the problems was the entire communications system and not just the much-maligned radios, I would get angry all over again, or long to be back in there fighting for what I believed in. I knew it wasn't healthy, but I couldn't let go. I had been gone from the job for months now, but I was finding less peace, not more.

It seemed strange and frustrating that my emotions hadn't settled down at least a little. It was, after all, nearly a year after the attacks, and the world was beginning to move on. However haltingly, I was living in that future I'd once found impossible to imagine. My family was doing well. My youngest son had gotten a big break in his theater career when he was cast in a starring role on Broadway. I had a new granddaughter in Kansas, and she was (of course) the light of my daughter Pam's life. My brother Roddy, like many firefighters after the World Trade Center disaster, had retired from the department, which should have made its concerns even more remote to me. Many of my own close friends from the fire department had moved on to different careers.

At the new office, I was learning the ropes as a consultant, comfortably surrounded by old friends and colleagues from the Giuliani administration. September 11 no longer dominated our conversations. Our work focused on clients, while our small talk tended to be about city politics and national affairs. The nation's focus was shifting to Iraq. Even the fire department, while dealing with the aftermath of the tragedy, was in some ways returning to normal, grappling with budget cuts and slipping back into old bad habits.

I rarely traveled to lower Manhattan, but when I did, I saw that the World Trade Center site, which had been a dispiriting mass of rubble, was now a clean, quiet place, more or less unchanged from week to week. To be sure, it was an enormous gouge in the earth, but at least it was calm and surrounded by traffic and air and crowds that seemed almost as they had been before. That day of ash and death and papers flying and workers fleeing, though fresh in my mind, was being displaced by newer images of more recent days.

So why couldn't I get on with it? Why wasn't I feeling better? Why did the grief not just pass, but hang on, revealing layer after layer, drawing me deeper and deeper?

All too soon it was the first anniversary of the attacks, a day I faced with dread. There was one more ceremony at the site. All of us returned yet again to remember.

The weather was not sunny and warm, as it had been a year before. Instead, a heavy wind blew all morning. The sand and grit stung our eyes, a nasty and unnecessary reminder that this place, once dominated by man-made structures of concrete, steel, and glass, had returned to a more elemental stage. Many people whispered that the wind was made up of all the spirits who had come to rest there.

I stood near the stage, next to Mayor Giuliani. Like many others there, he and I had been asked to read some of the names of those who had died. Hundreds of family members and friends from eighty-three countries stood around us. I heard many different languages being spoken. A lot of people held up pictures of their lost ones.

They all looked so different, every one an individual with a story. All they seemed to have in common was losing their futures in one horrible, random, senseless moment.

The ceremony made the familiar events, by now written about and witnessed over and over, seem fresh, vivid and all too new. Reading all the names took nearly three hours, far longer than it had taken the towers to plummet to earth. Many people cried the whole time. For the families and friends, no speeches, no talk of heroes or pride, however true or deeply felt, could fully erase the deeper void.

But as I stood there, feeling the emotions pass through those gathered there, I suddenly realized how much we all truly shared. Grief knows no boundaries. Skin color, age, income level—the differences that had stood out a few minutes earlier now seemed minor. Everyone who had died that day had a mother or daughter or sister or lover who mourned his or her loss. Everyone felt the same sense of emptiness. The feeling was universal.

Looking back, if that day recalled all the pain yet again, it also served as something of a milestone that helped me better grasp the scale of what had happened. In the middle of the disaster of September 11, I hadn't fully absorbed the wide-reaching impact of the events of that day. Writing this book had helped, but even then I had been largely absorbed with the challenges and losses confronting the fire department.

But being back at the site after some time away, the wind whipping up dust all around us, I was reminded that everyone there was just one tiny piece of a gigantic mosaic, and that all of us, and hundreds of thousands of people around the world, were somehow bound together forever by the tragedy, and that a larger chain linked us to many others who had experienced tragedies. Whether the mourners at the site were doing okay or were miserable, angry, and grief-stricken, they were there, together, to bear witness to those who had been lost and to share those emotions. The effect was powerful.

Before that last ceremony in a year of ceremonies, I had been to countless funerals and services, had cried at many of them, but never taken much comfort from them. I had been inspired by the strength in people, but had felt paradoxically too close to everything and a little distant too. I could let myself go, for a minute or two, but I always held something back, keeping it together and moving on as best I could.

Now, stripped of all the duties and responsibilities of the past, I didn't need to do anything but grieve. And looking around, I saw that to feel grief, despair, hatred, or anything else, even after a year, was understandable, *normal* even.

It made sense when you thought about it, that all those emotions would be churning under the surface and might only come out after a long while. How could they not? How could there not be a lot of pain buried deep down inside? How could the enormity of that day be forgotten quickly by anyone? How could you begin to come to grips in just a year with all those lifetimes lost?

Under the best circumstances, only the barest, tiniest

384 THOMAS VON ESSEN

piece of what happened on September 11, 2001, can ever be understood. Many of the stories and individual trials can never be known or told. The likelihood is that the grief, pain, and confusion will never fully go away.

Someone, I don't remember who, told me that you have to learn to let the pain live alongside you. I have discovered that's all you can do. There's nothing good about such pain, not in any way. I'll never buy the argument that it makes you stronger; I'll never believe that this kind of loss has its good side. But feeling it is part of what makes you human.

Now, as I write this, over eight months have passed since that day of remembrance, and we are within sight, unbelievably, of the second anniversary of the attacks on the World Trade Center.

The image of the falling towers is receding into the past now, replaced by more recent images of war. With our talent for adaptability, we've grown used to a new New York City skyline, in which the tallest structure is the Empire State Building. Images of the towers have been cut out of movies and TV shows. They live on only in memory and on city streets, hawked on buttons, postcards, and photographs. The pictures of the planes ramming into the spires have been replayed again and again on TV, to the point where they have become familiar images of our times. For many people, they are slowly losing their power to shock, like the moonwalk or the Zapruder film of JFK's assassination.

September 11, 2001, or "9-11" as we have now come to casually shorthand it, is gradually going from being a current event to a piece of history for most people. My grandchildren, growing up all too quickly, have no firsthand memories of that day. The pit that remains at the site, and whatever eventually takes its place, is all they will see. They'll never know what it was like to walk through the World Trade Center or ride to the Windows on the World. My stories, and those of my children, will probably seem like yesterday's news to them.

Things have returned to normal in our national affairs. The country is still fighting its war on terrorism, and it looks like we will be for a long time. U.S. soldiers in Iraq have demonstrated the same strength and nobility as the firefighters and police officers that died in New York, underscoring again our country's basic strengths. But the resolve of those early days is gone, and we are back to politics as usual. The feeling of common purpose we felt after September 11 has rapidly given way to the old bickering and dawdling that we saw before the tragedy. Watching from the sidelines, I've been frustrated that more hasn't been done to improve safety and protect our nation, and disgusted with many politicians in both parties. I am glad to see that the safety and preparedness of our rescue workers have become a topic of national concern, but I still worry about how equipped we will be for the next attack. And I'm certain there will be a next one.

In my own life, there have been, and continue to be, many blessings. Being away from the job has allowed me to spend much more time with my family. I don't know if they realize how much that has meant to me. Without me working such an intense job, my wife and I are closer than we have been in a long time. My children and grandchildren are all healthy and happy.

As I've said before, my pain paled next to that of the people who lost a spouse, child, or parent. Their strength continues to be a source of amazement and admiration to me. Mary Geraghty misses Eddie deeply, still feels the shock and pain of his loss. When I see her and the boys, my stomach aches thinking how much they too must miss Eddie, how much his advice, strength, and love would have meant to his sons as they grow. But recently I talked to her and heard hope in her voice too. She has moved to a new home and is throwing herself into the project of remodeling it. It can't make up for what she's lost, but it has given her something to look toward. And the boys love it.

Beth Petrone gave birth last spring to a healthy baby girl. We don't see Beth around the office as much any more, and she and I don't talk often about Terry or that day. I know she still has a very hard time of it. But that baby is some kind of miracle. She named her Teri, by the way.

Tara Stackpole remains, not surprisingly, a model of strength, perseverance—and humor. She has an amazing ability to find laughter in situations that would destroy most of us. As she asked me one day, when we talked about the difficulty of moving beyond September 11: "What am I going to do—leave the kids at McDonald's, throw my hands up, and run?"

After months of adjusting to life as a single mother, of learning to make decisions and carry responsibility for her family alone, she is growing in confidence and taking steps to build a solid life for herself and her kids. She is a new grandmother, thanks to her oldest son Kevin, and she recently moved to a house in Belle Harbor to be closer to her family. She says she isn't leaving her old life behind, just learning to live with it in a different place. And she tells me she's beginning to see through the fog and envision joy again. I hope it comes for her soon.

As for me, not a day passes that I don't remember September 11, and I don't think one ever will. Reminders can come from anywhere. Recently I was cleaning the house, packing away mementos, when I found a card from Pat Brown's wake. I was a wreck the rest of the day. Pat Brown was one of the many, many outstanding leaders lost. A highly decorated Vietnam Marine and highly honored member of the FDNY, Pat had taught and led by example. Fiercely supportive of his troops, he was at the same time loyal to the mission of the FDNY and its leadership. How would the department replace the void left when he and so many like him were lost?

I still get cards or calls at least once a week from widows and parents, and they almost always bring a tear. But I can say that sometimes I get up in the morning and September 11 is not the first thing on my mind. And that's something. Maybe we never fully move beyond tragedies. At best, I feel like I'm still in transition. But transition, at least, implies becoming something new.

It is a hard lesson to learn, that the old saying is not

true—that time does not necessarily heal all wounds. They are there now, and will be tomorrow. But the wounds do fade. Strength does return. And, somehow, some way, you go on.

Thomas Von Essen
May 28, 2003
New York

Listen to

BERNARD B. KERIK'S

New York Times bestseller

THE LOST SON

A Life in Pursuit of Justice

Performed by

RON MCLARTY

ISBN 0-06-008393-X
$25.95 ($38.95 Can.)
6 hours/4 cassettes

Available wherever books are sold,
or call 1-800-331-3761 to order.

HarperAudio
An Imprint of HarperCollins*Publishers*
www.harpercollins.com

LOA 0902